DON'T SET

To Steve

I HOPE You ENJOY READING ABOUT
MY ADVENTURE. THE RUNNING
WAS A LOT EASIER THAN
THE WRITING

BEST WISHES

Stephen Fry

WARNING:
THIS BOOK MAY CAUSE DROWSINESS!

DON'T SETTLE FOR GOLD

Stephen Fry

Published by Baildon Publishing

A CIP catalogue record for this book is available from the British Library.

ISBN 978-1-7394375-0-3

Book layout and cover design by Clare Brayshaw

Prepared and printed by:

York Publishing Services Ltd
64 Hallfield Road
Layerthorpe
York
YO31 7ZQ

Tel: 01904 431213

Website: www.yps-publishing.co.uk

For Evie Rose, my granddaughter

Dear Evie,

Always strive to do the right thing, but forgive yourself if you make a mistake, because you will.

Try to do your best in everything you do. You are only cheating yourself if you don't.

Finally, and most important of all, dream big and encourage others to do the same. You will be amazed at what you can achieve.

Contents

Author's Note

On the 6th January 2022 my daughter Vicky passed my wife Angela an envelope saying, "I was hoping to have this for Christmas, but it only arrived this week." Angela opened the envelope, gasped in surprise and let out a beaming smile. It contained a picture of an ultrasound scan. Turning to me, Vicky said "Dad. you're going to be a Grandad in July, so if you have plans to do any more daft, long distance challenges, you will need to get them done before then because after that, you're on babysitting duties." She didn't realise but she was watering another seed that had already been planted. Three months later, I was on the train to Penzance hoping to run the length of the country.

I hadn't intended to run for a charity but felt it was a waste to run so far and not use the opportunity to try and help someone. About this time, I read an alarming statistic. Every two hours, somewhere in the UK a man between the age of twenty and fifty takes his own life. I found this incredibly sad, so decided to support a charity called *Andy's Man Club*. This was set up by a man called Luke Ambler, and his grieving mother in law, after her son took his own life. Their aim was simply to get men to open up and talk about their problems. I contacted them, told them about my run and set up a fundraising page.

For most of my journey I was alone, probably only talking to a handful of people each day, and yet some of their stories tugged at my heart strings. These conversations were offset by fabulous folk, some stunning scenery, motivating messages and cake. Lots and lots of cake.

During my journey some of the people I met told me I should write a book. A teacher from Kent who I didn't know contacted me to say she heard about my run on Facebook and had read my updates to her class, adding how they were all willing me towards the finish on the last day. Another lady told me how she read my posts to her children at breakfast. They had enjoyed my journey but once I'd finished missed the daily tales of my trials and tribulations. She said, "the way you told your stories was wonderful. You really must write a book."

Five weeks after finishing, Angela and I were walking near our home. A man came cycling towards us then braked to a sudden stop beside us. We both looked up in shock as he said:

"Congratulations on your epic run Steve. That was absolutely inspirational."

The cyclist was Alistair Brownlee. He stopped to chat for a few minutes. Once he'd gone Angela said.

"Maybe you should write that book. After all, it's not every day a double olympic gold medallist tells you you're inspirational. Besides, it will be nice for our future grandchild to read in years to come."

I wasn't sure my writing capabilities could do the journey justice, but then decided I was trying to shy away from the challenge of writing a book. Having finished it, I am as proud of the book as I am of the journey. I hope you enjoy my adventure, but most of all, I hope my efforts in the running and in the writing, inspire you to take on your own challenges, whatever they may be.

Foreword By Boff Whalley

A story in which Stephen runs almost 1000 miles from Lands End to John O' Groats, solo and carrying little more than some not-very-waterproofs and a phone with a knackered battery. And while it's a tale well-told of adventure and challenge, it's as much about life's day-to-day and down-to-earth experiences – the people we meet, the food we eat, the chip shop that closes before you get there...

Talking of shops, Stephen begins this epic journey in a voice that reads as if he's nipping to the Spar for a packet of biscuits; which makes the ridiculousness of the challenge even more fascinating. As he writes himself, "I have never professed to be normal." We tend to think of the people who complete these kind of madcap ultra-ultra-ultra-marathons as being the visible component in a crack team of organisers, sponsors and support teams, whereas Stephen simply sets off on his own, seemingly driven only by a handful of disarmingly daft Yorkshire theories: 'if it rains, run topless, that way you'll have a dry shirt to wear when it stops.'

The book is a litany of cheap breakfasts and friendly cafés – yes, food is a nagging constant throughout the journey, with Stephen refusing to carry much more than a packet of peanut M&Ms and the occasional muesli bar. The hunt for an open café is ever-present; the smell of coffee that leads to a freshly-brewed cup becomes a daily treasure. And somehow, beneath all this understandable obsession with eating, there's the almost superhuman effort it takes to get up at the crack of dawn day after day to run, run, run.

The people he meets along the way tell their own story, of a nation made up of mad, abusive drivers who give this lone runner the middle finger and friendly, welcoming folk who offer rest, sandwiches and drinks. The daily conversations with strangers are a life-line, a recurring link back to the real world outside this self-driven, moving, eating bubble of madness. I say madness, but Stephen's version of it isn't some fierce, obsessive madness: it's simply a will to do the thing he loves, achieve something on his own two (sore) feet, and to complete it with a down-to-earth simplicity. It's all, dare I say it, and in the best possible way: very Yorkshire.

The challenge is carried out with little fanfare or chest-beating, with Stephen raising money along the way for Andy's Man Club, a charity that encourages men to face and talk about issues and problems they might have. Several times during the run he is told stories by people who have lost friends to suicide, and this raw emotion becomes ever more entangled with Stephen's own emotions as he hobbles through painful injury to cover the last few days into John O' Groats, where finally, a fitting last frame has him slumped over a coffee in a café, shedding tears of exhaustion. It's a place he's run a long way to reach.

It's a book about running, of course it is. But more than that it's a book about what we choose to do with our lives and how, across the length and breadth of the country, we relate to each other.

Boff Whalley May 2023

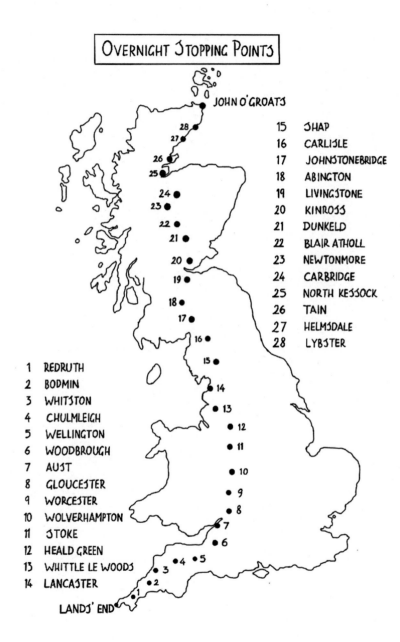

OVERNIGHT STOPPING POINTS

JOHN O'GROATS

1	REDRUTH
2	BODMIN
3	WHITSTON
4	CHULMLEIGH
5	WELLINGTON
6	WOODBROUGH
7	AUST
8	GLOUCESTER
9	WORCESTER
10	WOLVERHAMPTON
11	STOKE
12	HEALD GREEN
13	WHITTLE LE WOODS
14	LANCASTER
15	SHAP
16	CARLISLE
17	JOHNSTONEBRIDGE
18	ABINGTON
19	LIVINGSTONE
20	KINROSS
21	DUNKELD
22	BLAIR ATHOLL
23	NEWTONMORE
24	CARBRIDGE
25	NORTH KESSOCK
26	TAIN
27	HELMSDALE
28	LYBSTER

LANDS' END

CHAPTER 1

April Fool

Day 1 – 1st April 2022 – Lands' End to Redruth

I was standing outside a hotel in the dark. It was 6.30am on a cold April morning. April the 1st in fact. Some would say a perfect day for a fool on a fool's errand. A chilly Northerly wind was blowing, not too strong, but it brought the temperature down below freezing. The cold and dark had heightened my senses, creating an eagerness to be on the way and yet, there was a moment of hesitation as I stood there shivering.

In all my planning I'd rehearsed the moment over and over in my head, searching for the right words. What would I say when the time came? Now the moment had actually arrived I'd frozen, only metaphorically of course, but if I didn't do something in the next few minutes, maybe literally. I phrased the sentence in my head again, but it sounded like a joke. A line from a novel or film, not something that happens in real life. However, this was real. The cold, the dark, the butterflies of anticipation all meant it wasn't a dream, it was actually happening. With every detail planned, like a child at Christmas, I too had counted the number of sleeps to that time. The stage was set so drawing in a deep breath, I stepped forward and opened the taxi door.

"Take me to Lands' End please."

I climbed in and was soon being driven along narrow twisty roads in the dark. The car ride was about nine miles and lasted twenty minutes, and took me to start a much longer journey. A month-long run, on foot, that I had hoped would finish with me at the other end of the country in John O Groats. I had planned my route using the Ordnance Survey's mapping App according to which, the total distance was nine hundred and thirty-three miles. The aim was to finish in April making it a proper challenge, and most sensible people would question if a sixty-one-year-old man was actually capable of running almost one thousand miles in a month. To paraphrase William Blake, would those feet in modern times, stand up to England's mountains green?

As the taxi sped along the narrow lanes of Cornwall, I had scrutinised every turn, concerned that very shortly I would be running on that very road where for the most part, there was no footpath. It worried me as no driver would expect a lunatic from Yorkshire, or a lunatic from any other county for that matter, to be running along that road so early. Especially on a cold morning. So, I was looking to ensure there was some sort of 'safe haven' at the edge of the road if cars got too close. Mostly there was, but there were a few places where the road was right up to the wall. If the road was straight, they were OK. I had a bright orange tee shirt with reflective strips, two lights, one for the front, one for the back, and a head torch, so I hoped I would be visible from a good way off. However, I was in Cornwall where the road is rarely straight or flat, so any bends or undulations would be blind spots if the road came right up to the wall, and highly dangerous places. Drivers would have no view of an approaching pedestrian so at those points I would have to listen carefully and be prepared to get well out of the way. I hoped the sales of electric cars hadn't gone so well at that end of the country.

The taxi arrived in front of the Lands' End tourist attraction at 6:55am. I paid the driver the twenty pounds fare, climbed out and watched as he disappeared into the distance. No going back now. Clear skies overnight meant it was bitterly cold. I was keen to set off and warm up, but before I could get going, I needed the obligatory photograph of myself in front of the famous sign. Once that was done, I could announce my plans to friends and family, as so far only a handful of people knew what I was about to attempt. I had largely kept the whole thing a secret, but earlier in the week had posted on Facebook that I would be undertaking another mad ultra challenge soon and would make an announcement on Friday 1st April at 7am. My plan was to take a few photographs, make a short video, upload it all to social media and set off running. I made my way to the back of the buildings that appeared deserted. I looked out to sea then up and down the coastal path. There was absolutely no one around and I had the whole tourist extravaganza to myself. I found the iconic signpost and took the photos, then made a short video which I uploaded to Facebook. I took a last look at the sea and set off running leaving Lands' End at precisely 7am as planned.

Running past the shops and cafés towards the road, I hoped everything else would fall into place as easily over the next twenty-eight days. Then, without the shelter of the buildings, the icy blast of the freezing northerly wind hit me full on, waking me to the enormity of what I was undertaking. Ten minutes later, just to ensure I was fully roused and ready for the running, I was getting pebble-dashed in the first of three hailstone storms to hit me during the first hour. Welcome to Cornwall.

My phone started pinging with incoming messages from friends and family who had seen my social media post. Most were messages of good luck or playfully questioning my sanity. A few however, noticing the date had suggested it was some sort of April fool. In the past I had been known to play the odd practical joke so there was some justification for the scepticism. Luckily, I'd envisaged this so had asked a friend, Andrew Nicoll, one of the moderators of our running club Facebook page, to post a message on there explaining my run was genuine and circulating the details of the charity I was raising funds for. This is the message he posted.

It's April Fool's Day.

Given the date and knowing the man concerned, many of you will think the below to be an April Fool, however honestly, it's not. Earlier today Steve Fry set off on an epic adventure many of you will want to know about. Stephen's R.U.N. – L.E.J.O.G.

Today he is running 30 miles from Lands' End to Redruth, the first day of a monumental multi day challenge he hopes will take him all the way to John O' Groats.

Over the years Steve has taken on a number of epic challenges, some with myself, Dave Stephenson, and others and some solo. Events such as running 3 times around the Yorkshire 3 Peaks in a day, running the Pennine Way, the ludicrous Alpine P.T.L, the Tour of Mont Blanc, running across England, trekking the length of the Pyrenees, his grand day out running 127 miles along the canal from Liverpool to Leeds and more recently, the 42 mile Home from Holme run to support a homeless charity. These events have forged friendships, inspired some to get out and run, raised funds for numerous charities, and created lots of wonderful memories for himself and many in our club. Well now our nutty friend has set off on his biggest challenge yet and aims to cover his entire route in April. A distance of almost 1500 km or 930 miles which will mean an average of 31 miles per day. EVERY DAY for 30 DAYS.

At the age of 61 some may think that's mental, well ironically Steve is hoping to highlight the issue of men's mental health and raise funds for Andy's Man Club, a charity giving men a place to open up about issues and problems they may have. You can track his progress by following him on Twitter @ StephenFryRuns.

Dave Stephenson has set up Steve's Garmin to send a live tracking link to Twitter showing his position whilst he's running. Also, Steve says he will be posting daily updates on his Facebook page, WIFI permitting. Steve's technical (in) capabilities are legendary so let's wait and see on that score. Lol.

These were fine words from a man with whom I had undertaken many challenges over the years, not to mention hours of training. This time however I was on my own. No support crew, no pre-prepared parcels posted ahead, just me, myself, and my shadow, for company. I would be carrying everything I needed in 2 x 3 litre bum bags. These would fit around my waist and hold my entire stock of kit, clothes and equipment for my month-long meander. Everything else I needed such as food, drink and accommodation I would buy along the way. I had booked into twenty-eight guest houses or hotels to enable me to carry the absolute minimum.

By setting out on this journey, I was actually living the dream, and given the chance wouldn't you want to realise your own dreams? But how could a sixty-one-year-old man possibly think he could run almost one thousand miles in less than one month and carry everything needed in the process? It was a good question and yet there was absolutely no doubt in my mind that I would finish. Whilst that may have seemed overly optimistic or a little brash, my point of view was this. I had been running all my life, certainly for as long as I could remember, so it wasn't really the start of a journey, it was the culmination of a life spent running. A life on the run.

CHAPTER 2

Early Life

I was born in December 1960, the eldest of five children, and before I was six, my poor mother had given birth to all five of us. A family production line with Anne born in February 1962, Michael in March 1964, Maureen in May 1965 and Angela the youngest in October 1966. Actually, mum had given birth six times, as one year before I was born, she had a still born child who went the full term of the pregnancy, a boy, Peter. She was told the day before the birth that Peter was dead and yet she still had to go through all the trauma of labour, knowing there was nothing at the end of it. I can't imagine how painful and devastating that must have been. I have always been grateful that she decided to try again as a year later I came along. Mum always said I was more trouble than the other four children put together. My response was to tell her this was because my siblings all learned from my mistakes, and we would tease each other in a loving way. My sisters say I was mum's favourite. I don't know if that's true, but my mum is and always will be an absolute hero to me. To me a hero is someone who changes their world. Someone ordinary who does something extraordinary. Here was an ordinary housewife doing all the ordinary things, with next to no money, never seeking glory or prestige for herself but doing all those ordinary things brilliantly well. She would tell me often, "If a thing is worth doing, it's worth doing well," and do it well she did, seemingly all the time.

When I was young, we didn't have a car. If we wanted to go anywhere, we either caught the bus, or walked. Seven of us going on the bus was pretty costly even then, so if we went anywhere, we mostly walked at least part of the way. Now all that's OK if you're being pushed along in a pram, but once my sister Anne and brother Michael had been born, there was no longer any room in there for me. From then on, I was walking. Everywhere. On Tuesday mum would go to the post office and collect the family allowance. She would then go to the local shops as there was no supermarket nearby. She would stretch the family budget as far as she could: Fish from the fishmongers, bread from the bakers, meat from the butchers, fruit and vegetables from the greengrocer. She would move from shop to shop with me trying to keep up, which because she walked so fast was not that easy. Even from that early age it was more of a jog than a walk. She would hold my hand at the main road crossing but in between I was on my own, tagging along behind and had to keep trotting to keep up, I would be aged three and three months, and so began my association with running. On Friday when my dad got paid, we would go to a grocer's shop called Hanson's. My memory recalls this as being exactly like Arkwright's store in 'Open All Hours'. Mum would hand over a list and the shopkeeper would pack the groceries in a box. A young lad would then deliver them on his bike. Somehow, they all seemed to fit into the basket on the front. We would then rush back the quarter of a mile to try and beat him to the house and I was allowed to run ahead.

In January of 1966 I started School. St Anthony's Catholic School in Clayton, Bradford. This was almost two miles from our house. Each morning and afternoon the journey was made on foot. I was five years old. I didn't really like school and in the first week I came home at lunchtime twice, much to the dismay of the teachers. I wasn't supposed to and the first time the whole school was out looking for me. I seem to remember mum letting me stay at home for the rest of the day the first time, but on the second occasion she marched me back to the school and I was given a dressing down. Firstly, by mum, then by my teacher and finally by the headmistress, a severe looking nun called Sister Raphael.

The school was at the bottom of a big hill so on the way home each afternoon I was allowed to run, racing other boys to the top. Two boys in particular were David Bland and Peter Burgon. David lived not far from me, and Peter lived along a street just at the bottom of the hill but would still sometimes race us to the top. I became really good friends with both of these lads. We all ended up playing for the school football team, David as centre forward, Peter as right wing and me at full back. Out of the three David was the quickest sprinter, Peter and I were better at longer distances and would outrun David if we went further than fifty yards. This was pre decimalisation. David was an only child, but Peter was part of a large family with six children. As we went through school our families grew up together and there was a Fry and a Burgon in every class at St Anthony's for a few years. I also met Peter's older sister Catherine on my very first day at school. Each morning at break we would have a small bottle of milk. As this was handed out two older girls came in the class. One was holding a box of biscuits. Cadbury's chocolate fingers. Catherine was one of these girls. Over the years Catherine has supported many of my endurance runs so has spent almost sixty years looking after my nutrition.

When I was about six, I was given the responsibility of collecting our Saturday bread order from the local bakers a quarter of a mile away. Mum would give me sixpence for the two loaves and then she would time me to run there and back. I would set off as fast as I could and reach the shop breathless. I would hand over the money and a bag made of string, the lady would put the two loaves in the bag and hand it back. I would then race back as quickly as possible. Sometimes I don't think the bread was actually edible after I had finished bashing it about. I remember one snowy day mum gave me two old threepenny pieces. These were small twelve-sided brass-coloured coins, about the size of today's one pound coin. On the way I slipped in the snow and lost one of them. I returned with only one loaf. Over the years I would be sent on many errands like this, usually running there and back. When I started work aged sixteen, my boss, when learning that I was a runner, would send me to the shop for pipe tobacco and expected me to run there and back, which I did. Even now aged sixty-one, I still run rather than walk to the shop if we run out of something, however we do only live one hundred metres from a co-op.

When my two younger sisters Angela and Maureen were born, they took their places in the pram. This was a big wheeled thing made by Silver-cross. One that David Bland and I would later cut up with a hacksaw, attach to the base of an old kitchen unit, tie on a piece of old washing line for steering and hurtle off down the end of the street in our homemade Go Kart! We used our heels for brakes. What could possibly go wrong? Luckily nothing did although I wouldn't bother trying to get that past a Health and Safety committee in this day and age.

With Maureen and Angela installed in the pram, Michael and Anne had to walk but were each holding my dad's hand. I had to stay in front so mum and dad could keep an eye on me as if left to my own devices I would end up in some kind of scrape or other. So, I was running at the head of the pack and if I didn't stay two paces in front of the pram wheels, they would crash into the back of my heels. It was hard for my mum to see my little legs from the handle of the pram, especially if it was raining and the large hood was up. As the size of the family increased so my pace had to increase to avoid being run over. Thus, running became just a natural thing to do. It was very much part of my life, and that's ultimately what has led me to this point.

This point, or rather where I was at that moment on my first day, was actually on the A30 two miles outside Penzance, running in the third of the three heavy hail storms since I had left Lands' End. It was early days so I told myself to remain positive and call it a refreshing start, hoping it wouldn't be like that all the time recalling words on a poster that had hung on the wall in the office of my first boss, the pipe tobacco man.

'Out of the gloom a voice said unto me,

Smile and be happy, things could get worse.

So, I smiled, and I was happy and behold,

Things did get worse.'

I told myself that I must be mad, thinking that a prolonged spell of cold weather could mean there would be snow when I reached the Cairngorms, and hoped I was worrying unduly. We would have to wait and see. For the moment, I just needed to get to Penzance and the first of the day's refuelling points. Following the route, I made a right turn and headed down through the outskirts of Newlyn to the seafront, arriving as the sun was breaking through the clouds. There was a wonderful view across the bay and I stopped to take a photograph. As I looked out to sea, I saw two ships which reminded me of my work colleagues back in the office. The vessels were container ships, moving freight around the world and that had been my job for most of the last forty-five years. Hence, I thought of my colleagues taking up the slack whilst I enjoyed myself running the length of the country and hoped my month-long holiday wouldn't be detrimental to the country's economy. I turned left and ran along the promenade towards Penzance. Today's route from Lands' End to Redruth actually went right past the front of the hotel I'd stayed in the previous night. It had seemed daft to take all my kit with me, so I'd left most of it in my room.

I arrived at the hotel at 8:30 having covered 10.6 miles in ninety minutes. Not a bad start. I wiped my feet and removed my shoes, then made my way to my room. After removing my running kit, I placed it on the towel rail. It was damp from the hailstones as opposed to my body's own heat as I had been too cold. I drank two glasses of tap water, made a cup of tea then had a quick shower. Once dry I climbed into bed and ate breakfast as I checked social media. I noticed the tracker hadn't started so wouldn't have allowed anyone to track me but couldn't work out why. After sending my friend and IT guru Dave Stephenson a message about the tracker, I uploaded the pictures I'd taken to Facebook, then placed my phone on charge. I finished my breakfast consisting of a cherry yoghurt, a banana and a crunched-up Muesli bar, all bought from the co-op the night before, and all nicely washed down with a cup of sweet black tea. I then set my watch alarm for 30 minutes and laid down for a quick nap. I was out like a light.

I woke up after twenty minutes and felt refreshed. After retrieving my kit from the towel rail, I got dressed again, enjoying the warmth of the heated clothing. I then turned my attention to my running shoes and grabbed the hairdryer. I switched it on, placed a sticking plaster over the button and wedged it inside one of the shoes. Whilst it was drying my shoe, I packed the rest of my belongings into my two bum bags leaving two muesli bars at the top. I then moved the hairdryer into the other shoe and filled my water bottles with tap water. These were just ordinary bottles that said Harrogate spring water on the side. I had three, each a third of a litre, and packed one into each of my bags. The third went into a bottle holder that my daughter had made for me. This was attached to the left side of the waist strap of one of the bags. I then retrieved my phone and put that into a waterproof neoprene phone pouch that was attached to the right side of the waist strap of the other bum bag. I removed the hair dryer from my now dry shoes. Then I deposited the sticking plaster in the bin as I placed the hair dryer back in its wall mounted holder. Once I had laced up my steaming shoes, I carefully positioned the bum bags around my waist so they went one on top of the other but so they wouldn't go too high up my back.

Many will ask why I didn't just take a rucksack. The truth is I find it a lot more difficult to run with a rucksack. Also, I had read that the body carries weight better, the nearer it is to the hips. Having tried various options over the years I found this to be true. It felt lighter and more comfortable, rather than if it was higher up my back or near to the shoulders. Also, by loosening the waist strap of my bum bag, I could reposition it or one of them, to the front of my body, allowing access to the contents, without having to stop or remove the pack at all. Another reason was space. The more space you have the more you use. How many of us have a garage or loft that's partially filled with things we no longer use. If I carried a twenty-litre rucksack, I would fill it with twenty litres of kit. Most of it would be 'just in case' kit, i.e. kit that I didn't need. A piece of advice I read in a backpacking book years before said: After a few days on the trail, every ounce (25 grams) that you carry, will start to feel like a kilo. I had therefore been ruthless in what I had brought. If I didn't definitely need it, it stayed at home.

Refreshed and reloaded, I made my way to the hotel reception, placed the key card in a box on the counter and went through the hotel's front door. I emerged into a morning boasting a blue sky and bright sunshine and made my second start to the day.

CHAPTER 3

On the Road Again

The hotel was opposite the train station. I crossed the road and made my way through the station car park at the other side of which was a tar-macadam coastal walkway. This walkway forms part of the Southwest peninsula coastal path, the longest of the county's recognised long-distance footpaths. Once on this path I began to run, enjoying the moment. In some ways the early morning run from Lands' End to the hotel had seemed like a normal training run. Something I did most days before going to work or starting the day proper so to speak. This was the real thing now. John O Groats here I come. Somewhat excited, I started to sing.

"You take the high road and I'll take the low road and I'll be in Scotland afore ye."

Then once I ran out of words I followed up with a few lines from Kate Bush.

"I'm running on that road, I'm running up that hill, it doesn't hurt me."

I was ecstatic and at that moment everything in my world seemed perfect. My tee shirt displayed L.E. 2 J.O.G. On the front and on the back were the words 'Yorkshire Runner'. Like most Yorkshiremen, I am immensely proud of my home county, so was delighted to have that wording on my back, but it wasn't my idea. Yorkshire Runner is the name of the shop where I got the shirt printed. I was going to buy it but when the owner, Steve Brooks, a former international runner and national junior cross-country champion, heard what I was doing he kindly supplied it for free.

The sunshine was very welcome after the hailstorms of earlier and the day warmed up nicely. There was still a stiff breeze blowing into my face, but I told myself, "Hey Ho. You get what you get," and the competitor in me drove me ahead to set about passing a few dog walkers and other pedestrians in front. The path was quite busy, and I made a point of saying hello or good morning to everyone I met. Some acknowledged and replied but many didn't which I always find incredibly strange. When people don't respond to a friendly greeting, I think to myself 'Come on, friend. We are all on life's journey together. Will it cost you anything to reply?'

After a few miles the path ran through a car park. I saw a cyclist sitting on a wall. He was eating something from a bowl with a fork. I wished him "Bon Appetit." He smiled back and nodded. I had passed him before I noticed the two bulky panniers on his bike. They made me wonder if he was going to John O Groats, or maybe he was heading south on his way to the finish. I regretted not stopping and asking. I would have liked to congratulate him if he was on the home run, and I resolved to stop and chat to people I suspected were fellow End to Enders.

The path emerged from the car park and joined the coastal road. After a further three hundred metres it turned left onto a quiet lane, then shortly after, left again on to a bridleway. For anyone unfamiliar with this term, a bridleway is a route permitting horse riding, cycling and pedestrians, but not motorised vehicles. I heard wheels behind me and turned to see the cyclist from the car park fifteen minutes ago. I asked him if he was doing LEJOG, which is an abbreviated term for going from Lands' End to John O' Groats all in one journey. He confirmed that was his intention, although when he reached Bristol, he was going into Wales and taking a more circuitous route than I planned to. We travelled together side by side chatting for a few minutes, initially acknowledging how nice it was that the hedgerow to our right was sheltering us from the chilly headwind. After a few hundred metres we shook hands, and he cycled off ahead. A few minutes later I reached the end of the bridleway, arriving at a bend in a road. Turning left I went through an underpass that carried the busy A30. I could hear the traffic overhead as it whizzed by. At the end of the underpass the road became a narrow lane and soon all was quiet again as I left the motorised mayhem behind. However, it was not quiet for long as after a few moments the roaring of a diesel engine closed on me from behind. Technically I was on the wrong side of the pathless road, and I turned to see a parcel delivery van speeding up the lane. The driver had his phone, or some other similar device, in one hand and was holding the steering wheel with the other. He glanced down to the handheld object. There was no time for me to cross so I stopped running and pushed backwards into the hedgerow as far as I could. At the last minute the driver looked up. Then, having seen me, swerved slightly to the right holding a forefinger up as some kind of acknowledgement or apology.

He passed by and I moved myself out of the hedge then felt my new tee shirt catch and click on the branches.

"Bugger" I said out loud to no one but myself.

"This has to last me a month" and then set off running again. The road was slightly uphill, going round a long sweeping bend to my right. So, by being on the left-hand side, although I had my back to the traffic I could see more of the road ahead. I had to work a little bit harder up the hill and run a little bit further because of the bend. Suddenly I heard the almost imperceptible fizz of a bike approaching at speed and immediately three cyclists came down the road in quick succession. If I had been on the other side of the lane, it's likely we would have collided. It reminded me I was following a cycle route and would have to ensure I concentrated constantly.

Now here I am going to potentially alienate any cycling fans but please hear me out. I have nothing against bikes. I have a couple of bikes myself, and have many friends who cycle, several to a very high standard. However, in the dog eat dog, law of the road jungle world we live in, it's the poor old pedestrian who's at the bottom of the food chain. So, whilst I know cyclists get a rough deal from other vehicles, believe me it is the poor plodding pedestrian who is catered for less and less. If walking or running on a country lane where there's no path and a high or overgrown hedgerow, in some ways bikes are more dangerous than a car to a foot traveller, as you will usually hear a car whatever the weather. You may hear a bike if it's a calm still day, but if it's slightly windy or there's a lot of background noise, bikes can be upon you in a breath with devastating consequences for both runner and rider. In fact, the cyclist is likely to come off just as badly, if not worse than the pedestrian as they are travelling faster and have further to fall. So, whilst I don't want to spoil anyone's fun, sport, pastime or pleasure, we all have to be mindful of the possibility that there may be other road users around the next bend we can't see or hear. They have just as much right to use the road. My concern is that sometimes a dedicated cyclist will get their head down and the wattage output up, but in doing so they give no thought to the fact that around the next bend there could be a slower sauntering soul who can neither see nor hear them. I have had numerous near misses with those I now refer to as 'Silent Assassins.'

I continued on a series of quiet country lanes, following the well waymarked route without incident and arrived at the outskirts of Hayle. As I approached the town centre, the footpath was closed as there were some major road works. A diversion sign pointed me left but I must have misread it as I ended up in an ASDA car park at the wrong side of a narrow river. I retraced my steps and realised that I had turned too early. Sixteen miles and I had just made my first navigation error and wondered how many of those there would be before I finished. I ran along a pleasant strip of grassland between the river and a road before turning left over a bridge.

This crossed the river that flowed into what appeared to be a manmade lake. Once over the river, my route turned right onto a long driveway to a sailing club. The driveway had a walking and cycle track running beside it and was lined with rhododendrons. It was really pleasant. The running was easy, the scenery pretty and I had made excellent progress with eighteen miles done in total and it was only 11am.

The cycleway went around the head of the lake, bringing me back out to the main road I ran alongside earlier. The route then went straight across the road and up an unmade track at the back of a row of houses. Suddenly things became a bit more urban. At the top of the hill I turned left and down a normal residential street with semi-detached houses on both sides. Not quite what I was expecting, and it seemed at odds with the path to the sailing club only fifteen minutes earlier, but at least it was quiet. At the end of that street, a right and then a left turn, brought me to a roundabout on a dual carriageway with the entrance to an industrial estate directly opposite. I crossed the dual carriageway via a pedestrian crossing and stopped at the entrance to the estate and scoured the map thinking I was in the wrong place. My route was hidden by a large truck parked near the entrance to the estate. It was approaching 12 o'clock and there were several trucks parked along the lane with drivers eating lunch. This reminded me that I should be eating, and I munched on one of the cereal bars which I washed down with a bottle of water. I had one bottle left and was going to need to refill my water supply soon.

Another hour went by as I weaved my way along and shared my route with all manner of small birds. Gold finches, sparrows, blue tits and birds I didn't recognise all made an appearance as they darted in and out of blooming bushes bordering these twisting country lanes. Views were limited because of the high hedgerows but the bird life I saw was more than a fair exchange. Eventually I met a lady walking her dog and asked her how far it was to Cambourne. My stomach was telling me it was lunch time. She told me Cambourne was only about two miles away. I then remembered my tracker wasn't working so asked her if she was on twitter. When she said yes, I explained what I was doing and asked if she could help me by posting something to say she had seen me running and to tag me in so followers would know how I was doing. I provided her with my twitter name and thanked her as she turned into her gateway. I ran the remaining two miles to Cambourne arriving about twenty minutes later at 1.15pm.

The town was bigger and busier than I had expected. Eventually I found a small café and went in for a well-earned lunch. I checked my messages whilst waiting and saw the tweet from the lady I'd just met. It had already been liked by several of my family and numerous friends who seemed eager for news. This also reminded me that the tracker hadn't worked so I went through various checks as my lunch arrived. A ham salad sandwich, a piece of carrot cake, a pot of tea and a chocolate milkshake. Excellent. I put my phone on to charge and tucked into my meal.

Fifty minutes later, with both runner and technical apparatus recharged, I was ready to leave. As I was paying, I asked the lady if she knew the best way to get to my hotel in Redruth which was still about 3 miles away.

"I'm staying at the Inn for all seasons," I said.

"Oh yes, I can recommend the roast chicken."

She explained that she visited regularly for Sunday lunch and gave me directions.

I stepped out of the café and was momentarily blinded by bright afternoon sunshine. To use a footballing analogy, this day had been 'a game of two halves.' Frosty at first but warmed up nicely in the second half. I tried to run but my legs had stiffened up and I was forced to walk for the next ten minutes, although any running I had managed to do at that point, would at best have been intermittent. The route was along a busy main road and the pavement was thronged with shoppers. Also, there were cars parked at the curb all the way along the road so there wasn't really anywhere to escape to and run. Eventually I came to a major road junction where the pavement was much wider, and I was able to pass people. Once across this, I got back into my running but now had less than two miles to go. The route went uphill along the side of a busy dual carriage way but with a wide grass verge on my side of the road. I passed a large school with a queue of empty double decker buses entering the school which appeared to be about to finish for the day. The queue of buses extended from within the school grounds back onto the road and blocked the inside lane of the carriageway blocking my path in the process. I counted over thirty buses and was taken aback, pondering just how much it must cost each day to hire them.

I turned off the dual carriageway and followed a small path that went behind a hedge, then across grassland to what looked like a dead end but led to a gap in another hedge. This emerged onto another busy road I had to cross. According to my map I was only two hundred metres from my hotel, and I could see what I thought was the turn into the hotel car park but turned out to be the entrance to Aldi. My hotel was another one hundred metres further on. I ran the last few paces of my first day, the wind still blowing in my face and arrived just before 3pm having covered thirty-one miles. Day one done. Only another twenty-seven to go.

I checked into my room and took a much-needed shower. After that I washed my running kit, all of which I wrung out as much as possible before placing it on the radiator. I got dressed in what I referred to as my going out gear. I then walked back to the Aldi and bought supplies for breakfast plus a packet of biscuits for the afternoon. I noticed just how busy the road was. It was a dual carriageway and the start of my route the next day. There was a good wide path at that point, but a mile further along it went to a single carriageway with no footpath for about five miles to the small town of Chacewater. I thought I might have to consider an alternative because this looked a bit too busy. I didn't want to take any chances on such a busy road. I've had one major traffic accident in my life and that was enough for me.

CHAPTER 4

Nine Lives of a Volvo Crash Test Dummy

In 1993 I had a really bad car crash on one of the country's busiest roads. This caused my work colleagues to christen me 'The Volvo Crash Test Dummy.' after the Volvo adverts from the 1980's. Here's what happened.

It was a lovely sunny July day. I was driving in the outside lane of the A1. It was about 11am and the road was busy. I was approaching a roundabout at a place called Norman's Cross near Peterborough. Today, the road is now a four-lane motorway without any roundabouts, but in those days was a two-lane dual carriageway with a series of three roundabouts in less than one mile. I was in the outside lane. As I pulled away from the middle roundabout, I saw on the opposite carriageway a long line of stationery traffic. It was East of England show day and the entrance to the show was a left turn off the roundabout I had just passed. The two lanes of traffic stretched back a long way. On my inside was a Dutch articulated lorry. I had been driving alongside this lorry for about half a mile as the traffic in front of me was backed up nose to tail. My car was level with the truck's cab, and behind my left shoulder was all thirteen and a half metres of the attached trailer. I was underneath the truck's wing mirror, a blind spot because it was a left-hand drive vehicle. Thinking about it now, it was a stupid place to be.

Without warning or indicating the truck started to pull across into my lane, crushing my car against the safety barriers between the two carriageways. Almost immediately there was actually a short break in the barriers giving access to the southbound carriageway for emergency vehicles. I was driving at 40mph and had three choices. If I went through the gap in the barriers I would plough into the stationary traffic, if I did nothing or tried to brake, I would plough head long into the end of the barrier where it restarted. This would most likely push the engine or part of it into me, or I could steer left and try to accelerate in front of the truck before I hit the end of the barrier. I wrestled with the steering wheel turning it slightly to the left, fighting to hold my line and stay on the Northbound carriageway. The truck, seemingly still unaware of my presence, kept coming across into my lane, pushing me to the right. I hit the accelerator and sped in front of the truck and momentarily thought I had made it to safety. That was until the front right corner of the truck's cab caught the back left corner of my car, just after the crash barriers restarted. The result of this was to turn my car sideways and suddenly it was being pushed up the road by the lorry.

The drama didn't stop there as my engine was still in forward gear, so the car then smashed into bars that were welded to the side of another articulated lorry that was travelling in the inside lane. The Dutch vehicle having pulled out to pass this truck, was now completely in the outside lane, as was the back half of my car. As the Dutch truck continued forward it spun my car around to complete a one-hundred-and-eighty-degree turn ending up facing the traffic that had been behind me. At this point the bonnet of my car had crumpled into the shape of a triangle in front of my shattered windscreen. I could see nothing. Horror-struck I realised the car was now facing the wrong way and although I was braking as hard as I could, I was about to be heading blindly down the middle of the two lanes of traffic that had been following me. This wasn't likely to end well. Suddenly the back end of my car lifted off the ground and immediately became wedged between these two massive trucks. It felt like the world was raining down on top of me. Glass flew everywhere, and the sound of twisting metal scraping against more metal filled my ears. I let go of the steering wheel as I no longer had any control of the car which was now being dragged backwards. This turned out to be a good thing, as a few seconds later everything came to a standstill. The driver of the truck in the inside lane, seeing what was happening, pulled off the carriageway and into a lay-by to get out of the way. This was really lucky because in those days there was no hard shoulder on that road and the laybys were few and far between. Also, really lucky for me was the fact that a bar that is welded to the back of all trailers to prevent cars going under the wheels, had become wedged into the rear wheel arch of my car as I had been spun round. The driver in the inside lane had therefore unknowingly towed me and the remaining wreckage of my vehicle to safety.

When I came to a stop, my car, an Audi 80, was a pile of twisted metal. There was neither glass nor tyres left on or in the car. All four wings, the bonnet, and boot were all just twisted pieces of metal. The two passenger side doors were crushed into the seats. The door behind me had a large gouge in the outer skin caused by the truck's rear bar that had caught the door before wedging in the wheel arch. Miraculously the driver's door was unmarked. I opened it and climbed out completely unscathed. I will never forget my dad's words to me when I told him what had happened.

"Well son. You're going to have to be careful from now on. I think you've used all of your nine lives now."

First there was the time I repaired the electric fire. This was fixed to the wall in the corner of the dining area in our kitchen. The fire ran diagonally across the corner joining both walls. It had a guard grill on the front and a small metal switch at the right-hand side. It had two heating elements, one on top of the other. Each element was a wire coil that looked like a spring about a foot long. The top element was broken. I have no idea when or how this happened, but it didn't work. So, for some reason I decided to fix it. I was three years old, and I believe this is my earliest memory. Mum was cooking at the other end of the room. It was time for tea, so she was busy. If I could just reach the element, I am sure I could fix this and won't mum be pleased when I make it work. It was obvious to me the two ends of the element just needed joining up. I put my small hands through the metal grill and held the two broken ends together in my right hand. So far, so good. I then reached across my body with my left hand and flicked the switch. Hey presto! It worked, and I still have the burn scars to prove it. Eventually the ambulance man arrived resplendent in his blue jacket and matching flat topped peaked cap. He came in happily puffing on his pipe surveying the scene. I was seated on the sofa with a wet tea towel wrapped around my sizzled hand and seared wrist as between sobs, my poor mum fought back tears to tell him what had happened. When she'd finished her struggle to tell the tale, he removed his pipe and replied,

"Well I don't know why you're crying love; he should be bloody dead."

Shortly after this my dad pulled the fire out of the wall along with the structure holding it in place. These were breeze blocks and a timber frame. This was before household waste sites or people hired skips so all the debris was stacked in the back garden until another use could be found. How exciting and more for a young lad and his mates to play with. So, we did and sometime later myself and Peter Jennings built a small shelter with some of the wood resting on bricks and blocks. I sat underneath and all was great until it wasn't and the whole thing came crashing down on my head. Of course, this meant another ambulance ride to the infirmary to have my head stitched up. Very painful. Of course a week or so later mum had to pack the pram and take us all on the bus again to the infirmary so the stitches could be removed. All in all, I had my head stitched up three times before I was eight. If this happened now, relatives and friends would call me Rambo. My dad just called me a daft apeth. However, if you think that's daft, wait until you hear about the holiday to Bridlington.

Twas the night before our holidays. The cases were packed and stored under the bed I should have been sleeping in but I was too excited to sleep and was out of bed rummaging in the cases. Exploring, I came upon treasure to a child. Sweets. I opened them and ate one. They tasted great, so I had another. With everyone else asleep there was no one to share them with, so I just kept eating them until they were all gone. I never gave a thought to how much trouble I was going to be in when mum or dad found out. To this day if I open a packet of sweets, biscuits or a bar of chocolate, I will usually eat most of the packet in the one sitting. I don't actually remember what my mum said. In fact, I don't remember much at all but believe that having finished my midnight feast I laid down and went to sleep. What I do know is that I had eaten my way to a whole heap of trouble.

Looking back, it's hard to distinguish dreams from reality. In my dream I was flying along horizontally on my back at speed whilst looking up at bright lights, lots of bright lights. One after the other. In reality I was staring up at a series of fluorescent lights illuminating a long corridor as I sped along horizontally, supported by a hospital trolley that rushed me from an ambulance to the intensive care unit at Bradford Royal Infirmary. I loved the taste of Aspirin, but you're not supposed to eat the whole bottle in one go. I can remember a burning sensation in the back of my throat as hospital staff forced a plastic tube down into my stomach, pumping out the contents. I know my throat was sore for days, and although we were still allowed to go to Bridlington I was confined to bed.

Eventually I was well enough to be allowed outside but only with mum or dad present because apparently, I was really quite ill. It was towards the end of the holiday that I was allowed to go to the beach. I can remember having a new orange towelling shirt. I think mum bought me the orange one to make me easier to spot as I was prone to exploring, or as she called it, wandering off. As we walked on the beach, I got ahead of everyone. I remember there was a massive oil slick which I avoided by walking a higher line on the drier sand, whilst my parents and siblings stayed closer to the sea. They mustn't have seen the oil and continued until eventually they were faced with either walking through it or turning back and taking the route I'd taken. I arrived at a wooden walkway which cut across the sand and climbed up then began to make my way along it. Looking back towards my family, I waved and shouted to them, telling them to hurry up. I continued, looking over the edge as the arid sand became firmer, then slightly moist and was eventually covered over by the sea. Mum and dad were waving, I waved back. Sea spray splashed me as I enjoyed the fresh air. I looked back at my family again. Dad was shouting. He seemed cross. I was thinking one of my siblings must have walked in the oil. I was glad I hadn't got oil on me as I didn't want to be in trouble again. I kept walking, looking at the clear blue sea in front of me. Glancing at my family again I saw Dad had now left the others and was running fast in my direction. Don't go that way Dad I thought, you will get covered in oil. Oh no, too late! He ran towards me through the treacle textured tar. It was then I realised he was chasing me, and it was a game. He was trying to get to the end of this wooden jetty before me. I set off running as fast as my little legs would go. Suddenly there was an unbelievably loud shriek.

Have you ever heard your name screamed? I mean really screamed, a noise so piercing it seems to make all other sounds stop and time stand still. The call of Raksha, the mother wolf from Jungle Book, protecting her cubs. Somehow my mum seemed to have made the earth stop on its axis and I dare not move another step. I turned to face her and our eyes locked together. Her steely stare sent signals, warning me that all was not well. If I didn't stay put, I knew I would be in deep trouble but had no idea why. I'd been heading for the edge of a jetty that went thirty yards out into the sea. Realising I was oblivious to this Mum had gained vital seconds. This enabled my breathless father to arrive in the nick of time and pluck me from the jetty edge into the safety of his arms. Too tired to chastise me, he lifted me up and hugged me to his chest. "Dad! You've got oil all over my new tee shirt now." I don't remember being allowed out of the caravan again that holiday.

Dad was always up early and on Saturdays, if he wasn't working, he would take me hiking with one of his workmates who had a car. He loved to get out on the moors and would carry me on his shoulders up to many of the high points in our local area. Baildon and Ilkley Moor, Beamsley Beacon, Simon's Seat and many of the hills around Wharfedale. I loved it and felt special, but it was probably because I was awake, and the others weren't. Sometimes we would go later, and all the family would come. This was difficult with no car. I remember one trip which ended with me having another near-death experience when I fell down Otley Chevin.

We got a lift to the car park at the top of the Chevin, known as surprise view. From this point the whole of lower Wharfedale opens out in front of you and on a clear day you can see York Minster, or so they say. We set off walking down into Otley, descending the steep grassy bank to reach the woods. Here the path joins some old Victorian stone steps set into the wooded hillside. Once again, I was out in front. I would have been seven or eight as we started down the steps that day. I have no idea what happened, if I just went too fast, if I slipped, or tripped, but before I knew it, my feet were moving so fast I couldn't stop and suddenly I was off the ground. Anyone who has ever been down those steps knows just how steep and rocky they are. Once I lost touch with Terra Firma it was unlikely to end well. Behind me my mum and sisters screamed as my dad shouted at me to slow down. How could I do that? I was actually flying through the air and could do nothing at all to stop myself. Later dad described the scene to me.

"You were airborne" were the words he used.

In front of me was a man walking up. I remember this as though it was yesterday. He had blond hair, a light-coloured polo style shirt and a grey jacket over his shoulder. Hearing the screams, he looked up. I can clearly see him throw his jacket on the floor, spread his arms out wide and brace himself for impact. Somehow, he caught me, the force spinning him around and he fell sideways, still clutching me in his arms. He sat me down on the ground and reassured me by repeating;

"You're alright, you're alright."

I didn't feel alright, in fact I felt quite sick and sat there crying. My family arrived and my sobbing Mum hugged me. Dad shook the man's hand and thanked him. I don't think they asked his name, and he went on his way up the hill. We all sat down on the spot for a few minutes, trying to take in what had just happened. Everyone except Dad was crying. If I am making it sound dramatic that's because it was. It could have had a very different ending but thankfully it didn't. Someone somewhere was watching over me. Eventually we continued down into the town. We were all still shaken but we howled with laughter when out of nowhere a pigeon landed on my Dad's head. Now that is lucky.

Sometimes In quiet moments of contemplation I think about that man. I wonder who he was, where he was going and what became of him. I would have loved to have the opportunity of meeting him in later life. An unsung hero who's name I never knew. He possibly saved my life. He certainly saved me from another trip to hospital, although by now I'd probably qualified for some kind of frequent flyer discount, and you can guess it wasn't long before I was back there again, but this time for a longer stay, however more of that later or we are never going to get to John O'Groats.

CHAPTER 5

More Energy Required

Day 2 – Saturday 2nd April 2022 – Redruth to Bodmin
On the evening of my first day, I had spoken to a few Redruth residents who confirmed that when the road turned from dual carriageway to single carriageway it was not advisable to run along it. I gave this quite a bit of thought as I was planning to set off early and it was Saturday so maybe it wouldn't be that busy. In the end I decided not to take the risk, so I plotted a safer but slightly longer alternative. This would meet up with my original route at Chacewater and I estimated it as about one mile longer. However, it should certainly be more scenic as it was along a series of bridleways, forest trails and country lanes. Whilst it looked an interesting route, it would require careful navigation, unlike my first day which had been mostly along a recognised and well waymarked cycle route and I'd barely used the map. Today was going to be completely different.

By 7am I was running down the hotel driveway, too early for my hotel breakfast which didn't start until 8am. I made do with yoghurt, blueberries and a crunched-up muesli bar purchased from the Aldi store the day before. A light drizzle meant day two was another refreshing start but it was nowhere near as cold as the previous morning. Turning left out of the hotel I retraced my steps from the day before. After fifty metres I turned left again, into a deserted industrial estate. Almost immediately the way was unclear. There was supposed to be a footpath, but it wasn't evident as I entered the estate, so I got my phone out and opened up the mapping tool. There was no footpath sign where the path should be. Instead, there was what looked like a driveway to a private house. I walked across the road looking at the map again, as a few droplets of drizzle landed on the screen.

This was a relatively new phone for me. I'd managed for years with an old Nokia, but having decided to take on this challenge, I'd invested the price of my first car, in a not quite as old iPhone. I could now download maps onto this phone. This made a lot of sense as opposed to having to carry all the different maps. It would also be better than carrying my old phone and additional mapping device, adding weight and possibly some other kind of charging adapter. So somewhat overdue I had ushered in the twenty first century and bought an iPhone eight. I purchased and downloaded the Ordnance Survey map app and road tested it several times in the spring. It was clear and easy to use. Another brilliant function was that by pinching the screen or zooming out, the map scale changed, so I could switch from the 1:50000 scale to much more detailed 1:25000 scale and my plotted route would just switch automatically to the new scale. No more painstaking hours at my kitchen table with a magnifying glass, maps cello-taped together and a series of highlighters to mark my route. Fantastic.

So here I was at just after 7am on a drizzly Saturday morning, in a bright orange tee shirt and shorts, standing suspiciously at the entrance to what looked like the driveway of a private house. I had my expensive new phone in my hand and pinched the screen for all I was worth. Nothing was happening. For some reason I couldn't switch to the larger scale map to see if the path actually went through this garden or not. As no one was around to ask, I would just have to take a chance and hope I was right or that they didn't have some kind of man-eating guard dog. Nervous and yet frustrating moments and I was peeved that having paid all this money I couldn't get it to work. I took a few hesitant paces down the drive and saw that off to the right there was indeed a small path. It was a little overgrown at first but then cleared and emerged onto playing fields. Great, I was up and running but when I arrived onto the playing fields there was no visible path. I looked to the corner in the direction I thought I should be going, but the early morning drizzle limited the visibility. I lifted the phone again just to confirm I was heading in the right direction. Frustratingly as I did this the phone's screen saver kicked in and I had to punch in my code. Two or three droplets of rain landed on the screen, and this must have affected one of the numbers of my passcode because the phone would not open. No matter how many times I tapped one particular number of the code it didn't register, and the phone refused to work.

I stood there for two minutes trying hard to ensure the screen was dry and my fingers were warm enough to make the touch screen register. Eventually I managed to dry it and my fingers properly, enabling me to open the app again. This time it worked, and the little red arrow confirmed I was on the right line but it was now over fifteen minutes since I'd left the hotel and had only covered a distance that should have taken me less than five. I hoped this wasn't going to be an ongoing feature of the day, or it would take me about twenty hours to reach my hotel in Bodmin.

Once across the playing fields I emerged onto a residential street and my route was clear and obvious, continuing onto a tar surfaced snicket. The snicket ran downhill bringing me to Redruth railway station. Suddenly my way was no longer obvious, and I was now back on the phone. I had this inside a plastic zip lock bag, and that was inside a waterproof phone holder fastened to the strap of my bum bag so it was easily accessible. If I was running the phone was perfectly dry but the touch screen would not work whilst inside the plastic bag so had to be removed. I tried putting my hands into the bag, but my hands were damp and all this did was make the inside of the bag damp. It seems unbelievable now to say this, but

I realised that all my testing of the mapping app had been on dry days. I had not tested it in the wet. I had never given a thought to the screen not working when it was raining. It never happened with my old Nokia.

I asked a man walking his dog if he could direct me to the cemetery. He looked at me with suspicion until I explained that a bridleway I needed started near the gates and he then kindly showed me the way. Once on the bridleway, navigating was easy for a while. The bridleway was a mile long and emerged on a quiet lane. I turned left and followed the lane to the village of St Day. Here I joined another bridleway which climbed up to a ridge forming one side of a steep horseshoe shaped valley. Across the valley I could see a number of small chimneys that reminded me I was in tin mining country.

The running was pleasant, and the scenery was pretty with bright yellow gorse on the opposite hillside. At a path junction I had to stop to recheck the map. The drizzle had stopped and the day was drying out. However, the battery on my phone was down to 50%. How could this have happened? It had been fully charged when I'd set off and I had only been going about forty minutes. I still had another thirty miles to cover. I found the correct path which descended almost two hundred feet to the valley bottom. There was a broad track there that ran the length of the valley, and I could see a runner making his way along the broad flat track. It looked easy to run on as opposed to my route which had suddenly become significantly more difficult. To reach the valley bottom I had to negotiate a series of small boulder fields. Boulder fields is a slight exaggeration. It was in fact a series of scree strewn sections. Each of these looked like the rock had been blasted into small tennis ball size lumps that were not conducive to running over. A turned ankle or twisted knee at this stage could prove disastrous so I tip-toed over the testing technical terrain like Bambi on roller skates and was grateful to arrive at the valley bottom unscathed.

My route went straight across the broad track and immediately headed up the other side of the valley, entering a walled pathway that wound its way up the hillside. To begin with it was clear of underfoot debris as it climbed through woodland, and although steep it was pleasant. I could see horses' hooves in the soil so I was a little surprised when halfway up the hill I had to climb over a series of fallen trees, then like a long-limbed limbo dancer with arthritis, had to scramble under low hanging branches. Eventually after negotiating the challenging woodland assault course, I arrived onto a narrow road that contoured around the steep hillside. After consulting the map again, I turned left and 50 metres later, right onto another bridleway. Again there was evidence of recent use by horses and the fresh floor contents stuck like cement to the bottom of my running shoes. After a few hundred metres it was like running in builders' boots and I was forced to stop and use a stick to scrape off as much of the sweet-smelling sticky substance as I could.

After about a mile along this muddy track I arrived at another road. Here I was to turn right and about a mile later this would bring me to Chacewater but, to ensure I was correct, I checked the map again. I was shocked to see the phone battery was showing only 21% charge remaining. How could that be? Suddenly the phone pinged, and a message popped up saying power was now down to 20%. I opened the phone and turned everything off except my map app, then headed off to Chacewater hoping there would be a café where I could recharge the phone. It was evident that the battery was running down very quickly. After one hour and twenty minutes and only seven miles I arrived in Chacewater rejoining the original route, but the phone battery was now down to 14%. It was not yet 8.30am and there was no café to be seen. There was a pub but that of course was still closed so I looked around for a shop. It crossed my mind that unless I could find somewhere to charge the phone I was stuck.

Twenty metres from where I was standing, there was a man unloading fruit from a van. I called out to him asking if there was a café nearby. He spoke. "No but you are welcome to have a coffee here," and he headed through a door that was partially hidden by his van. I followed him into a short narrow passage to another door that opened into a courtyard that was covered along one side. The covered section was supported by six stone pillars. There were about a dozen tables laid end to end along the length of the covered area. Each table was stocked with all kinds of fruits and vegetables, whilst against the back wall of this covered area was a row of fridges and freezers all stocked with meats, cheeses and dairy products. There was a break in the middle of the row where a desk stood that held various piles of papers, a radio, a coffee machine, a stack of paper cups, and the owner's phone which was charging.

"Help yourself to Coffee," he said and pointed to the machine. I thanked him and told him what I was doing, then asked if it was possible to charge my phone, explaining how my maps were all on there but the battery was almost out. He immediately unplugged his phone and put mine on to charge. All the time he was emptying boxes of stock and setting it all out on the tables and all the time he asked me about my run, about the charity I was running for, about me, what I did for a job, my family. We talked about the village and about lock down and how it had affected the place. In the few minutes I had been in the area I had noticed that some of the shops were closed and derelict.

I finished my coffee and felt I should be on my way. It had been twenty minutes since I'd arrived and I was starting to stiffen up, but my phone was still less than 50% charged. That was not going to be enough so I waited another ten minutes, trying to keep warm. Eventually it was time to leave but when I tried to pay the man for the coffee, he refused to accept anything. After he directed me on the first part of my route and wished me good luck for the rest of my journey. In turn I wished him good luck with his business. He obviously worked hard and was trying his best to cater for the needs of the locals. The place was a real oasis, it was well stocked and he deserved the local people's support. What he was doing was more than running a business. He was providing a public service to all the people who didn't have transport. I hope they knew the value of what they had in their midst and gave him their custom.

My route now consisted of a pathless B road for two miles. It was now around 9.15 am on Saturday morning so there wasn't a lot of traffic, but what there was came hurtling along as if auditioning for a grand prix. I didn't enjoy the next twenty minutes and was glad to reach a small retail park where the footpath restarted for one hundred metres going to a large roundabout at a junction with the A390 and a 'park and ride' car park. Once across this I joined another quiet lane where the running was easy and carefree. Two miles of running through wonderful woodland brought me to the valley bottom and the running got tougher and complicated. For two hours a series of tracks, trails, twists and turns eventually brought me to the back of the service area on the A30 at Carland Cross. It was 11am and I thought about stopping for lunch but the running was easy, the weather perfect and I really was enjoying the day. This made it seem wrong to stop so I pressed on for another hour.

At exactly 12 noon I arrived at the village of Summercourt. The village store and Post Office sold hot food so obviously a traditional Cornish pasty was the order of the day. Once again, the phone was completely out of charge and the shop owner kindly allowed me to use his electric and charge it up. There was not a lot of room in the shop, which was quite busy for Saturday lunch time, so I stayed outside sitting on a stack of bread baskets. Before I started to eat, I bought a litre of water, drinking half the contents immediately. After the Cornish pasty, I had a piece of fruit cake and washed this down with a cup of tea. Almost as soon as I finished my meal it started to drizzle so I went back into the shop to retrieve my phone. Unfortunately, it was still only 50% charged. I didn't think that would be enough based on the morning's performance and there was no obvious place to recharge it between here and Bodmin. I would definitely need to use the maps later in the day, so I bought another cup of tea, two snicker bars and another litre of water for the afternoon then returned to my breadbasket bench. I put on my rain jacket and bottoms, wrapped my gloved hands around my warm drink and hunkered down in the dreary drizzle to see out a further twenty minutes before reclaiming the phone and hitting the road again.

Anyone who had witnessed the finely tuned athlete that entered the shop at noon, could have been forgiven for not recognising the man with the tin legs who emerged in full wet weather gear an hour later. My legs had stiffened up so much I walked along the street with a similar gate to war time fighter pilot Douglas Barder and laughed to myself saying, "Good God man, this is only your second day. What will you look like in another week?" It took a good half mile before I got running but once I did, I was fine. I followed the main street out of town and reached another bridge over the A30. After crossing it I stopped to remove my waterproofs as I had started to warm up. The sky however showed signs that rain was on the way again, so I tied the jacket around my waist to keep it handy. Following a series of country lanes and quiet roads that more or less ran parallel to the A30, I eventually reached the small town of Indian Queens. This was significant for the fact that Indian Queens was the end of day one in a journey of 18 days laid out in a book I had read whilst researching my route.

The book is called 'End to End Cycle Route, A Safer Way' by Royston Wood, and I would be largely following the route in his book. I had been forced to make a few route changes in places where I had been unable to get accommodation, and a few more where I considered that even the 'safe' cycling route to be too unsafe for a pedestrian. The traditional cycling route between the two well-known points is almost exclusively on public roads. Wood claimed to have cycled the traditional route several times and having more than one near miss with vehicles. Then, shortly after successfully finishing one of his LEJOG journeys, he read about another cyclist who died on the A30 when a lorry driver fell asleep at the wheel and killed him. This prompted Wood to seek out a safe route and having found something suitable he put pen to paper. Where possible this safe route utilises canal tow paths, disused railway lines, woodland bridle paths or genuinely quiet country roads. This was the route I would largely be following. Thus, having reached Indian Queens, I only had another seventeen sections of his route to go. Unfortunately averaging over 50 miles each day was a bit too much for me to run. I mean come on, I am on holiday after all. I would therefore go along at a more sedate pace of thirty two miles per day and take a little longer over my running excursion.

I passed through the small town before turning right onto a network of disused railway tracks. Railway tracks are usually flat, so I hoped for more easy running all the way to the next village which was called Roche. Here, after crossing the A30 again, I'd join the 'old coach road'.

The sky grew darker and it started to drizzle again. The drizzle matured into heavier rain and the tracks, which were a mixture of mud and gravel, became a sea of silt, stubbornly sticking to the soles of my running shoes like crusting concrete. This was worse than the earlier equine excrement as stone filled sludge encased the soles and outer edges of my shoes. It flicked up behind me as I ran. It stuck to my shorts, the backs of my legs and eventually the insides of my calves and knees. The bits around my knees then acted like the serrated edge of a bread knife as one knee passed close to the other knee during the running motion. As they passed close together the small stone fragments moved against the other knee and gradually began to rub each other raw. Every few hundred metres I had to stop and scrub the soles on vegetation at the side of the trail.

I met a couple walking in the other direction with their hoods pulled up tight and their dog, a springer spaniel, looking decidedly bedraggled and uninterested as it slowly but faithfully followed. The damp dog's demeanour seemed to indicate that he thought the bad weather was going to be with us for a while. Eventually I arrived at a junction in the path. Which way? I took out my phone. Once again my hands were wet and when I pressed the touch screen nothing happened. Very frustrating. Left, or right? I took a chance and went left which seemed the right direction. I looked at my watch noting the time and distance covered. Sixteen minutes later something was wrong. I came to the end of the track onto a small road and asked a walker if I was on the right route. He opened out his own waterproofed paper version of the map and showed me where I was. Nope I was miles away and should have turned right earlier and then immediately left, arriving shortly after at a different road. This meant I had run two miles in the wrong direction. I retraced my steps to the junction and went the right way. Very frustrating. An extra four needless miles.

Once back on the correct route, the road took me to the village of Roche. From there it went back across to the other side of the A30 via a surfaced, pink coloured cycle path next to the road and a busy roundabout. Thankfully it had now stopped raining. I joined the old coach road. This was long and straight. It stretched out in front of me for the next few miles and unlike the busy A30 there was not a single car on it. In fact, it was deserted apart from a lady walking about two hundred metres ahead. As I got closer, I could see she was rather a large lady and was wearing a heavy woollen overcoat. The sun was out again, and it was now warm and pleasant. I said hello as I passed, and she returned my greeting. She smiled and then said. "I wish I was as fit as you, how can I get fit?" I stopped and walked, chatting to her for a few minutes.

She explained that she was really trying desperately to lose weight and went for a five mile walk every day with lots of clothes on. I told her to stick at it. "It's not easy when you get to my age", she said, adding "I'm sixty now". I laughed and told her I was sixty-one, but I don't think she believed me and just looked at me in a questioning sort of way. I wished her good luck and set off running again.

Three miles out of Bodmin the rain started again. My energy levels had plummeted, and I had eaten the last of my food. The old coach road merged into a busy A road that connected the A30 to Bodmin and suddenly there was no path. There was a series of narrow strips of long grass pressing up to the trees and hedges on either side of the road. This appeared to go on for almost two miles to arrive in the outskirts of Bodmin. It was late on a Saturday afternoon that under the heavily laden sky had suddenly become dull and quite dark. Cars with their headlights on, were flying along creating a lot of spray. I was not going to be able to jog gently along this road but there was no alternative as far as I could tell. There was nothing for it, I would have to battle with the traffic and use gaps in the hedgerow as refuge points and sprint along the road from one to another when the traffic was less heavy.

I waited for a gap in the traffic, looking up the road for a safe haven. I estimated the distance and time it would take me to get there. I then wait for that last vehicle to pass before sprinting for all I was worth to the next safety point to catch my breath. This was not how it was supposed to be. I repeated the process, clad in a high viz jacket and two flashing lights. I made myself as visible as possible. It amazes me how some drivers prefer to bray on their horns to tell you that it is dangerous to be a pedestrian on a road where there is no footpath and yet make absolutely no attempt to use their brakes or brains.

Just to add to my pleasure the last half mile was up a steep hill but thankfully at that point there was a grass verge worthy of the name, and I was able to get completely off the road. I arrived at the top of the hill to be greeted by a sign that read 'Welcome to Bodmin' and a pavement that for me was more of a welcome than any sign. There was a petrol station here and I sought shelter and sustenance spending the £5 minimum card payment on a magnum ice lolly and bag of wine gums. It's funny, I was wet and cold and yet the ice cream was absolutely delicious and rejuvenated me. They body gets what the body wants, and I was off again in search of three hot B's, Beverage, Bath and Bed. I arrived in Bodmin town centre at 5.30 and noticed a phone shop that was just closing. The owner took pity on me, and I was able to buy a power pack for £9.99. This was to prove a wise investment in days to come. The day was not over yet. I still had to find my hotel. Typically, this turned out to be at the far end of the town, still another mile away and of course it was at the top of a long hill. I arrived bedraggled and exhausted after a day which ended up being eleven hours and thirty-nine miles. Never mind, two days done, twenty-six to go and tomorrow would bring Bodmin Moor.

CHAPTER 6

Diamonds and Pearls

Day 3 – Sunday 3rd April 2022 – Bodmin to
West Nethercott Farm, Whitston

Day three started a bit later than the first two days. Well, it was Sunday after all. Plus, the overnight temperature was minus four, so an extra hour in bed was the order of the day. I was still up and running by 8am on what was a clear crisp morning. I contoured around the valley on quiet streets to pick up a country road called Helland Road. This would take me up the hillside. The name Helland Road reminded me of Leeds United's home ground which is Elland Road, so I photographed the name plate and sent a picture to a misguided work colleague who for some inexplicable reason supported them and smiled at the friendly rivalry we shared.

The road climbed gently, with open fields on both sides and even though it was early, the sun began to warm me a little. After a mile and a half, the road entered woodland and immediately descended steeply, crossing a stream in the valley bottom. With the place surrounded by trees and totally in the shade it became very cold. I could see my breath in the frosty air. I took a buff from my bag and pulled it over my head, to cover my mouth and nose in an attempt to warm the air a little before filling my lungs with it. Catching a cold on day three would ruin everything. After fifty metres the road began to climb again and became very steep, the increased effort immediately warming me. I reached a fork and checked the map. Bearing left I emerged from the trees into bright sunshine with open views across the valley. The road descended again, and I arrived at the small hamlet of Helland Bridge. It looked very pretty in the spring sunshine. Here, running at right angles across the road were old rail tracks. These were set into the tarmac, a legacy from bygone days when there was a train service through this valley operated by London and South West Railways. This has now been converted to a cycleway called the Camel Trail. This is an eighteen-mile marked route that starts in the coastal town of Padstow and follows the disused line from the Camel Estuary, through the Camel Valley. My route would take me along approximately five miles of this pleasant pathway.

I turned off the road and through a gate stepping onto the gravel surfaced tree lined trail. Blossom was budding on the trees as the sun shone through. Birds were singing and could just be heard above the sound of the river. It was a lovely morning and a real pleasure to be here running in this stunning setting. I stopped to take off my windproof jacket and trousers having now warmed up. As I was stuffing them into my bum bag, I heard the gate open and close. I looked behind and saw another runner approaching. John, a tall dark-haired guy in his mid-thirties, was out for a Sunday morning run. We ran a few miles together. He was a bit too quick for me but it was nice to have company so I worked harder to keep up, especially when he said I could have coffee and cake at a café a little further along the trail. He told me the café had been set up by cycling enthusiasts and they also hired bikes. After about twenty minutes John turned around to head home. He had run for an hour along the trail and would now retrace his steps. We took the obligatory selfie, shook hands and said farewell. I continued, buoyed by the idea of a second breakfast, my first being of yoghurt and blueberries at 07.30. I had been running for eighty minutes and covered seven miles when I arrived at a wooden cabin which housed the wonderfully named Snail's Pace café.

The well stocked woodland wonderland was warm and welcoming. The owners were just setting up. The countertop was lined with eight massive cake stands, each displaying a different homemade cake with the name of the mouth-watering fare marked on the glass cover in white crayon. Victoria sponge, carrot, coffee and walnut, lemon drizzle, orange and almond, raspberry frangipane and chocolate brownie. There was also a tray of scones, fresh from the oven and I salivated as I watched the lady taking them off the baking tray. Just as my eyes had been drawn in by the sight of the cakes, my nose had also been accosted by the wonderful aroma of brewing coffee. I stopped my watch. There was no way I was passing up this opportunity and reminded myself of the importance of supporting the local economy when visiting these little places. I checked the battery on my phone which was already down to 60%. Time for a recharge.

"A piece of raspberry frangipane, a large americano and a glass of tap water please."

After a twenty-minute recharge, a few photos and coffee and cake consumed, I was back on the trail. Two hundred metres further on I reached the end of my excursion on the Camel Trail. I now left the valley and turned right, heading up a quiet lane that would take me on to the moors. Once again, the road was steep. I shortened my stride, lifted my head, and let the tap tap tap of my feet beat out the rhythm of my run, percussion as I sang that Kate Bush's song again.

"I'm running on that road; I'm running up that hill, It doesn't hurt me, do you want to know how it feels? It doesn't hurt me".

Eventually it did start to hurt me. My heart rate began to climb as my lungs went into oxygen debt. The leg muscles were now demanding more oxygen enriched blood to flush away the acid waste produced by the muscles. I slowed my pace and straightened my back, trying to ensure I was as upright as possible so as to engage my glute muscles. This would also ensure I didn't lean forward as that would constrict my diaphragm and thus restrict my breathing. Eventually though, the gradient won, and I succumbed to walking when the rate of my hard-working heart reached one hundred and seventy beats per minute. A person's maximum heart rate depends on lots of factors, one of which is how fit they are but as a rule of thumb or rough guide, if they are in good health, it can be calculated by subtracting their age from two hundred and twenty. This meant my maximum heart rate should be roughly one hundred and fifty-nine, but I wasn't unduly worried. In training it had been as high as one hundred and ninety. One minute of walking and it was back down to one hundred and twenty-five and I was back running again.

The gradient eventually eased and having reached the top of the climb I was treated to stunning views of Bodmin Moor. In the distance was a noticeable peak which I wrongly thought to be Brown Willey, the highest point in Cornwall. I stopped to make a short video and had just finished when a couple walked along the road. We chatted and the man explained that what I thought was Brown Willey was actually the second highest point in Cornwall and hid the larger peak.

Every so often I would meet one or two people. Most were either cycling or horse riding and there wasn't an opportunity to talk, but all in all the area was quiet which surprised me as it was a perfect day to be outside. This suddenly changed when I reached a disused airfield. The road stretched about two miles in front of me. On each side of the road were large, unfenced areas of close-cropped grass. There were groups of people dotted all over. Some of the groups were quite large but it was such a wide-open space they were almost lost in the vastness of the location. The first group of about thirty people seemed to be holding some kind of horse fair. Further on was what looked like a small car boot sale. Then there were a dozen people flying model aircrafts. There were various family groups walking dogs or playing football. I passed one family of four and watched the parents trying to teach the children to cycle. Dad was running along holding the back of a little bike for his young son to get up to speed before letting go. They tried a few times and eventually he was away. I applauded as I ran past. The mum and daughter were close to the roadside.

"That's it now" I said. "It could be the Tour De France in a few years." The mum smiled and said "Hopefully, we just need to get this one off now" and looked down at her young daughter who was clutching her mum's leg. I said to the young girl.

"I bet you will be faster than your brother." Her eyes sparkled like diamonds as she smiled then looked up at her mum saying,

"Will I mummy?"

I wished them good luck and carried on checking the map as I had a turn coming up. I saw the place about a quarter of a mile ahead. The road rose up twenty metres and I started to walk. The sun was hot on the back of my head, and I took my shirt off and drained the last of my water. I still had about twelve miles to go today and would need to find water soon. I arrived at the turn and noted the route on the map. It was a straight road of about three miles to the village of Hallworthy where hopefully there would be a shop or pub so I could get a drink.

There is an old saying 'It is better to travel hopefully than to arrive.' This was to become almost a mantra on the journey as it was filled with a series of small disappointments, but it's also true to say that when I needed some kind of help, something always turned up. This was such an occasion as when I arrived in the village, I could see neither pub nor shop to quench my thirst. I looked up and down the road, nothing in sight. Nothing shown on the map and no one about to ask. Should I make a detour and go searching? Or should I stay on the main route and just trust luck, fortune or whatever divine power was looking after me? I chose the latter and carried straight on.

On my left was a row of cottages, all except one with a manicured front lawn. The odd one out was at the far end of the row and looked overgrown from a distance. On closer inspection, the garden was so filled with pots of wildflowers and herbs, that it was almost impossible to see a pathway to the house. At the side of the cottage was a colourful gypsy style caravan. I could hear bees buzzing as they foraged for pollen in this insect's supermarket. I stopped to take a photo, moving right up to the garden wall. An old lady I hadn't noticed looked up. She was on her knees tending one of her pots.

"Hello," she said. "Can I help you?"

She stood up but still seemed lost among the mass of plants, many of which were as tall as she was. Her accent sounded to me like she was from the Black County.

"I was just admiring your caravan. Is it OK if I take a photo please?" She gave me permission and moved nearer to the wall. It was then that I noticed she was holding a small watering can. She watched me as I took the photo and asked me how far I had run. When I told her I'd come from Bodmin that morning she gasped saying

"That's about twenty miles, I know because I have to drive there to do my shopping." I explained I was running from Lands' End to John O' Groats, adding that today I was finishing at a farm near Whitston, which she informed me was a further 10 miles away. Pointing towards the watering can, I asked if she had a tap in her garden and would it be OK to refill my bottles.

"Of course," she said and reached forward, taking them from me before disappearing behind the caravan. When she came back, she asked me about my run and if I was doing it for a charity. This became a common question. It was the first thing people asked. At any other time, I would have found this irritating. If you are running, why must you be running for a cause? I smiled at her and began to explain.

"Well, yes I am, but that wasn't originally my reason. I'm doing it because I want to see the country, but it would be a missed opportunity to do all that and not try and help a good cause so I'm running for Andy's Man Club."

"I don't think I have heard of that," she said. I explained what the club did. How it had grown and now had over 100 clubs around the country, informing her of how it had been started in 2016 by a lady whose son committed suicide. She looked at me and said in a quiet voice.

"My brother committed suicide last year."

The bees were suddenly silent. Birds stopped singing. There were no traffic noises and time seemed to stand still. My eyes started to water as my throat filled with words that got stuck somewhere between my voice box and my lips. What seemed like an age later I managed to mumble, "Oh, I'm so sorry. That must have been awful." She shrugged her shoulders and said. "I think that life just got a bit much for him." I didn't really know what to say. I would have been glad to run off down the road but didn't just want to leave at that point. It felt somehow cowardly. A newspaper headline flashed into my brain as I stood there, drowning in a pool of inadequacy.

'Old lady kills herself after conversation with runner!'

"Are you OK?" I asked, quickly adding "I bet this garden keeps you busy?" and immediately followed this with, "where are you from? Your accent doesn't sound local."

She confirmed she was in fact from Wolverhampton but had lived here a long time. I told her I would be running through Wolverhampton in about a week's time. She asked if she could give me some money for the charity. I had already decided that I wasn't going to start collecting cash on route. It would become unworkable, so I had taken the decision to only accept donations on the just giving site. I explained this but as the words left my lips, I guessed this would be a world of mystery for her. She confirmed this by saying,

"I don't do the internet."

"Me neither, if I can avoid it." I said,

We smiled at each other finding common ground in our technical ineptitude. I thanked her for the offer of the cash but asked her to give it to the next homeless person she saw when she was next in Bodmin, and she agreed that would be a worthwhile thing to do. Out of the blue she asked.

"Would you like a sandwich?" I had now been standing there for about twenty minutes. Time was marching on, and I really wanted to be going, so I thanked her but declined politely and thanking her again, I set off running. After a few seconds I looked back to see her standing at the wall. We waved to each other, and I turned to carry on. Tears welled up in my eyes. I was blown away by her kindness. What a nice lady. A real diamond. Suddenly I felt guilty that I didn't accept the offer of the sandwich. She was probably lonely and glad to have someone to talk to. This made me smile as in my head I could hear the words from several of my friends.

"Bloody hell! She must have been desperate."

It's good to have friends who appreciate your talents. I am grateful for mine, friends and talents and I was grateful for the water too which I guzzled greedily as I ran off down the road.

An hour and a half later I finished the last of the water as I struggled up another steep hill bringing me into the village of Weeks St Marys. I was now only about two miles from my evening lodgings and had agreed to call and give the landlady an estimated time of arrival. The place I was staying was a working farm and the lady said she may be out milking the cows, depending on what time I got there. I pulled out my phone and dialled the number. I told her where I was, and she gave me directions.

"Down the road to the crossroads. Turn left and carry on until you see the recycling bins at the end of the track. We are half a mile up there" and those famous words "You can't miss us."

She confirmed it was no more than two miles in total and I told her I would be there in about twenty minutes. I had plotted the route into my phone on the OS maps and the lady's description of the route looked the same as I had plotted so all seemed fine although there was no West Nethercott Farm named on the map. There were lots of buildings that looked like they may be farms and two with a name that included Nethercott, one of which was written in italics on the map. This indicated that it was very old, and I had asked the lady if the farm was named on the map and if the farm was very old and she confirmed yes to both so everything seemed to be OK. How wrong can you be?

I headed off down the road and a mile later arrived at a small crossroads with a farm lane on both sides. Each lane was surfaced with concrete. Was this the place I asked myself? The lane on the left certainly took me to the place called Nethercott I had marked on the map. I turned left and ran past two other farms both with waste bins at the gates but neither of them had names that included Nethercott. The smaller place was new and wasn't shown on the map at all.

After another quarter of a mile, I arrived at a five-bar gate which was longer than a normal farm gate, more like the width of three normal gates. Whilst the sign had Nethercott in the name, it didn't say West Nethercott Farm and didn't look right but there was nowhere else on this track that it could have been, so I decided to knock and ask the owner. My only other choice was to go back one mile to the main road which seemed stupid without checking first. My unease was added to with another sign on the gate that read 'Caution! Dogs running free.' I slowly opened the gate and walked down the shrub lined driveway that curved round to the large house about thirty feet below me. I walked up to the big heavy, metal studded front door and gave my best effort at a knock. What a waste of time. From where I was my feeble knock sounded like a dried pea landing on a drum. No one in the house would hear that. I barely heard it. I tried again and this time I was heard as the deep base notes of barking dogs came booming from the back of the house. I could hear them approaching. A lady staggered around the side of the house, bent double as she tried to hold on to the collars of two German Shepherd dogs. They stopped barking and looked at her for approval.

"Can I help you?" she said.

As I started to speak the dogs started barking again and it was obvious that she couldn't hear me, so she shouted at the dogs to be quiet. They obeyed instantly. Just then a man followed her round the corner. He was holding his phone to his ear and in his other hand held two dog leads. He handed the leads to the lady and thankfully she clipped one to the collar of each dog. I breathed a sigh of relief and walked towards them.

"I'm sorry but I seem to be a bit lost. I'm looking for West Nethercott Farm. The owner gave me directions which have led me here. This isn't right, is it?"

"No it's not," the lady said, then asked "What's it called again?"

I repeated the name of my intended lodgings to which she said.

"I've never heard of it, but my husband may be able to help" and she nodded to the man who was still listening intently to whoever was on the other end of the phone. The lady turned and walked the dogs back around the corner, leaving me to wait for her husband. I stood feeling very conspicuous in the middle of their driveway in my bright orange tee shirt and shorts, sweat dripping from my nose and flies circling around my head, like hungry vultures hovering above a stricken beast in the last throes of life. From the conversation I could hear the man was talking to his father. It was the way he kept saying "Dad! Dad! Dad!" that gave it away and reminded me of telephone conversations with my own pater. This man's father either couldn't hear him or didn't really want the call to finish. Eventually the man raised his voice and said,

"Right dad I have to go. There's someone to see me." There was a pause then, "No, I don't know who it is." Another pause "No he has just arrived." Yet another pause, "No, I don't know what he wants. I don't actually know anything about him or why he's here."

I felt like an intruder about to feel the cold steel of an Englishman defending his home, or at least the frustrations of a son having a difficult conversation with his father which I certainly could relate to. Time to exit stage left. I held my hand up in apology and started to back away to the gate. The man moved the phone away from his mouth and called to me,

"Just a minute". I stopped. He put the phone back to his ear "No not you dad, I was talking to the man" and then "As I said I don't know who he is". Then with a real sense of frustration in his voice "OK, OK, I will call you back when I've spoken to him."

He finished the call by pushing the off button so hard I expected it to come out of the back of the phone. He put his hand to his forehead and wiped it down his face then took a deep breath before looking at me. In my head I said to myself 'Here it comes. Both barrels.'

"Sorry about that, he said very politely." What is it you wanted? "

I repeated my plight, missing out the fact that I had done a mountain leadership course and prided myself on my ability to navigate my way around the mountains, even in the dark or mist. Nor did I share the fact that it was my intention to get myself all the way to the end of the country. I didn't mention that bit either. I just stood there dripping on his private pristine pathway, feeling out of place and unbelievably uncomfortable.

"No Sorry I have never heard of West Nethercott Farm" he said. I began to think I must be absolutely miles away and in a voice that bordered on panic I explained it was a Bed and Breakfast in the hope this may ring a bell with him, and did he know of one close by? This didn't resonate either. How could I have got this so wrong? Apologising, I returned to the gate. I don't know why but I was expecting him to call me back, having had a sudden realisation of where the place was, but he never did. I closed the gate and jogged off down the track, looking across fields trying to spy other buildings. At the road I turned left and thought back to the day before. Just like yesterday I had done more wasted miles.

I ran down the road feeling hungry and certainly ready for a hot shower. After a further half mile there was a proper crossroads, I turned left. The road was signed to Whitston, and this was definitely correct. I realised my error and felt foolish and angry with myself at the same time. Three hundred metres further along was the promised farm track, unsurfaced and with four recycling bins lined up. I could see the farm a few hundred metres up the track. I looked across the fields and could see the house I had been to just a couple of fields away.

As I ran up towards the farm I noticed the front door looked out onto a field full of lambs. I walked to the side door which opened onto the farm track. The owner, Pearl, who I later found out to be seventy-six, greeted me with the words,

"You're here?" As if to say, "where have you been?" A perfectly justifiable question as I told her I would be about twenty minutes and it had actually taken over an hour. Pearl instructed me to go around and enter through the front door, saying she would meet me in the hallway, adding that she didn't like guests walking through the kitchen. I did as instructed, removing my shoes before entering. She then showed me to my room promising tea and cake in ten minutes downstairs once I had unpacked. She then asked me

"Where's your bag, is someone bringing it for you?"

"No. This is me. I have everything I need right here.

What you see is all there is" I replied "Oh right" she said and frowned which conveyed a message telling me either she wasn't impressed or thought I was some kind of nut job, or both.

"So, you have no support at all?"

"No, well not until I get to Lancaster on Good Friday which will be around halfway.

My wife and some friends are meeting me with a change of clothes and a few other bits. Until then I'm on my own." This was followed by another.

"Oh" and a sort of disbelief and then, "Are you running for a charity?"

"Yes I am. I'm running for a mental health charity set up by a lady in 2016. She started the charity after her son committed suicide." Pearl replied,

"My husband's brother committed suicide about five years ago." I gulped and replied,

"Oh, I'm very sorry to hear that" but for the second time that day I was stunned. Pearl didn't say anything, she just shook her head and closed the door.

I showered and washed all my kit including removing and scrubbing the insoles of my shoes but didn't wash my shoes today as there was no hair dryer. However, as I had been on roads all day and had washed them yesterday, I decided they were OK. I hung my damp shorts and tee shirt out of the window and lined my socks on the stone window ledge which was still warm from the afternoon sun. I was in the room above the front door and spent a few minutes watching the new lambs in the field then remembered the tea and cake. After plugging in my phone to charge I rushed downstairs, eager for tea and cake and arrived just as Pearl was carrying a tray from the kitchen with a large slice of Victoria sponge and a large teapot. I followed her into the dining room and sat down at a table already laden with cups, milk and sugar. Pearl asked me where I had run from today. When I replied that I had come from Bodmin, she responded,

"Oh you've come from Cornwall have you?" I was a bit taken back by this and asked,

"Does that mean I'm in Devon now?" Pearl confirmed I certainly was now in Devon, and this brought a big smile to my face. I had run through Cornwall. She asked me what time I wanted to eat and if roast chicken, potatoes and vegetables would be OK for dinner. I tried my best to hide my excitement but replied with a big hearty

"Yes Please". She then asked,

"Is there anything you don't like?"

"Porridge and rice pudding." I responded, following up with. "I like most other things but feel that porridge and rice pudding should be used to fill in potholes in country roads." Pearl laughed and promised neither would be on the menu. She then added,

"I've discussed it with my husband and we won't be charging you for your evening meal but would like you to put the money to the charity. Will that be alright?" I replied

"Of course it will be Pearl. Thank You, that's very kind of you. I will ensure it's shown on the fundraising page."

"Right," She said "I'll leave you to your tea and cake and see you at 7.30 pm. Just knock on that door if you want more tea" and with that she disappeared into the kitchen. I polished off my tea and cake then returned to my room where I retrieved my phone and called Angela, updating her on the events of the day. I expressed the shock at the fact that at least two of the nine people I had spoken to had experienced bereavement to suicide, but tried to end on a brighter note with the good news that I had ticked of my first county.

After the call I checked for messages on social media. I then slept for an hour by which time it was the appointed hour for the promised roast dinner, and I returned to the dining room. Pearl was as good as her word. Roast Chicken with all the trimmings and trifle and cream for dessert. I had already explained to Pearl that I would only want a light breakfast of tea and toast and would like to pay before going to bed. Transaction complete. I returned to my room and wrote a report of the day. To save time the following day I packed everything into my bags except my toothbrush, my phone, my watch, their respective chargers and my almost dry running kit then climbed into bed.

Another day exceeding thirty miles. The views were great. I had run well, eaten well and hoped to sleep well, but the people I'd met had made the day even more special and shone out like diamonds and pearls in the murky waters of life.

CHAPTER 7

Oven Ready

Day 4 – Monday 4th April 2022 West Nethercott Farm to Fox & Hounds Chulmleigh

I awoke to be greeted by low clouds and drizzle. Yesterday's sunshine was now just a memory and the murky miserable weather looked to be in for a while. However, the drizzle had changed by the time I set off. Changed to heavy rain and this continued for the whole morning. I said goodbye to Pearl who seemed much less chatty than the day before. I had spent five minutes with her over breakfast asking about a path that ran up the farm track and across the fields at the top. Was it passable or would it be overgrown.

"No, it is certainly passable and will save you from running up the road as it can be busy before school," she said.

I made my way up the track and after two hundred metres came to a gate in the right-hand wall leading into a field full of cows. At this point the track became thick with mud and a very wet greeny brown substance that wasn't mud. It was in fact, how should I put it? A sea of steaming $£*t stretching from five metres before the gate to five metres past it and all across the track. Wall to wall shit and enough to mean I was going to have to wade through it or go back to the road and add another mile to my journey, which today was planned to be thirty-five miles. I chose to press on through the fragrant festival of fertiliser and if you will pardon the expression, just suck it up! Having spent many years running around Yorkshire I have passed through many cow fields and farmyards so It's not my first excursion through a pile of bovine excrement. I shrugged my shoulders and pressed on, grateful for the fact that I hadn't bothered to wash my running shoes the night before. I thought back to my Facebook post earlier that morning advising followers that it was raining but stating that I was merely advising them of today's weather and not complaining about it. I had added the comment 'You get what you get and have to embrace it.' Now I actually said to myself "Shut up Stephen."

Two hundred metres further on, the now dry stoney track came to an end with a five-bar gate leading into a field empty of livestock. I went through a narrow stile to the right of the gate and was met by knee high soaking wet grass with no visible path. It was about one hundred metres across the field, leading to another stile and another field with more of the same. By the time I emerged on the small lane at the other side of the second field, there was no sign of any cow dung on my shoes at all. My waterproof pants however were stuck to me and were littered with grass seeds. "Hey ho". Like I said you get what you get.

I turned right and ran the remaining few hundred metres to the village centre and a crossroads. My route was supposed to take me straight ahead, and then to follow the road for about five miles, but there was a road closed sign blocking the road. Just as I stood there a Lady came out of a shop at the junction and opened the door to a Land Rover which was pointing as if she had come from the direction I was heading. I asked her where the road was closed and if it was possible to get through on foot. She explained that about two miles further on there was a big hole, three quarters of the way across the road but I could get through on foot. Good news as the alternative would have added another three miles.

I made my way along the road. The rain was absolutely pouring down and large puddles had formed in places at the side of the road which meant that I was running in the middle, at the top of the camber to avoid being up to my ankles in water. I put my fingers into the hood of my jacket and tucked the edge of the hood behind my ears so I could hear any traffic approaching from behind. Well unless they're electric I thought. I will only hear them as I hit the floor as they drive over the top of me.

Being a long-distance runner generally means spending quite a bit of time on your own. This gives you a lot of time to think and sometimes it raises a few questions. It struck me as I was thinking about electric cars. Would they work as well in the rain? I was of the opinion that nothing is actually fully waterproof so if water somehow got into the electrics would it stop working, or worse still would it set alight, self-combust and somehow burst into flames. My thoughts were interrupted when I heard a vehicle racing up behind me. I turned to see a car approaching at speed. I moved as far over to the right-hand side of the road as possible. I knew what was going to happen, but the driver didn't appear to.

Like me the driver wanted the centre of the road. His wheels were touching the edges of the water channels on both sides, so whichever side of the car I stood on I was going to get wet. He was spraying a lot of water to the side of the road as he sped along, making no attempt to slow down. Sure enough, as he passed me It was like a fairground log flume, and I got a soaking from the waist down. I used a few Anglo-Saxon adjectives under my breath and watched the driver disappearing up the road. In order to retain some faith in humanity I told myself that he was oblivious to what was going to happen and must have other things on his mind, but it is possible he knew but just didn't care and actually thought it good fun.

The car stopped suddenly about half a mile away. Just beyond it, I could see orange crash barriers across the road. He had reached whatever was obstructing our route and began to reverse before turning around in a farm gateway. He was now heading back toward me at speed. Once again, he was in the middle of the road but now, having moved back to the top of the camber as soon as he passed , so was I, and I planned to stay there. Although I was already wet to my skin, I didn't really want another drenching. It somehow seemed humiliating. Not the drenching particularly but the fact that I knew it was coming and that it was avoidable if the car driver drove in the correct position in the road, rather than in the middle of the road. Anyone with a brain could see that if he drove through the water at the speed he had earlier, anyone walking along the road was going to get a soaking. If I just accepted a repeat of the same, it would feel humiliating. Like saying, "Yes, thanks for your first act of stupidity but don't worry you can do the same to me again." "Sorry pal, not this time." I held my position as he drove towards me. He was about forty metres away when he flashed his lights at me. I didn't move from the central position. I was still running towards him, and he must have thought I was playing chicken with him. I suppose that's exactly what I was doing but I just wanted him to show a bit of consideration for another road user. I had moved well out of his way and given him the whole road earlier, but he showed me no consideration in return by making no attempt to slow down and drive at a speed the conditions dictated. As he got nearer, I was still in the central position so he honked his horn but started to slow a little. He then moved right over to the left-hand side of the road, the position he should have been and would have been if a vehicle had been coming towards him. The water level now came several inches up the tires and either he slowed, or the water slowed the car down. I moved slightly to my right, positioning myself in line with the wing mirror of his driver's door. At the same time, I stuck my arm out and began waving it up and down, flagging him down. I was holding an orange buff in my hand like a flag. I had been wearing this on my head. There was no mistaking that I wanted him to stop, which he did about ten feet in front of me. I walked up to his window and indicated a winding down movement. He didn't oblige but shouted through the window.

"What do you think you're doing?" I shouted back my reply

"Can you help me please?" He then opened his window a tiny bit.

"What do you want?" I wanted to say, I want you to drive a bit more considerately, but decided it would be a waste of time.

"Is the road blocked up ahead please?"

"Yes," he replied, "and It's going to mean a ten-mile detour." Wow I thought, no wonder he's in a rush.

"Is it possible to get through on foot?"

"Yes, you will be alright," he replied.

I thanked him and moved out of the way and we both went our separate ways. I felt pleased with myself for avoiding another wetting. Now some of you will be thinking I acted like a bit of a pratt and maybe I did, but If it had been this man's mother, wife, child or someone else he cared about walking along that road in the pouring rain, or someone about to get in his car, I doubt very much he would have driven so fast as to send a bow wave over them.

I reached the barriers and could see that the gas board had dug a big hole that stretched right across the road. It was possible for a cyclist or pedestrian to pass but nothing else. I went around the hole and before I reached the end of the road two miles ahead, I had flagged down three other vehicles and informed them of the problem, saving them all time and saving me another drenching. All three drivers thanked me, so it was a win-win. Once again, the rain played havoc with the touch screen and I was not able to open the correct map easily nor zoom in and out. This was proving to be a nightmare situation which could derail the whole project if the wet weather continued. I reached a crossroads with no road signs at all. From memory I should be heading straight on but straight on looked to be just a farm track. I either had to go left or right. It was not possible to see very far in either direction as both options had a blind bend within fifty metres, so I had no idea which way to go and really needed to open the map.

Directly opposite me, at the junction of the farm track and road, was a wooden structure about waist high. It was a doorless cupboard or more accurately a wooden honesty box holding eggs for sale. The bottom shelf was raised about eighteen inches from the ground. It looked like it had been made from pallets, so the top had gaps. Rain dripped down onto the top layer of eggs although they were covered by a plastic sheet. I saw a possible solution and walked across to the structure. Having removed the phone from the outer case I initially tried holding it with my hands still inside the zip lock bag, but I couldn't read anything as the bag was either scratched, greasy or somehow misted up. I removed the phone from the bag and held my hands on the shelf where the eggs were. I tried in vain to open the maps. Nothing! Drizzle still landed on the phone and drips through the gaps in the top self either landed on the phone, or dripped onto my hands which were now very cold.

The lower shelf where the eggs sat, was built at knee height, but the underneath was protected by the plastic sheet. I knelt down as underneath that self the ground was dry. However, when I placed my hands under the self I couldn't actually see the phone at all. I ended up laid on my back with my head and shoulders under the lower shelf as my legs and feet laid across the farm track. I could now see and read the screen, but it took an age to open the correct map due to my cold damp hands, but eventually, I found the correct route and was on my way again, but not before I took screen shots of the next two sections. It was easier to open photographs than it was to open the mapping application. Fifteen frustrating minutes had passed before I was running again, so from that point, I would take screenshots of each map section of my next day's journey in case I had another wet day.

After nine miles I reached the small town of Holsworthy. Not to be confused with Hallworthy, the tiny village I had passed through yesterday where I had spoken to the lady from Wolverhampton. Holsworthy was a completely different and much larger place. I sought shelter and breakfast in a café. I removed my now filthy 'non waterproof' waterproofs and stood dripping on the café floor, apologising to the staff and customers. I placed my order and retreated to the toilet where I removed my sodden tee shirt and shorts. I replaced the tee shirt with a dry running vest and then wrung the shorts out over the sink before holding them under the hand dryer until there was a knock on the toilet door. I put my shorts back on and added a down jacket over my vest and opened the door. There was no one there. I went back into the café and immediately an old chap stood up and headed for the toilet. Walking up to the counter I held up my damp tee shirt and asked the owner if they had a heater, I could drape it over. The lady took the shirt from me and disappeared into the back.

After a well-earned breakfast and an hour drying out it was time to be moving again. The heavy rain had eased to a fine drizzle once more. I went to pay the bill and the lady returned my now dry shirt. It was lovely and warm.

"Wow thanks," I said, "That's really great." She then told me she didn't have a heater but could see I needed help so had stuck the shirt in the oven. It certainly did the trick. I was warm and at least my top half was dry. For the moment anyway.

I was off again and heading for the picture postcard village of Hatherleigh. The first section was on a disused railway line and although it was still drizzling, I was protected from the worst of the weather by a good covering of trees and running on the level sheltered path was pleasant. I met a few people walking dogs. After about three miles I joined the main road again. This was an A road, The A3072, a busy road, the first one of several I would have to run on that did not have a footpath. I would be running along this road for about six miles. There was an overgrown grass verge on either side, filled with nettles, brambles and pieces of litter. The road was long and straight, and I could see that after a few hundred metres it was covered by large trees and becoming dark, as though entering a tunnel. Unfortunately, it had started to rain again, so I was faced with a dilemma of whether to put on my rain jacket or not. The jacket has reflective strips which are picked up by the headlights of approaching vehicles. It's great for running in at night but is actually grey, and not the best colour for running in during the day on the road. Also, the back of the jacket was now covered in dirt from laying under the wooden honesty box earlier in the day. Despite the rain it was actually quite warm, so I didn't really want to be wearing a jacket at all. Time to put one of my personal theories into play. Well actually several theories rolled into one.

So here is the first theory. If you're running in the rain when it's wet but muggy, with just a tee shirt, if you take the tee shirt off and run bare chested, when the rain stops you will have a dry shirt to put on.

Theory two. If you are running in a technical tee shirt that wicks away the sweat from your body, are you actually making yourself more dehydrated more quickly? Surely if the sweat is being wicked away and not cooling you down as nature intended, the body is going to produce more sweat to replace the sweat that's wicked away, isn't it? If these technical tee shirts actually do what the manufacturers' claim they do and wick away sweat, the answer has to be yes. So, if it is the case, that the body produces more and more sweat to replace the moisture that's been wicked away, it must be a never-ending cycle until you either finish the race or become completely dehydrated. So, the answer has to be that an ultra-distance runner will become dehydrated more quickly if they wear technical wicking garments for long periods. I have no scientific proof of this, but I can't come to any other conclusion if technical garments work in the way the manufacturers' claim. Following on from that. If on this journey I have to drink an extra litre of water each day to replace the extra water wicked away because I'm wearing a wicking tee shirt, that equates to an extra kilo in weight I have to carry every day. Over a month that's a total of 30 kilos. That's like carrying a sack of potatoes from Lands' End to John O' Groats. My intention was to remove my tee shirt at every opportunity but so far, I had only managed this for a few hours yesterday. Now would be a perfect time because of theory three.

Theory Three. I believe it's safer to run down a busy road with no shirt on, than it is to run wearing a shirt. This is because more people will actually notice me if I run bare chested. If I run along in a tee shirt, irrespective of the colour I will blend in as just a man running. Whereas if I have no shirt on, I will be noticed because it's unusual. I know that sounds crazy, but I believe it's true. So, if I want to increase my chances of not getting knocked down as I run down a busy road, I should run topless. It is just a theory and not proven but it's a feeling I have from many hours of personal experience. People may say "have you seen that idiot running with no shirt on in the rain" but if they have then seen me, proving my point. So, if the shock of seeing my skinny white frame makes them sit up and take notice, even if it's just to question my sanity it's a no brainer – topless every time.

So, as I was about to leave the relative safety of the cycleway, I removed my shirt and fed it under the strap of my bag. Attached to the bag I had two lights. One red and one white which I unclipped from the bag and switched to slow flash mode and held one in each hand as I set off running down the road. I tried to stay as close to the grass verge as possible. The road was long and straight, and I should be visible to vehicles from a long way off.

At frequent intervals all manner of vehicles came speeding along the road towards me. Cars, vans and the occasional articulated lorry. Once I saw them heading towards me, I looked behind to gauge if there was traffic coming in the other direction preventing them from moving out and giving me space. When that was the case, I stepped off the road into the overgrown verge, but it was impossible to run on the verge at first. It did get easier after a mile as the amount of tree cover had prevented the grass from growing. At those points I was able to step off the road and continue running on a surface of hard packed bare earth, although I had to be on the lookout for broken bottles, of which I saw several. I covered the six miles in just under fifty minutes which was way too fast, but it was downhill and I was running on adrenaline. I breathed a sigh of relief when I reached the next stage of the disused railway. I followed this for about a mile before it brought me back to cross the main road. My route now followed another series of country lanes passing small farms and some beautiful properties before coming back to the main road half a mile before the village of Hatherleigh which I reached at 2.00 pm. I had covered a total of twenty-four miles for the day but still had about twelve remaining.

Hatherleigh is a beautiful place with lots of thatched roofs and quaint shops, but I didn't want shops and once again searched for a café. I spied one up the street which was a steep hill. I salivated at the thought of sandwiches, tea and cake not to mention an overdue bottle refill and set off marching up the hill. My chin must have nearly hit the floor when I tried the door and saw the CLOSED sign because a man called to me from across the road,

"Café don't open on Mondays. Try the George."

He raised his left arm and pointed back down the hill I had needlessly hiked up. I waved my thanks and retraced my steps to the pub. I then noticed the village store a few doors down. I thought back to my coast to coast run in 2008 and the pub in Reeth where I waited 90 minutes for a meal, so decided to try the shop first. Entering, I asked the lady if she sold sandwiches, pies or pasties of any kind. She replied,

"No. Try the George." and raised her left arm pointing at the wall of the shop. I thanked her and went back outside. I looked at my watch. It was 2:10. With twelve miles still to go I needed to eat and further inspection revealed my phone needed to be charged, again! For some reason the battery definitely didn't last as long when it rained but I had no idea why that would be it now showed only 16%. So, 'The George' won by popular vote and I walked into the highly recommended pub. It proved to be a good decision and I spent forty minutes recharging myself and my phone. I chatted with a few of the locals and the pub actually sponsored me as did two of their customers. The pub also put a picture of me on their Facebook page telling customers what I was doing, although in the picture I was standing next to a large ornament that held pride of place on the corner of the bar. It was a larger-than-life sized cockerel, so no doubt there would be a few suitably worded comments, not for printing in this fine publication.

Leaving the pub at 2.50pm I started off up the steep hill out of the village but after only twenty metres remembered the place I was staying that night was in the middle of nowhere. There was no village or shop of any kind within three miles, so I returned to the store to buy something for the following morning. The first time I entered the shop it was deserted but now it was suddenly packed. School must have just finished, and I waited my turn patiently, respecting those in front of me in the queue. Frustratingly, it took almost ten minutes to make my purchases. The shop was also a post office and suddenly half the village wanted to send parcels.

At exactly 3pm I began my last stint, and the twelve miles to the Fox and Hounds Country hotel. The hotel is situated three hundred metres from Eggesford Railway Station, the nearest town or village is called Chulmleigh three miles away. It was actually a bit off the cycle way route but was the only place I could find with accommodation anywhere close to the route. It meant I would need to follow the map closely again, hence the need to recharge the phone. The stage started with a climb up a 1:5 hill for a quarter of a mile, but once at the top the views were spectacular. There was actually a monument at the top with a viewing platform. I continued along to the village of Monk Okehampton and was thankful I didn't have to write that place as part of my address. Far too many letters. Even though the roads were narrow, they got noticeably busier after 3:30pm and I had to stay alert. Especially going through the village of Winkleigh. I crossed the main road that ran north to south through the village and tried to start running again but suddenly my energy levels seemed spent. I drank some water and chewed on the last of a bag of wine gums I had bought at the petrol station in Bodmin. Just as well as once through Winkleigh I had another long climb gaining one hundred and fifty metres in height. I ran for fifteen seconds and then walked for thirty seconds and repeated this until I got to the top. Once there, the road levelled out and I set off running again. About forty minutes later I passed through the village of Wembworthy. It was 5pm. I estimated I was under three miles from my hotel. The road ran gently downhill passing a large area of woodland and it became almost dark. For the second time that day I switched on my two lights and set them to flashing. Ten minutes later my route turned right and headed steeply downhill in a long sweeping arc where I seemed to have to use all my remaining energy to fight the camber of the road in an effort to stay up right. Thankfully after only five minutes of this I reached the valley bottom where a left turn brought me to the entrance of the railway station car park.

The map showed the hotel was three hundred metres away, but once again I had to negotiate a pathless A road with traffic hurtling along no more than two feet from me. Luckily the driveway of the hotel was about two hundred metres long, so this latest near-death experience was over very quickly. I arrived at 5.20 pm having covered a little under thirty-five miles and an actual running time of six hours and fifty minutes. It was another day completed, and I was about to stay in the most expensive hotel of the whole trip so may as well enjoy it.

The day had been long and lumpy. When I finished the phone battery said 1%, which was 1% more energy than I had. There was also a message from Garmin apologising that they had some kind of power outage during the day and I added a screenshot of their message to the following social media post 'Interestingly I am not the only one experiencing power outages' and I finished my post with 'Tomorrow I will enter Somerset and I am really looking forward to the Somerset Levels'.

CHAPTER 8

Hot Air or Hot Gossip

Day 5 – Tuesday 5th April 2022 Fox & Hounds
Chulmleigh to Wellington

Today was going to be another big day, but one of my main concerns was finding food and drink during the early part of the day. I had searched the route on google maps, but nothing seemed to be available. So far on this trip I had mostly set off before the hotels served breakfast and would have preferred to do the same at this hotel. However, with nothing available nearby, I decided I should have a continental breakfast. They didn't officially start serving until 7.00am but I had spoken with the manager the night before and he agreed to leave some cereal for me. I was already seated in the restaurant at 6.00 when the chef walked through the door. He did a double take when he saw me sitting there munching on rice crispies.

I told him what I was doing and explained my conversation with the manager. The chef nodded and immediately brought me a steaming hot cafétiere of coffee. He said he would bring some pastries for me to take away. I thanked him for coffee but said he didn't need to bring pastries, adding I would be fine with cereal as I'm setting off in ten minutes. He said, "the pastries are in the oven already and will be ready in five minutes," then he walked back to the kitchen. Sure enough, exactly five minutes later he emerged with a basket filled with pain au chocolat, just as I was clipping on my bags and about to leave. He placed them on the table. "Thank you" I said, although of all the continental breakfast pastries, they are my least favourite. The chef stood there looking pleased with himself. It was clear he had rushed around to look after me, so I felt obliged to take two. I wrapped each in a paper napkin and thanking him again, I set off toward the reception.

In addition to the food issue, I was also concerned about the busy road outside the hotel. I had heard cars whizzing by as I dressed. I had to run past the train station I had passed yesterday, and a further two hundred metres to a road junction with a B road that would actually double back and climb the hill right opposite the hotel. I had looked on the map and from the hotel car park for a path through the woods but couldn't see one.

I paid the bill and made my way outside, still clutching the warm pastries, one in each hand. Walking down the hotel driveway I began to nibble on the first of them as I looked again across the road in the hope of finding a possible route up through the wooded hillside. I reached the end of the hotel drive and waited for a gap in the traffic before stepping on to the road. Directly across from me I could see the ends of the tree branches were broken off and there was a small gap in the grass, not so much a path, just a small foot long area of trampled grass. I couldn't see past the tree, but it looked to me as if someone had come through there. I crossed the road and pushed the branches back. Sure, enough there was a small trod evident on the ground. Someone used this as a path. Brilliant. Although it was a steep scramble of 30 or 40 metres, this would save me at least one kilometre, half of which was along the busy road. A positive outcome and good start to the day. I began the scramble, still chewing on the pastry, but as I climbed steeply, my breathing increased due to the gradient and suddenly I breathed in a flake of the dry pastry. I began to cough uncontrollably, my eyes watering and momentarily lost my balance. This resulted in me dropping the other pastry and I watched helplessly as it rolled out of the napkin and down the hill gathering dirt along the way. Once I had finished my coughing frenzy, I retrieved the napkin but left the pastry, which was now out of sight some thirty metres below me. I hoped the local wildlife liked flaky pastry and bitter chocolate. I carried on the remaining ten metres to the road before reaching for my water bottle and taking a long drink.

The coughing had made my eyes water so whipping tears from my cheeks, I set off running up the road still with half a pain au chocolate in my hand. I took a bite, and it took an age to swallow. I looked at the pastry but it had now somehow lost its appeal, so deposited it in a bin at the end of a farm track further up the road. I don't like throwing food away and this dampened my mood. I felt morose, moody and not at peace with the world. I am sorry to say that I do get days like that. I wake up tired and feel like I have to be in a bad mood. I have no idea why. Is it some kind of chemical imbalance that affects the brain? Some days I wake up full of the joys of spring and regularly drive my family mad as I walk around the house singing and smiling at them fondly with arms outstretched. To be quite honest I think they prefer me to be miserable in the mornings and that was certainly how I felt at that moment. I could quite easily have gotten into an argument if my mood hadn't improved. Perhaps I was still tired after the last four days and possibly not properly rested. The sky was overcast and filled with dark clouds as if it too wasn't properly rested and didn't appear to have decided if it was in a good mood or not.

Three miles further on I reached a small village of Chawleigh on the B3096. According to google maps this had a shop but when I had looked on google street view as part of my planning, the place where the shop should be was just a square of flat earth between two houses. I didn't know if the shop had recently been built, or if a previous shop had closed during the pandemic, which was a strong possibility. Also I knew that because of the housing shortage, some retail properties in rural places had been turned into dwellings, so it was perfectly possible the shop had been demolished so someone could build a house on the plot. That's the reason I had gone back to the village shop in Hatherleigh the day before. I had bought the two snicker bars but ideally, I would have also liked to have had some boiled or jelly sweets as they are the best for fast energy.

I looked at my watch. 6:50am. Even if the shop was there, it was unlikely to be open so early. Wrong! It was both there and open. I went inside and bought a half litre bottle of water and a bag of jellybeans. Jellybeans are like rocket fuel for endurance runners. Don't ever waste them on young children if you value peace and quiet.

I spent several minutes chatting to the shopkeeper and his wife. She was blown away by what I was doing. We talked about how Ian Botham had walked what was then referred to as 'the end to end' in the 1980's. Her husband recalled how Botham had the press and a film crew following him every day, with other celebrities joining him at certain points. She said I should also have a film crew following me. The couple gave me directions telling me to stick to the B3096 and not drop down to the cycle route I had previously been following but had left yesterday afternoon near Monk Okehampton to get to the hotel.

"If you go back to your cycle route you will have to drop down to get to it, only to immediately climb back up again. If you stay on this road you will save yourself the additional climbing and it will be no busier."

I thanked them and refilled one of my bottles with 300ml from the new supply. After drinking the remainder, I dropped the empty bottle in the shop's recycling bin, and with the sweets safely stowed, I set off again, smiling at my good fortune. I now had fuel for the next three or four hours and a less hilly route. I told myself to cheer up, it was going to be a good day as I trotted through the village and past the last of the houses. The road was free of any traffic, and I suddenly felt much more at ease with myself. I thought about the lady's suggestion that I should have a film crew following me and this reminded me of the words 'playing a part in a picture show' from a song called 'Take the long way home' by a band called Supertramp from the 1980's, The words seemed to fit both the setting and my mood. In my head I could hear the mouth organ playing the first few bars and I whistled the intro and then started to sing.

"So, you think you're a Romeo, playing a part in a picture show,

Take the long way home, take the long way home.

'Cause you're the joke of the neighbourhood. Why should you care if you're feeling good?

Take the long way home, take the long way home'.

I was now in the zone and feeling much better. It was 7.10 and I was flying. I hoped to be having lunch in the small town of Tiverton by 12:30. It started to rain. I looked up at the sky and smiled as I remembered those words on that poster in my old boss' office. I held my arms out and smiled at the rain, singing even louder.

"There are times when you feel you're part of the scenery, oh the greenery coming down boy.

Then your wife seems to think that you're losing your sanity, oh calamity,

Is there no way out?

You take the long way home, take the long way home."

At that moment I was incredibly happy and wouldn't have swapped places with anyone. It was nice and cool for running and the quiet lanes of Devon were perfect. There was no one in sight and I didn't have a care in the world. My body was being flooded with free drugs and the chemicals were making me smile. Adrenaline being produced naturally by my body was releasing mood enhancing endorphins that filled my brain. I shouted at the sky. "Come on rain, is that all you've got?" A few minutes later it stopped raining, and I sang even louder.

"Take the long way home, Take the long way home".

I rounded a bend in the road and saw two teenage girls

dressed in school uniforms standing at the end of a farm track. They both looked away from me and stared down at their phones.

"Sorry for disturbing your peace" I said. "I'm just having a great day. I hope you do too".

They looked up and smiled weakly not knowing what to say. Why would they? Most people don't expect to see any normal person running along the road singing for all they are worth at 07:45 in the morning. Then again, I have never professed to be normal.

I continued to enjoy the morning. The weather continued to be unsure of itself and light drizzle persisted on and off for the next hour. I had the breeze behind me for the first time since leaving Lands' End, so I made good progress arriving at a junction, half a mile outside the village of Witheridge at 9:15. I was supposed to turn right here and head away from the village but saw a sign for a café and suddenly felt the need for coffee. I turned left and ten minutes later found the place, only to read the sign, 'closed on Tuesdays!' My heart was now set on caffeine, and I looked around for an alternative. I asked a passer-by who directed me to another pub. On the way there I passed a community centre that had a sign that read 'tea and coffee all welcome'. It was now 9.25. I had been on the go since 6:10 and had covered almost seventeen miles. I had earned a break so in I went.

Two old ladies were sitting at a table at the far end of the room. Hearing the door, they looked up at me, resplendent in my sweaty running kit.

"Hello" I said, "is it OK to come in for coffee and cake please?" One lady replied saying

"We're not actually open until 10am but you're welcome to come in and wait inside," after a tiny pause she finished the sentence with, "Where it's warm!"

I thanked them and closed the door. It seemed darker and certainly a lot colder in the room than it was outside. I noticed they both wore woollen overcoats, and still had their hats on. I pulled my down jacket from my bum bag and put it on. I added my waterproof pants. The ones I had spent forty minutes removing the grass seeds from the night before, which was not easy as the seeds were stuck onto the Velcro straps and fastenings. The lady said they were waiting for the boiler to heat up and that it would be about fifteen minutes but promised that as soon as it was up to temperature, she would bring me a cup of tea. At this point I didn't say I wanted coffee. I just sat on my hands and waited in the cold. The silence of the large almost empty hall was shattered by the booming "tick tock" of a clock on the far wall.

I asked permission to plug my phone in and decided to phone Angela but had no signal so checked the phone for messages. I had started getting a lot of messages on Facebook and twitter as more people began to hear of my run. Despite wearing the down jacket, I started to shiver and remembered my tee shirt was damp. I suddenly felt really cold in the hall, so I attempted to dry my shirt under the hand dryer in the toilet. The warm air on my body felt fantastic. I calculated that if I sat on the floor under the hand dryer, I would still be able to reach the button. Yes really! and for what I thought was only two or three minutes but turned out to be much longer, I sat there with warm air blasting on my head and shoulders. Looking back, it sounds ridiculous that I was sitting on the floor of a public loo to have a shower of warm air and yet it felt so uplifting at the time that I was reluctant to get up and my mind drifted for a few minutes. Eventually I returned to the hall and one of the ladies stood up saying the boiler was ready and asked me what I wanted.

"Coffee please, white with two sugars and do you have any cake please?"

"Cake? No, I'm sorry, but we may be able to rustle up a few biscuits." She returned a minute later with a cup of coffee and three biscuits. The coffee was only just lukewarm, and I gulped it down in under two minutes having already polished off every crumb of the biscuits. I noticed it was almost 10:30

meaning it had been an hour since I came in. I had lost some time somewhere and suddenly realised I must have been sitting on the toilet floor for over half an hour. I was certain that I must have actually nodded off whilst in there. I stood up, gathered my gear and walked over to the counter to pay.

"How much do I owe you please?" The lady replied

"It's just one pound please." Then she said "You spent a long time in the toilet! We were just deciding which one of us was going to go in and check on you."

"Yes I'm sorry about that. I was just trying to dry my shirt. You had better take another pound for the electric." I passed over a £2.00 coin. "Please keep the change and thank you so much for letting me come in early."

I looked around and waved at the other lady, still only the two of them there. Walking over to the door, I was embarrassed at the thought that they probably presumed I had fallen asleep actually sitting on the toilet but feeling that may be less embarrassing than owning up to sitting on the floor. "Thanks again," I said. As I made my way outside another elderly lady was just going in and I held the door for her, noticing she was clad in a similar woollen overcoat and warm hat. No sitting under the hand-dryer for this lady either. I smiled and shook my head thinking of the story she was probably about to hear from her two friends. The village seemed almost deserted. I laughed thinking that my toilet tale will be 'trending' all over the village by teatime. Hot Gossip.

I left Witheridge retracing my steps for the first half mile along the B3137. It was going up to 11am and suddenly the road seemed busier. Although it was pretty flat and straight it was once again pathless, and the traffic was going fast. I suddenly wasn't happy with this situation. About a quarter of a mile northwest of a village called Normansland I had a very close call. Actually, it was the only one of the whole journey but it shook me up. It could have ended differently for all concerned.

There was a narrow grass 'verge' at the side of the road between the tarmac and the wall. It wasn't really a verge as such, but more likely where grass had grown wild with other weeds and forced its way up through the edge of the road next to the wall. It was tussocky, very overgrown, and only about one foot wide. But the wall was only about 18 inches high, whilst at the other side it dropped down four or five feet to fields, and the area close to the wall on the other side was littered with fallen stones. I was running along the road facing the oncoming traffic, exactly as stated in the highway code. A car was speeding towards me. At this point the road was covered by the national speed limit, but the car was coming out of a 40mph zone although it certainly seemed to be travelling a lot faster. There had been a number of heavy goods lorries coming along the road, travelling in both directions and I could hear another one coming from behind. I turned around and saw the large lorry then realised the car driver wouldn't be able to see the truck because I had just come around a small bend that was more of a kink in the road. The car driver would be able to see the road a long way after the bend, but the area immediately before it was hidden by a large barn and the slight bend in the road. It was a blind spot. The car saw me and moved across the white line but seemed to make no effort to slow down. Realising what was going to happen I stopped running and stepped up onto the narrow strip of grass, pressing myself up to the low wall but wobbling on the tussocks. I felt like I was going to topple over the wall, so I placed a foot on top of it, whilst grasping strands of the long grass in both hands to maintain my balance. I looked back and saw the truck round the bend. The truck driver, obviously seeing the car coming towards him, immediately engaged his brakes and his horn. I looked at the car which was only a few metres from me and saw him swerve back to my side of the road as he too hit his brakes and horn. He actually gesticulated at me with one hand as he passed. I was incensed and shouted at him.

"Just press your foot on the middle pedal a bit earlier you complete f*<kwit" I almost fell back into the road after he had passed and stood looking at the car as it disappeared round the bend. Neither of the vehicles stopped. I turned and began to walk along the road feeling pretty shaken. "Get off this bloody road" I said to myself and made an adrenaline fuelled sprint to a small lane 300 metres up the road.

I sat on a stone plinth showing the distance to the nearest water hydrant and retrieved my phone. I had to find an alternative route to Tiverton avoiding this road. I opened the map and checked my location and began working out a route when to my horror I noted the phone battery was down to 15%. It must not have charged at all back at the village hall. To make matters worse I had left Facebook, twitter, WhatsApp, text messaging all open and immediately closed them all. I phoned Angela as I needed her help. I had maps for my entire route saved onto my iPad. I had used the iPad to plot all the routes but made them available so I could access them on the phone. So, it was possible for Angela, who was working from home, to access the maps and guide me if I was stuck. I called her saying

"I've got a big problem. My phone battery is almost out, and I might need you to access the maps on my iPad and guide me part of the way." I looked at the screen again and told her, "The battery is now down to 13%. It was 15% before I called you so I'm going to have to turn it off and save it for emergencies. So I need you to open the map app and select the map for day five and keep it open in case I call you for directions." There was a long silence at the other end of the phone, so after this pregnant pause I said.

"Please!" It's funny how when you are in the thick of things you sometimes lose sight of the simplest of solutions. There is a story told by Sir Alex Ferguson, the former Manchester United manager, that beautifully emphasises this. It shows that even the most experienced of people can sometimes overlook the obvious.

Ferguson was a few years into his management tenure at United, but things were not going well, and it was rumoured that he was going to be sacked. He was sitting in his office when Sir Matt Busby walked in and asked him how things were going. Ferguson said that things were not too bad. Busby asked him why he seemed so down. "It's the press boss. The papers are crucifying me." Sir Matt looked at him and simply said. "Don't read them." Ferguson recounted this story during an interview I watched. He said after he stopped reading the papers, this immediately improved his positivity and soon the results changed. The rest, as they say, is history. My wife had her own Sir Matt moment when she simply said,

"And have you used up that new battery back you bought?"

"Er No. No, I haven't, I completely forgot about it. I will try it now and see if that works. Thanks love" I said, adding "You're a genius. I knew there was a reason you married me"

"Was it because I was attracted to idiots?"

"Harsh but accurate. No it was that knowing you're much cleverer than I, you would always be the winner at scrabble," I replied.

"You never play me now."

"That's only because you deserve a better level of opponent. Right, I will try the new charger and ring you back if it's not working. Otherwise, I will call you in about two hours. Hopefully from Tiverton whilst I'm having lunch," and with that I rang off.

Just like Sir Alex my spirits were lifted. I delved into my bag for my battery pack and plugged the phone in. I clipped the bag to my front so I could check on the phone more easily and set off running. I had only gone a few yards when an elderly man came round the corner walking his dog. I started to walk towards him and said,

"Excuse me. Could you help me please? I'm trying to get to Tiverton on foot. Would you be able to suggest a route that doesn't involve running along that road?" I pointed back to the road I had just come from. He actually gasped saying,

"Whatever you do, don't go along that road. They come along there at sixty or seventy miles per hour. It's like a racetrack. Right then let me see." He thought for a few minutes and I started to think he didn't know a better route when he said

"OK here you go." He gave me a few short specific instructions and two specific landmarks, adding in the name of a village called Calverleigh. He said that this route would take me to one mile outside of Tiverton. I thanked him and was about to go when he said.

"One more thing. How are you with steep hills"?

"I'm from Yorkshire so we have one or two of those there". I replied.

"Yes but these are Devon Hills", then with a big smile he said. "They're not to be underestimated." I smiled back and replied. "I will give them the respect they deserve." Holding out my hand, I watched as he removed a thick leather glove before grasping and shaking my hand like old friends.

"Thank You. I really appreciate it. That road is a suicide mission" I said, pointing back to the road.

"Yes," he said, "you will be much safer this way. Good Luck."

I was on my way and his directions were absolutely perfect. They took me across seven miles of country lanes, and I never once felt uneasy about where I was. I did come across the hills he mentioned. A small village with a steep descent, probably about 1:4 and an equally steep climb back out. The funny thing being that when I arrived at the top of the first hill the road had temporary traffic lights on. The telecoms company Openreach was installing fibre optic cabling. Two men were at the top of the hill. One was climbing down into a hole and the other was holding a big coil of cable. As I got nearer to the bottom of the hill, I could see another man standing above another hole and another guy bent double in the hole. Suddenly there was a shout from behind me.

"Shove your hand right up and grab hold. Then give it a right yank and keep pulling."

I looked at the guy standing on the road and we both laughed. He said in a strong West Country accent,

"I don't suppose he should really be bellowing that over the village should he." I replied,

"Well, it does give the impression that your mate in the hole is actually a vet with his hands in a cow's backside." He laughed and shouted down to his mate in the hole.

"Ere Dave. There's a bloke here who wants to know if you would prefer to have your hands up a cow's arse." From the bottom of the hole, we heard Anglo Saxon expletives and both laughed.

"I think that's a definite No!" I said and set off running up the hill with the workman still laughing and suggesting other animals his mate may prefer to inspect if he decided on a veterinary career.

The hill was steep and seemed to go on forever but eventually I reached the top and was rewarded with fine views. The road was empty, the sun had come out and once again it was a pleasure to be running. It was now all downhill to the outskirts of Tiverton and I arrived in the town at about 1:15pm having completed a further ten miles since the hand dryer experience.

I found a lovely little café where I had lunch. When I pulled my phone out, the battery said 88% and the new pack had worked a treat. I called my wife again to give her the good news and she reminded me how lucky I had been in my choice of life partner. How could I possibly argue? It turned out the café owner had lived in Bradford in the 1980s and actually worked in offices in the same building I worked in. It's a small world.

Refreshed, I began my afternoon run at just after 2.30pm. I had a further ten miles to go to reach the Somerset town of Wellington. The good news was that most of the run was along a canal. Flat running and despite a brief altercation with a Swan that wasn't exactly friendly, I arrived in Wellington at about 4.30 but not before I stopped for a photo of the Somerset sign as I crossed the county boundary. My arrival in Wellington had similarities to my arrival in Bodmin in that my accommodation was in a retail park. Of course, it was right at the far end of the town. That night I totted up the miles for my first five days and realised I had completed one hundred and seventy-two. Not bad for a sixty-one-year-old.

CHAPTER 9

Beefy's Footsteps and
The Road to Endorphia

Day 6 – Wednesday 6th April 2022 – Wellington to Winscombe

I intended to be running today by 7am. I'd thirty-seven miles to cover, and hoped to be on the outskirts of Bristol by tea time. The good news was my route was almost flat so after an uninspiring overpriced pastry and coffee that was so strong you could probably have run your car on it, I was on my way. My journey began with six miles of road running, along the A38 to Taunton. Not very inspiring but certainly direct. On the outskirts of Taunton, I looked at my watch noting that I had been running fifty-seven minutes, covering four point eight miles.

My pal Adrian Netherwood, had really put me through my paces in the early part of my training. Adrian, who served on submarines in the Royal Navy led me on run after run, taking me up every hill in our local area, the Aire Valley. I cursed him every time we ran together as he dragged me up Carr Lane, Gaisby Lane, Emm Lane, Long Lane, Shay Lane, Lee Lane, Cottingley Cliffe, Cottingley Moor Road, Ghyllwood Drive, Park Road, Hope Hill and many more. These are all just names to most of you, but to me these are routes all marked with my blood sweat and tears, each providing painful memories of an unfit body morphing into something almost resembling a runner.

Adrian had been based in Plymouth so spent many days running in the hills of Cornwall and Devon. He knew the terrain was rarely level, so my preference for running along canals or flatish moorland paths was just not going to get me through the first week. He had also advised me that even when I got to Somerset and the terrain flattened out, I must not get carried away, and try to maintain a pace no faster than five miles per hour, as going too fast in the first week would burn matches I would need in the last half of the run.

Just before the time on my watch clicked over to the hour, I pulled out my phone and took a picture of the details. At exactly one hour, the distance read five point zero one miles. Right on target. I stopped in Taunton for twenty minutes at Greggs buying a two-pound special offer of coffee and bacon bap, whilst sending Adrian a picture of the watch readings.

Buoyed by the brief breakfast, I set off running along the Bridgewater Canal. This took me past Somerset's county cricket ground and once again I was reminded of the exploits of their cricketing legend Sir Ian Botham who was I suppose the first person to make me aware of this challenge. Seeing his exploits in the Eighties made me think that must be some achievement, and though it wasn't on my personal radar until many years later, I think it's fair to say 'Beefy' had definitely planted a seed that would eventually blossom into my own attempt at an End-to-End excursion.

Without doubt the second thing that made me consider this undertaking was a book I read called 'Road to Endorphia: Running and Ranting from John O'Groats to Land's End'. It wasn't actually the route or location that attracted me to the book. By that I mean I wasn't looking for a guidebook or advice on how to undertake an End-to-End run. Instead, it was the wonderful title I was attracted to. Like a running equivalent of Indiana Jones, in search of the lost city of Endorphia.

Over the years I have read it many times, although on the first occasion I nearly put it down before I got going, but once I got past the references to religion on the first page, I thoroughly enjoyed it. I recommend anyone to read this book and please don't let that reference to religion put you off, as actually it becomes clear that he is referring to an inner spirit in the same way a sportsman may talk about heart, courage or bottle. The author, Joe Donnerchie hails from Glasgow and the description "Running and Ranting" is right on the money. He comes across as a milder running version of Frankie Boyle. The book is both humorous and thought provoking. Humorous in its reference to his personal slant on incidents and happenings on the journey and thought provoking with his take on how running has such a positive effect on a person. It made me think that undertaking such a journey was not really a challenge, but actually a normal and thoroughly natural process. Over the years I have read numerous books of this ilk, but this is the only one I have ever read a second time. In fact, I have read it several times. I particularly like what I can only describe as Donerchie's 'no frills' ending but you will have to read the book to find out what I'm referring to. If I told you, it would spoil the surprise.

After nineteen miles I arrived in Bridgewater and found a café in the centre of town overlooking the river. I enjoyed an all-day breakfast, two pots of tea and an Ice cream sundae. One hour later I was on my way again, but only at a walking pace for the first mile to let my marathon meal melt into fuel. I walked down a narrow street on the opposite side of the river from the café, at the far end of which was the A38. This would now be my route for the next ten miles. I was not particularly thrilled that I would now spend the next two hours at the side of this very busy trunk road, but I was safe in the knowledge that there was a wide footpath all the way to the point where I turned off. I knew this for a fact because Joe Donnerchie had told me. He had run from John O'Groats to Lands' End and had used the A38 on his personal 'road to Endorphia'.

As I was leaving Bridgewater, I passed a massive distribution warehouse for the Morrison's Supermarket chain.

This made me feel ever so slightly home sick. Morrison's was started in my home City of Bradford. In the middle of the 19th Century Bradford was reported to be the richest City in Europe, and whilst it may have fallen on hard times in recent years, I am extremely proud to say I come from Bradford.

I am proud to belong to a city which has given this country so many things. Things that have had a significant positive effect. Such as, the present F.A. Cup. Yes, this was made in Bradford in 1911. The first free school meals. The formation of the Independent Labour party. The formation of the Barbarians rugby team. The first (and last) electric trolley buses in the country operated in Bradford from 1911 to 1972. Two of the oldest running clubs in the country, Bingley Harriers founded in 1893 and Bradford Airedale, originally Airedale Harriers, which is actually about ten years older.

There are also numerous sports stars, actors, pop stars, and TV personalities who hail from our great City. Cricketing legends, Jim Laker and Jonny Bairstow, From the world of entertainment, Ade Edmondson, Art Malik, Peter Firth, Timothy West, Anita Rani, One direction's Zayn Malik, Kimberley Walsh, Kiki Dee, Gareth Gates, 70's band Smokie, Harry Corbett, the creator of Sooty and Sweep, One of the original presenters of changing rooms Linda Barker, and the mind muddling magician Dynamo. Kaiser Chiefs frontman Ricky Wilson is also a Bradford lad. Yes, I know he may support Leeds United, but he was born and grew up in the BD post code. The late Harry Gration and his weather forecasting friend Paul Hudson. Bruce Bannister a former footballer and the man behind what is reputedly the world's largest running shoe retailer, Sportsshoes.com, selling running shoes and sportswear to over 130 countries. The Brontë Sisters, J.B Priestley and David Hockney. It really is a long list and I could go on but will finish by adding the Brownlee brothers. Now I know you're going to tell me they're from Leeds and are proud to tell you so. I have no issue with that as its true and I believe a person should take pride in the place they come from, but whilst they may have been born just over the border in Leeds, they went to school in Bradford, and so it was the place where much of their running and endurance ability was forged, on the hills, trails and woodlands in and around Bradford Grammar School.

Some people reading this from outside Yorkshire, may think Bradford is just a small town in the North. From the way it is portrayed in the National media this is perfectly justified, but actually it is the sixth largest city in the U.K. having a population exceeding 500,000. That's right, over half a million people. This makes it much bigger than lots of other UK cities you may have thought larger. Cities such as Belfast, Bristol, Cardiff, Coventry, Edinburgh, Leicester, Liverpool, Manchester, Newcastle, and Nottingham. Bradford is bigger than all of those, and actually over twice the population of places such as Aberdeen, Derby, Plymouth, Southampton, and Swansea.

Views of Bradford are seen on millions of T.V. sets all over Britain several times each week, as Bradford City Hall is regularly used for scenes in Coronation Street and Emmerdale. Much of Peaky Blinders was filmed in Bradford at the UNESCO World Heritage site in the district of Saltaire, 3 miles from the city centre. Within that same city centre, we are proud to host the National science & media museum. This building is just across the road from the beautiful Alhambra theatre which is just one of a large number of the City's elegant structures, as believe it or not, Bradford also has more grade two listed buildings than every other UK city outside London, Bradford is far from a small town in the North.

Now I am not implying all of the above celebrities are guilty, if guilty is the right word, of what I'm about to say, but everyday I hear people criticising Bradford which I can accept to a point, but what really saddens me is that too many of this City's sons and daughters, when asked where they originate from, now seem to disown their Bradford heritage and purport to come from Leeds. Not that there is anything particularly wrong with Leeds. It's all right, if you like that sort of thing, but it's not Bradford is it.

Bradford became a city in 1897, two years later, William Morrison started his business as an egg and butter merchant in Bradford's Rawson Market. At the time, this was the main food market in the city. I wonder what William would say if he was able to see the size of this distribution centre . You could just about fit Rawson Market into the playing area of a school football field and yet you probably could fit Wembley Stadium into this warehouse three times over. Is that really progress?

I trotted on, passing through the town of Highbridge. A few miles later the A38 turned right heading for the M5. The traffic had become noticeably busier, but thankfully I left the A38 at this point, and continued along the A370. This goes to the holiday resort of Weston Super Mare. The weather had been in a holiday mood most of the day and I had enjoyed a perfect afternoon of bright sunshine but with pleasant temperatures for running. Suddenly that had changed. The wind had increased a lot in the last few minutes. Up ahead the sky had darkened. My wife, an avid viewer of TV decorating shows and student of Dulux colour charts (Other paint brands are available), would probably describe it as cornflower. Suffice to say it looked threatening with its heavy shade of dark blue with a hint of purple and a rainbow taking centre stage. There was definitely a storm coming. Time to put the rain jacket on. I was pulling this out of my bag when I realised I must be very close to the point where I turned off the main road, so thought it best to check the map first, as if it rained before I opened it, we could have another episode of what I had now christened the 'map app pantomime'.

I pulled out my phone and punched the code in. The map opened immediately and thanks to the wonders of modern technology, the little red arrow showed my position, confirming I should be turning right in less than two hundred metres. The first spot of rain hit me in a big wet droplet and was followed immediately by several more. Rain crept along the road in front of me, approaching like the spray from an automatic car wash. I stowed my phone as quickly as possible and was struggling to get my jacket over my head when the rain arrived. I was engulfed by a short sharp shower that saturated my shirt, shorts, socks and shoes. I began running and a minute later reached the turn onto Bristol Old Road and the village of East Brent.

Once through the village I was out in the country again. The rain stopped almost as suddenly as it started but I kept my jacket on hoping this would warm me up more quickly. A few minutes later, a lady on a horse approached me. She was as wet as I was. Smiling I said;

"Well that was certainly refreshing" She smiled back saying "Yes. That's certainly one way of putting it." We laughed, both slaves to our choice of hobby.

Looking up the lane I noticed a marked hump. I realised that I had not gone up a noticeable hill all day. The hump turned out to be a bridge over a railway line and I knew I was nearing the end of the day. I estimated I'd fifty minutes to go, but I also knew that the last three miles would take me up a long hill with the same incline as the nearby Cheddar Gorge. I reached the hill and considered walking but after all the flat terrain, running up actually felt comfortable and before long I arrived in the Bristol suburb of Winscombe. I was just about to check my map when another runner caught me up, so I asked him for directions. He was called Chris, and said he was going to pass by the hotel in question so would run with me. It took about ten minutes and whilst we ran, Chris asked me the usual question,

"Are you running for a charity?" He seemed blown away when I told him I was running for a men's mental health charity and told me he was a junior doctor at a hospital in Bristol and spent quite a bit of time dealing with some of the effects of men's mental illness. When we arrived at the hotel, he shook my hand and said he would be in the bar later and would buy me a pint. He was as good as his word and came to find me at about 8:30pm. Unfortunately, by this time I was falling asleep into my sticky toffee pudding. So, I had to reluctantly decline his kind offer, and by 9pm I had crawled into bed and was exploring the mythical land of Nod.

CHAPTER 10

Easily Diverted

Day 7 – Thursday 7th April 2022 – Winscombe to Aust (Old Severn Bridge)

Once again, I set off early, continuing my preferred habit of foregoing the hotel breakfast. The weather forecast predicted a dry day, but with strong winds from the West in the afternoon. In the early part of the day, I was going Northwest to Clevedon and across the Southern end of Bristol to Portbury, none of which should pose any problems. However, around lunchtime I would have to cross the river Avon and later follow the Severn Way coastal path. At these points I would be exposed to the Westerly winds. These were predicted to be gusting to gale force, and I hoped it wouldn't slow my progress. I was booked into a Travelodge at the motorway services at the English end of the old Severn Bridge. Today's journey would bring my first week to an end which seemed a significant milestone that I was looking forward to ticking off.

The route started downhill on the road before picking up another cycle path along a series of disused railway lines. The good thing about old railway lines is there is usually a good covering of vegetation running along each side meaning, there is both shade from the sun, and a degree of shelter from the wind. This proved invaluable on this day.

After about forty-five minutes there was a diversion, and the route took me through the carpark and around the perimeter of the Thatchers cider factory. I felt this warranted a photo but in doing so noticed that once again the phone battery was already down to 60%. It had been 100% when I set off. I immediately closed down every program and turned it off. Once I'd negotiated the route through the cider factory, it was left down a lane for a short while and then back onto the disused railway track. This went on for several miles during which time I saw only two people, both cycling in industrial clothing with large headphones. Neither acknowledging my presence.

Every now and again there was a break in the railway to cross a main road, but apart from that, there was nothing more to report. Ninety uneventful minutes later I arrived at the district of East Clevedon. It was just after 8am. I had covered ten miles. Earlier I'd decided that Clevedon would be my first port of call or more accurately, my first refreshment stop. My plan was to go into the Town Centre and have breakfast, but I was a little earlier than expected, and the morning rush hour traffic coming from the town was nose to tail. I didn't really want to run the extra mile into town and back out again alongside all this heavy traffic. So, I decided on a change of plan.

Where my route turned off this major road, there was a petrol station advertising fresh coffee under the guise of the 'wild bean coffee shack'. This sounded to be just what was required. I ordered an Americano and a pecan Danish pastry which I was confident would see me through until lunch. Whilst adding milk and sugar to my caffeine of choice I got chatting to a really nice guy called James Llewelyn. James asked me if I was running to work. "Not exactly "I replied, and explained what I was doing. He asked if I had a charity or web site, I gave him my twitter address and two minutes after leaving received a good luck message from him. It turns out he was a bee farmer and the owner of a honey company called Waggle and Hum.

I wished I'd been aware of his occupation when we were chatting. I have always found bees pretty interesting but even more so following a conversation I'd had with my son a few weeks before setting out on my trip. We had been watching a kestrel, and I commented about how fantastic it was to watch them hovering in the air. He replied saying whilst it was impressive, it was less so than the fact that bees could actually fly at all. He explained that because of the size of a bee's body in relation to its wing size, it should mean it just wasn't physically possible for bees to fly at all, and actually contradicted what are the general principles of aviation. I was fascinated by this so began to research how they managed this improbable feat. Apparently, they can only get off the ground because of the amazing rate at which they flap their wings as opposed to speed of forward velocity in relation to the wingspan. As we know from my Otley escapade explained earlier in chapter four, once an object's forward motion reaches a certain velocity in relation to its shape and weight, lift is achieved by the speed of the air forcing the object upwards and off of the ground. This, however, is not the case for bees. Their bodies are too large and their legs too small to move forward fast enough. It is said that a bee can flap its wings at the mind-boggling rate of two hundred and forty beats per second or fourteen thousand four hundred beats per minute. No wonder they are called 'busy' bees. I would really have liked to discuss it with an expert.

After my refreshment and a fifteen-minute break, I was off and running again. The route went northwards, up a steep hill away from the main road. After a quarter of a mile there was a sign pointing right. A blue sign with a small red square. Inside the square in white writing was the number twenty-six, informing me I was following the number twenty-six national cycle route. The lane was again sheltered from the wind by a long line of trees. It was pleasant running. A quiet, sheltered undulating lane, initially flanked by fine houses. These were separated by large well cared for gardens and eventually the houses gave way to open fields and fine views. In the distance I caught my first glimpse of the sea since leaving Penzance.

I was still right on my five miles per hour schedule and as my watch clicked onto three hours, it showed I had covered fifteen miles. I photographed the watch face again and sent the images to Adrian telling him I was following orders.

More quiet lanes and cycleways brought me to a pleasant looking village which turned out to be Portbury and was definitely not what I had expected. The cycle route took me across the M5 on a narrow bridge and to the outskirts of Portbury docks. Here I picked up a narrow path, full of right-angled turns. This was supposed to be a cycleway, but it seemed clear to me that a non-cyclist had devised this series of twists and turns. I would certainly have had to dismount to negotiate some of the corners and felt there was no way two bikes travelling in opposite directions could have negotiated any of them simultaneously, and I questioned if it was actually fit for purpose.

The path formed a big rectangle around the perimeter of the docks along the side of some new fencing and it appeared to me this had been extended to accommodate the storing of hundreds and hundreds of brand-new electric cars. All the vehicles were a new make of car produced in China. The irony being that just a few weeks before leaving to start this journey, as part of my work I had been asked to arrange the importation, customs clearance and storage of five hundred new electric cars coming from China into Bristol. I contacted the Port authority to ask if we could store them there. They declined saying they already had around five thousand stored at the port. Most had arrived almost a year before, and so far, there was no sign of them being sold. The man I spoke with added, "Or of us being paid." I looked at the vast array of vehicles. Row upon row of them, almost as far as the eye could see, and was grateful to the man for being so forthright. This ensured my employer was not exposed to a possible debt of this magnitude. Big business is only good business if you get paid.

Shortly after, a split in the path had me heading in the wrong direction again. I had continued to follow cycle route twenty-six but should have switched to cycle route forty-two but failed to notice the turn off. This was because route forty-two went up a flight of steps that I hadn't realised was actually the cycle route so just ran straight past. At some point it occurred to me that I was going Southeast with a body of water to my left which didn't feel right. When I checked the map, I was following the river Avon inland, when actually I should have been going over it. I had only gone a few hundred metres so it wasn't a major issue. I retraced my route back to the steps and climbed them arriving at the Southern end of the Avon bridge. Once on the bridge I was suddenly bombarded with noise, as the cycleway that ran across the bridge shared it with the M5.

Six lanes of Friday lunch time traffic were speeding across the Avon Bridge, the first lane of which was less than five metres from me. There was a steel crash barrier and a narrow screen about six centimetres thick. This was about one hundred and seventy centimetres high, meaning it was at the height of my chin. The noise coming from the road was incredible, but what was also incredible was the force of the wind. This had really picked up as predicted and was coming from my left in forceful gusts. I would have loved to move as far from it as possible, but the cycleway was only five metres wide and on my right was a metal railing over which was a very long drop to the river. I can't tell you how high up I was, all I will say is it looked a long way down and the river below looked deep and wide, not to mention cold. As the wind was so strong, I ran as far over to the left as possible but every so often the strong wind buffeted me to my right and sent me closer to the railing. Suddenly a cyclist came alongside and shouted something. I didn't hear but I smiled and said sorry holding my hands up in apology. I felt like I was swaying across the lane and had probably made it difficult for the cyclist to pass by. After this I periodically turned around to check for bikes. The wind, the noise and the threat of silent assassins creeping up from the rear made it a nerve wracking ten minutes and I was glad to get across.

Arriving in the Kingswood area of Bristol at 12:30, I decided to seek out lunch. With no café in sight and the nearby pub not serving food, I settled for a Ginsters pasty, and washed it down with a bottle of Lucozade, with a Snickers bar to follow. Rubbish fare I know. Nevertheless, it filled me up and I sat in the midday sun having enjoyed my snack feeling sleepy and contended. I could feel myself starting to nod off but felt this was definitely not the place to be taking a quick nap so set off again at 1pm, Although the route was waymarked at this point, I seemed to be going in the wrong direction. Eventually the route turned right going behind a small school and along a tarmac cycle path. This led me to a road in a housing estate. There was a parade of shops across the road, and I noticed the café I had wished for earlier. The aroma of its lunch times specials wafted across the road, enticing me to enter, but I resisted the pull of its tantalising tasty tentacles. This journey is not an eating competition.

I ran past another school, this one a much larger senior education establishment. Noticing the name of the school I stopped and pulled out my phone, taking a picture of the school sign. The school was called St Bede's which was also the name of the school I attended from the age of thirteen. St Bede's Grammar School, Bradford played a significant part in my life. I made some lifelong friends, but it was also where my love of running was really forged. I was reminded of the final line of my school hymn and sang the last line.

"We shall not shrink, we shall not yield, we shall not fail."

Inspirational words that I hoped would help me to the far end of our little island.

The route took me around the school's perimeter, and past some allotments where the road ran out. It looked like a dead end and I began to think I'd gone the wrong way. It was only when I got right to the very end of the road that I spotted a small path through an area of undergrowth. This led to a narrow footbridge over what is best described as a large stream but was really just a murky, litter filled ribbon of slow-moving stinking sludge. At the other side of the bridge was a concrete underpass. I'm not sure what it was actually going under. It appeared to have nothing particularly over the top of it and from what I could tell, didn't lead anywhere particularly at one end. Graffiti adorned the walls, and the floor was littered with hundreds and hundreds of small aluminium cartridges and empty larger cans. At the other end of the underpass, was a road that appeared to have been recently completed. It was flanked on both sides by overgrown wasteland that looked like it had been cleared and flattened in preparation for building on but had been left to go wild again. Between the road and waste land were two drainage ditches, one on each side. Each ditch was filled with green slimy looking water, and every so often pieces of half-submerged debris. At the edges of the ditches were piles of household rubbish, old mattresses, wardrobes, discarded kitchen units and broken furniture. Clearly this was fly tipping territory. Much further up the road I could see large industrial units but here there was nothing. No buildings, no side roads, no car parks and no layby.

Further up the road a white van had just come around the corner and was facing me at the far end of one of the industrial units. It drove at speed passing the last unit and headed towards me. It got closer, finally slowing just before it reached me. The road was made narrower at this point by the debris, and I had to move behind a pile of rubbish so the van could pass. The driver wore a baseball cap and just before he reached me, he pulled the peak further down over his eyes. As the van passed, I noticed there were no markings on it. Clearly the driver was up to no good. I watched him drive all the way down to near the underpass, turn the van sideways and stop. He got out and walked around the back of the van but didn't open the door and continued round to the far side of the van where he was out of sight. I considered going back and asking him what he was doing, but apart from photographing the registration number there was not a lot I could do. I was surrounded by fly tipping. Surely the local council must be aware of this and could have installed a hidden camera somewhere nearby if they really wanted to resolve this issue. After a minute or so, I heard the van's engine start and he drove back up the lane. I moved as far to the side as possible again, allowing him to pass.

Just after the van had gone, I heard a small dog barking urgently from back down the lane. I turned but couldn't see anything. The barking stopped, I continued to look but still could see nothing. I turned to continue, and the barking started again but seemed closer and then it stopped again. A minute later it started again and this time it was coming from one of the ditches. I looked down and saw a wirehaired terrier swimming through the filthy slimy water. I looked down at the poor wretched animal. The dog looked up at me and climbed onto a piece of the floating debris. It then jumped onto the bank of the ditch and ran up onto the road. I held my hand down for the dog to come to me, but it was clearly too scared and shied away. I looked down into the dog's eyes and squatted down, slowly edging nearer. The dog seemed to be accepting me, so I held my hand out again. The dog immediately bolted past me, shooting off up the road and disappearing around the bend. I never saw it again. I have no idea what the driver was up to. Had he been going to fly tip but got put off seeing me, or had he tried to dispose of this helpless hound. It could all be a coincidence and perhaps the driver was a tradesman, desperate to take a call of nature and my discovery of the distraught dripping dog could just have been a series of unfortunate coincidences, leading me to think the driver was up to no good. I want to believe that it was all innocent, I really do, because I want to retain some faith in humanity and not fall prey to media hype that leads us to believe that everyone who just happens to be in the wrong place at the wrong time is up to no good.

I continued through the industrial area, arriving on to a busy road with lots of freight traffic and knew immediately I was near the route to and from Avonmouth Docks. On my left was the sea and the Bristol channel. Up ahead in the distance I could see the new Severn bridge. Although I couldn't see it, I knew that a few miles beyond this was the old Severn bridge and tonight's hotel. I had about five miles to go, It was 1.20pm, I should be there at around 2.30. Perfect.

Four hundred metres further along was a roundabout at which point I would leave the road and join the Severn way footpath. From here the route ran along the bank of the Bristol channel, and should present no navigational issues at all. I just had to keep the vast expanse of water on my left for the next hour and I would be there. Also, at that point I entered Gloucestershire and another county had been ticked off. This gave me a little boost, not that I had been feeling down, at least not yet anyway.

I passed the sign welcoming me to the new county, but my joy was short lived as underneath the boundary sign was a red sign diverting pedestrians away from the riverside footpath and along the road. Next to this was a large section of portable wire mesh fencing. This secured the entrance to the riverside path. On the fence was a letter from the environment agency advising that the path was closed for flood prevention work. There was a map showing the route of the diversion. The first part of this was along this busy road. I looked at the map and estimated the new route added almost two miles to my day's journey. It was a kick in the teeth, and I cursed under my breath then set off along the road. I brought up the map app and noticed a cycle route. The one I had been following all morning that I had somehow forgotten about in my frustration at the path closure. This should take me all the way to Aust, and I set off with renewed hope.

The lunch time sunshine had been replaced by threatening dark clouds which had been blown in by the blustery wind. There was definitely a storm coming and I hoped to get to the hotel before it hit.

I don't know how or why but somehow, I lost the cycle route and ended up on a small quiet street surrounded by residential houses in a place called Severn Beach. As the name suggests it was near the River Severn. I pulled out my phone again and saw that I was mid-way between my original route and the cycle way. A spot of rain landed on my phone then immediately another. Suddenly large droplets were hitting. On the map I saw there was a railway station about four hundred metres towards the river. Although this was in the wrong direction, I may at least be able to get some shelter and let the storm pass. I put my phone away and set off sprinting along the road as the heavens opened and the rain came down in an almighty deluge. I was thoroughly drenched as I approached the train station but right there was a small café and an opportunity for a hot drink.

The café was a real find with what my mother-in-law Maureen would call 'proper food.' Not pizza or paninis, but all manner of home cooked meals. Cottage pie, meat and potato, corn beef tray bake, fish pie, vegetarian lasagne. All good old-fashioned fayre with puddings and custard to follow. The café brought back childhood memories. Oh yes, this was just what the doctor ordered. Needless to say, I spent a happy hour sitting out the storm, eating a hearty meal and enjoying two tea pots of tea. I emerged feeling as though I was a stone heavier.

The little respite had allowed me to spend time looking at the map and I had worked out a route back to the cycleway. First though I wanted to look at the Bristol Channel so made my way left and walked two hundred metres to the coastal path that ran like a seafront promenade on the edge of the Severn. My original route would have brought me along this path had I travelled along the Severn way as planned. When

I arrived, I couldn't see why I'd been diverted because at this point it was definitely open. Confused, I decided to see how far I could go so I set off with the sea on my left. I could see workmen a few hundred metres ahead and some very large plant equipment. Sure enough, less than a quarter of a mile later the path was closed. I pulled out the map again and plotted a route past some allotments before rejoining the cycleway and going over the M49 motorway. As I write this today, I have no idea exactly where I went. I just remember a lot of twists and turns and eventually arrived at the edge of a very busy dual carriageway. I pulled my phone out to check the route again.

A father and son cycled past me and stopped at the gate of a house nearby. Opening the gate, they went in. I ran past and heard the father say,

"You go in and I will be back in a minute." The surfaced cycleway running past the house stopped about fifty metres further on, turning to a grassy footpath along the verge of the dual carriageway. A voice called to me from behind,

"Excuse me." It was the man from the house. "Where are you going?"

"Aust," I replied, "to the Tavelodge at the services."

"You can't go that way," he said.

I was about to say that I'm following the national cycle route number forty-two when he said: "You have about five seconds to make a decision!" This suddenly sounded very threatening, and as he stood there, something about his posture or the way he delivered the menacing message just rang alarm bells in my head. One word flashed up in my brain. 'Military.' There was a pause as I thought about how to respond. For a split second we just stared at each other. Then he lifted an arm and like the grim reaper he pointed past me.

"They have closed the cycleway at the other side of this dual carriageway so If you carry on, you will have to run a mile along it, but I wouldn't recommend it as the grass verge runs out in another one hundred metres. There's also a lot of freight traffic on this road and they all fly up and down at around eighty miles an hour."

"I've already run over thirty miles today. I can do without any diversions; I'm running from Lands' End to John O'Groats."

"Well, it's up to you, but if I were you, I wouldn't go that way. I can direct you across a series of field paths that will add a mile to your route, but you will get there in one piece, but the first one is twenty metres ahead so, as I said, you have about five seconds to make a decision."

I turned and saw a broken stile over a fence twenty metres away, and a muddy path heading into a coppice. He gave me directions adding, "It will be very wet but will get you there in one piece."

I thanked him for taking the trouble to chase me and help me out. I was about to set off, but my curiosity had been tweaked so said.

"Can I ask you something? Do I detect a military background?"

"Yes," he said. "Were you in the military?"

"No," I replied. "I did think about it when I was twenty. I even went to Sutton Coldfield and spent three days with the Army but decided against it. Over the years it's proved to be the right decision. I'm too much of a maverick and like to do my own thing. I'm not good at following orders if I don't agree with them, even from my wife."

"Ha," he laughed. "I know that feeling". We both smiled. Then he asked, "How long is your run taking?"

"A month."

"How did you manage to negotiate a month away from your family? I'm in trouble for doing a challenge of my own this weekend."

"What's that?" I replied.

"I'm canoeing down the Thames for the Help for Heroes charity."

"Wow, that sounds like a serious challenge. How far is it?"

"One hundred and fifty miles."

"ONE HUNDRED AND FIFTY MILES!" I exclaimed. "Are you kidding? Wow!

I did a raft race once that was less than two miles that nearly killed me. My pals and I still have nightmares about it. I can see where you get the shoulders from now" I said, nodding towards his massive frame. "Paddling one hundred and fifty miles. Wow," I added, shaking my head in disbelief.

"It's just a different kind of fitness" he said.

"Thanks so much for the directions and best of luck with the canoeing." and I held out my fist. He reached up and bumped his fist against mine saying,

"I wish you the best of luck too. It's an awesome challenge you have set yourself."

We shared a moment of mutual respect and then went our separate ways. Despite the disappointment of another diversion, I was lifted by another moment spent with another stranger on the pathway of life. At least until the latest pathway turned into a swamp.

The footpath ran at right angles away from the dual carriageway heading through a small area of woodland. To the right of the path was a drainage ditch and soon it appeared that the ditch was blocked. Water had spread across the path in front of me. A series of branches and bits of broken fencing had been placed along the ground as makeshift stepping stones, small islands of hope through the black, smelly ankle-deep water. I know it was ankle deep as I had the misfortune to slip off one of the branches early on and ended up with water spilling over the top of and into my running shoe. Not nice. The pathway ran for half a mile and eventually I emerged from the coppice. One white shoe and now one black shoe. Turning left I joined a lovely grassy path running through the fields, almost parallel to the dual carriageway, and arrived at a hedgerow. There was a gate in the hedgerow leading to more open fields, or it should have. Once again, my progress was thwarted as at the other side of the hedgerow, more sections of mesh fencing had been placed, adorned with yet another diversion sign. I was turned right and guided away from my destination to skirt around two large fields and eventually, after over ten minutes of running, I was brought back to a point no more than one hundred metres from the aforementioned gate in the hedge.

I was only about one mile from Aust, but over three hours ago I'd been only five miles from my destination. Thankfully this was the last of the day's four diversions, and I arrived at the Old Severn Bridge at 4.30. I was tired. It had been a long and challenging day. The strong blustery wind had made running much harder, but I had arrived. As I crossed the footbridge over the M49 motorway I realised there was no traffic going along the motorway. I looked along the road towards the old bridge and noticed that all the overhead signs read 'Bridge Closed.' It was too windy for cars to travel over, but not too windy for a Yorkshireman to run over thirty-four miles. You don't have to be mad to be an ultra-distance runner, but it will help if you are.

I'd completed my first seven days and had passed Bristol, a significant milestone. The Southwest had been conquered and tomorrow I would be heading for the Midlands. I'd covered a total of two hundred and forty-eight miles in seven days. I felt immensely proud and yet, I still hadn't equalled the miles run in an average training week of David Bedford, a running legend of the 1960's and early 1970's Bedford was reputed to run two hundred and fifty miles each week in training. He was Britain's top long-distance runner of the era but never won a medal at either Olympic or Commonwealth games, and yet held the world record for the 10,000 metres with his time of 27:31.

Some people reading this may be regulars at their local park run, a distance of five kilometres. My reference to the park run is to help people understand just how fast Bedford's time was, or 27:31 is just a number. If you've taken part in a park run, think back to how you felt when you finished. Could you have gone and immediately run the distance again? What was your time? An average club runner will aim to finish in under twenty minutes. If you run under eighteen minutes you are likely to be near the front. Under sixteen minutes and you are considered a local elite. I think the ladies park run world record is 15:29. My best time over 5K was 16:52, achieved aged forty-seven, and my last park run time was 22 minutes so 15:29 is like flying.

Bedford's time is equal to running two park runs back-to-back but running each in 13:46. He really was a true legend and someone who inspired me to take up the sport, but he wasn't the only one as the sixties and seventies were littered with sporting heroes who all played a part in my love for running.

CHAPTER 11

He's Catching You

In the summer of 1968, I was seven years old when the Olympic games were held in Mexico City. They were also held in a little street in Lidget Green, Bradford. Thanks to a local lad called Peter Jennings, sporting competition came to our little street.

Inspired by the events in Mexico City and the exploits of the newly crowned double Olympic Gold medallist Kipchoge (Kip) Keino, Peter organised a group of kids to hold our own little Olympics during the school holidays. Kip Keino won the 5000 metres and the 1500 metres, but our races were not that far. We had the short sprint, a longer sprint and then a longer race that involved a lap around the block. We lived on a crescent, St Wilfred's Crescent, and in those days, there were not a lot of cars, so the street was our playground. A full lap of the crescent was probably about 250 metres but seemed a lot longer.

Our Olympics also included a long jump and an improvised shot put which involved pushing a half brick, shot put style, across the road as far as you could. We would hold the events each day over one week and you would get points which were all added up over the week and on the last day, medals made from milk bottle tops and string were awarded. This was really great fun and although I didn't win, I always enjoyed the competition. A spark had been ignited.

Further up the street was a boy called Neil. I can remember that in my earlier childhood he played out with the rest of us but as we got older, he was not allowed to. The thing was he had some kind of learning difficulty and went to a special school. He was a bit of a gentle giant but didn't know his own strength, and there had been some complaints that he had hurt other kids. He meant no harm but his parents had decided to chain the garden gate up so he couldn't get out. That way he was less likely to cause or get into trouble. He would stand at the gates watching us play but was unable to join in. Now it sounds cruel and looking back he must have been very frustrated but that was just the way it was.

Shortly after our Olympics I was sent on an errand and had to run past Neil's house to the shops. Neil was at the top of his drive at the gate and saw me coming. As I approached, I could see he had a brick and was shot putting it down his drive as he had seen us do earlier in the week. Suddenly Neil hurled the brick over the gate hitting me on the head. The result was another ambulance ride to the Infirmary and more stitches.

The City of Bradford had its own cricket league and for those who are non-cricket fans, the standard in the Bradford League was very high, with many Yorkshire County players representing one of the Bradford League clubs. Lidget Green had a team in the league and each year the club organised a summer fete, 'The Children's treat' As the name suggests it was aimed at children's entertainment with stalls and activities for children to have a special day out. There were races too for ages seven up to twelve years old. They were sprint races, a flat sprint, an egg and spoon and a sack race. I entered all three and these were my first real taste of athletic competition.

Lining up on the start line was a nervous moment. I looked at the other competitors. I was on my own. No parents. No teachers. No team to help me. Just me against the rest. Was I their equal?

It's still the same today and the experience of standing on a start line heightens your senses. It makes you feel alive.

Silence descends. The butterflies are going. At that moment who really knows? Are you better than the person standing next to you, and if you think you are, are you mentally tough enough to prove it? At that moment it's not always about who is the best runner, but who can hold their nerve the longest. If you're on that start line, you're pitting yourself against your peers and even Olympic champions have come unstuck at this point.

BANG!

The gun goes and you're off. What's going to happen in the next few seconds? Well back in 1968 what happened was, I got soundly beaten in all three races, however I absolutely loved it. The whole experience. The anticipation, the excitement, the competition, right up to the point where I realised I'd lost, but I couldn't wait for next year to have another go.

Two years later the Commonwealth games were held in Edinburgh and Kip Keino was there. I sat glued to the TV watching the festival of sport. Scotland went wild when the relatively unknown Lackie Stewart won the ten thousand metres, however pride of place went to Ian Stewart who beat the Olympic champion to win the five thousand metres. Fantastic. Back on our street, Peter Jennings again organised our own version but this time with longer runs involving two laps and four laps of the crescent. Peter beat me over the two laps, but he didn't beat me over the four laps. I was champion and I loved the thrill. Shortly after this I asked my dad to cut my hair really short just like Ian Stewart, although that didn't last long, not when I was also a George Best fan.

Peter, who was two years older than me, was the instigator of many of the events we did on the street. In addition to the mini-Olympics, he used to arrange five a side football matches against teams from other local streets. We played in the local park on summer evenings calling our team Wilfred's Wanderers. I loved it and it really played a part in my love of sport. Peter was a good friend and role model. He used to give me his old football magazines, old football boots and kit he had outgrown. To this day he is still involved in running junior football teams in the local area, doing his best to keep young lads off the streets. I occasionally bump into him on Bradford City match days, and we talk about those old days.

Two years after those Commonwealth games I started at a new school where I was introduced to cross country running. This school was called St Edmund Campion and it was probably one of the happiest times of my life. My form teacher was also the head of the P.E. department and this couldn't have worked out better for a sports mad eleven-year-old. We had four lessons of PE each week and at least two of these involved us being sent on a cross country run. Most of the boys thought it was akin to torture, but I thought it was brilliant. I would usually finish in the first three and actually win most of the time, but not always. Later that winter I was selected for the school cross country team. The team of eight was made up of boys aged under twelve, under thirteen and under fourteen as we were running in the Bradford Schools under fourteen race, meaning I was running against boys almost three years older than me. I remember the race was held in Heaton Woods Bradford on a snowy January day. I finished thirty sixth in a field of over two hundred but was a long way behind the winner, Eric Walsh from St Bede's. However I finished as the second member of our team. My dad told me how proud of me he was and suggested I join a local running club. He must have made enquiries as a few weeks later he took me to Horsfall playing fields which had a running track and was the home of one of the country's oldest running clubs Airedale Harriers, Initially I only went along a couple of times, as it was a bit too far for an eleven year old on the bus on a school night. Instead, I started running before school, and two or three times each week I would run six laps around the block before School. Our postman nicknamed me David Bedford who had now become a household name for his flamboyant running exploits and running in his red socks.

I enjoyed my time at this school as they played a lot of sports. For boys it was football, rugby and cross country in winter, cricket and athletics in summer. They even had an inter-form rugby sevens tournament and I played that too. Although I was a bit small for the central rugby positions, once I got the ball on a full-sized rugby pitch with only seven players I was away and scored try after try in the tournament. I was selected for the school rugby XV playing on the wing. Our first game was at a public school called Rishworth. This is not too far from the famous farm in the middle of the M62 motorway, often mentioned on the BBC traffic reports as 'little house on the prairie.' Needless to say, we played there on a wild and windy winter's day when the westerly wind was not helping weedy twelve-year-olds hurl the ball out to the wing where I was. A freezing frustrated figure sprinting up and down next to the line to try and keep warm. As the rain grew heavier the sodden sleeves of my rugby jersey grew longer as the game went on. I think that is the coldest I've ever been. Thirty minutes felt like three hours in which I never touched the ball. Not once. It never made it out to me. The teacher substituted me at half time and sent me back to the changing rooms saying

"Fry. You had better go and get warm, your lips are blue."

I was also selected for the football team, and eventually made captain. We had football training every Wednesday after school in the winter, which meant I was home about two hours after my siblings. By that time they had already eaten and my meal would be plated up and covered by the lid of a poaching pan with the plate sitting on top of the simmering water. Wednesday in our house was baking day. Mum would make meals with pastry and usually it was meat and potato pie or sometimes corned beef pasty. Delicious. This was followed by either jam pasty or a sweet mince pie, both made in a baking tray and sliced into squares for our packed lunches. However, on baking day these were served with custard, all piping hot, and all eagerly wolfed down by a hungry energetic teenager who loved his mum's cooking. I loved Wednesdays.

One member of our team was called Barry Gallagher. Barry was a good footballer and eventually played professionally for Bradford City, Halifax Town and then in Malta, but was keenly chased by Everton before signing for his hometown club. As a boy, Barry was a great all-round sportsman. He was West Yorkshire Schools Javelin champion, a good sprinter and a decent long-distance runner. We played many football matches together and went to the youth club most weeks for two years where I never once managed to beat him at table tennis in all our visits. My favourite memory of him though is at cricket practice one night. Three teachers were supervising the session and Barry was batting. He'd been in for an age and no one could get him out. In the end one of the teachers, Mr Rayner, asked for the ball as he took his sweater off. He shouted to Barry that he was taking over the bowling and to be prepared. Barry took his guard as the teacher took a short run up and sent down a slow but accurate delivery. Barry was unflustered and easily drilled a cover drive, sending the ball to the boundary for four. He looked at the teacher and let out a hearty laugh. The ball was returned to Mr Rayner who took a slightly longer run up, coming in with more vigour than the previous attempt. Barry stepped forward and smartly drove the ball to the boundary again. Mr Rayner was not amused and stared down the wicket at Barry. One of the other teachers stepped up and asked to have a go. He took a much longer run up and came steaming up to the wicket, sending the ball towards the waiting batsmen. Barry stepped forward and with an almighty swing cracked the ball straight back over the teacher's head for six. He let out another hearty laugh. Five minutes later all three teachers were taking it in turns to come racing in and bowl the ball as fast as they could in Barry's direction. He stood his ground and one by one smashed ball after ball, all over into the school car park, over the fence onto the road, over the other boundary into local gardens, and after each boundary he let out a laugh, on a few occasions, saying "is that really the best you can do sir?" It was like the football scene from the film 'Kes' as the teachers grew more and more frustrated, trying even harder to get him out, but Barry was not to be beaten. It was brilliant and one of many happy memories I have from taking part in sport at school, even though it was only training. They didn't get him out that night and eventually we had to pack up, but I never forgot what a pleasure it was to be there.

The school was about three miles from my house by road, but there was a more direct route across a series of fields. This route however went along a muddy track servicing a working quarry. There was a way to avoid part of the service road, but this meant climbing over a six-foot wall and going through a cemetery. In autumn and spring I would sometimes run home this way having spent my bus fare on ice cream, still my favourite food today. I would try to beat the bus but would arrive home muddy and sweaty in my now scuffed school uniform, never giving a thought to my poor mum. Somehow she would get everything clean and presentable for the next day. To be honest I think by this time mum was already used to the fact that I was always going to come home dishevelled and must have had an early indication when, aged six, I caught and brought a frog home. I wrapped it in my new school coat and carefully held both in my hands as I ran home, whilst the rain poured down. Mum saw me as I approached the house and was probably confused as to why I was carrying my bundled-up coat and not wearing it. She was standing on the threshold at the back door as I arrived. I was soaked to the skin but had a beaming smile on my face as I opened up my coat to reveal the prize inside. She screamed as the frog leapt from my grasp, on to the kitchen floor that had been swept and mopped earlier that afternoon. Mum was not impressed with the present nor with the fact that my new coat was covered in a green slime. I was ordered to catch 'that thing' and put it back where I'd found it.

In my second year at Edmund Campion, I had again ran for the school in the Bradford schools cross country Championships. In the under thirteen race I finished in seventh place, doing my best to chase down six boys all wearing white running vests, each with a claret hoop across their chests. Their sports masters, Mr Tony Kingham and Selby Brock, encouraged them all the way. Bradford Grammar School has a strong tradition in producing top class runners. and its alumni include The Brownlee Brothers, Richard Nerurkar the world marathon champion from 1993, and Emile Cairess who recently broke Richard's European record for ten miles. They have always produced first-class runners and the team they had assembled in 1973 were no exception. These were to become my adversaries for the next few years. My teacher congratulated me for beating two of their team as their runners also filled positions eighth and ninth.

At the end of the academic year the school held a sports day and a two hundred metre track had been marked out on one of the football fields. Thankfully this sports day was only for our school so I would not have to contend with the Bradford Grammar School boys on this occasion. I was entered for two races, the eight hundred and fifteen hundred metres. A programme had been produced which showed the school records for each age group, distance and event. The fifteen hundred metres record was shown as five minutes and nineteen seconds and held by a boy I didn't know called J. Crowley. Reading the programme, it showed that J. Crowley also held the under seventeen records. His time as a thirteen-year-old was the fastest any boy who'd attended the school between ages of twelve and seventeen had ever run.

Lining up alongside me in the eight hundred metres was my friend from junior school, Peter Burgon. The gun went and we were off on our first lap of four. I got out in front straight away and was soon ten metres ahead. People often ask me what is the hardest race I have ever done. Without doubt it's eight hundred metres. It is basically a sprint for a distance runner. In most distance races the last lap is always the quickest. That's not the case with the eight hundred metres. If you analyse the times, you will see that the last quarter is the slowest part of the race.

As we started the last lap, I was out in front with a twenty-metre lead. Everyone was cheering. Someone shouted to me "he's catching you." Suddenly I was hot, and with eighty metres to go my breathing became laboured. With fifty metres to go I was far too hot, my legs were heavy, my mouth was dry. With forty metres to go, my lungs were bursting, and my legs no longer seemed to work and I was sure the back of my throat was actually on fire. With thirty metres to go it felt like someone had fastened a tow rope to me and I was pulling a tractor. I could hear someone behind me. He, whoever he was, was certainly catching me. With twenty metres to go my arms were now too heavy to lift and someone must have tied my feet together as they didn't seem to be moving either. Ten metres from the finish line a shadow on the ground seemed to pass me, five metres later the shadow became a person and my pursuer drew alongside me as we both crossed the line. It was Peter Burgon, my old friend. Had he beaten me? We shook hands as we collapsed on the ground, gasping for oxygen and lay exhausted on the grass, not knowing or really caring who'd won. Whilst Peter and I tried to get our breath, everyone else held theirs asking who won? The teachers deliberated and eventually announced the result. The race was a dead heat. We shook hands again and shared the prize. Over the years we shared many experiences. Playing in the same football teams, hiking, going for our first pint, going along to the job centre for the first time then meeting up after our first job interviews and discussing the merits of what we had been offered. Going on our first holiday without our parents. That's what sport does. It's not just the physical health benefits. Sport brings people together. It forms bonds and friendships that last a lifetime.

An hour after that race I stood on the start line for the fifteen hundred metres and won easily in a time of five minutes and seven seconds, beating the time of J. Crowley and setting a new school record. I didn't realise at the time but in fact records were broken in nearly every event that day.

CHAPTER 12

Lucky Man

Day 8 – Friday 8th April 2022 – Aust
(Old Severn Bridge) to Gloucester

It was a bright morning as I left the service area and headed towards the river. I followed the signpost for the Severn way, joining a narrow footpath that took me along a ridge and through an area of long grass. The path was overgrown with shrubs on both sides, but eventually emerged onto farmland, and a short while later onto a wide grassy river bank with extensive views across Britain's longest river. The close-cropped grass was a pleasure to run on. Sheep dotted at intervals were munching away and ensuring the grass was a perfect length for running on. It struck me that sheep were God's groundsmen.

It was about 7.30 and I sent a message to family and friends advising that I was on my way again. I remembered the words to a song from the 1970's by Manfred Mans earth band, called 'Davy's on the road again' and began to sing, changing the name and some of the words to fit my own circumstances.

'Stevie's on the road again,

'He's wearing the same clothes again.'

'Stevie's washing all his kit,'

'So he smells fresh and clean.'

I repeated this over and over as I trotted along the riverbank, amusing myself with the fitting lyrics. It was another bright clear day, but it was cold and there was a stiff breeze blowing south, which I was once again running into. I reached a stream that ran into the main river and crossed over a footbridge leading onto a small lane. The lane then followed the shoreline. I stopped for a brief comfort break. So far, I'd been running in my down jacket because the head wind was so cold, but I didn't want to run in this jacket all day. This was my 'going out' gear and supposed to be purely for evening wear. I took out my phone and reviewed the map. Originally I'd planned to follow this riverside path and coastline all the way to meet the Gloucester Canal at a place called Newton, but if I left the coastal path here, I could rejoin the national cycle route 41 in about a mile which would take me on country roads almost to the Gloucester canal and hopefully I could get some shelter from this headwind. I removed my down jacket and trotted up the small lane away from the coast and immediately felt warmer. I was a little bit disappointed to be leaving the nice grassy carpeted coastal path, but the cold headwind had been really sapping my energy. After only a quarter of a mile I arrived in the sleepy village of Oldbury on Severn. I felt out of place in my bright orange tee shirt, running past its picture postcard thatched roofed houses. I didn't see a soul as I made my way through the village. After another half mile I turned right and joined the cycle route. The sun was now doing its thing and warming the world. Wonderful. I was passed by the occasional cyclist but there was hardly any traffic, people or other road users at all. There was very little uphill and it was all a bit boring with nothing really to mention at all, but hey:

"You should write a book" they said,

"Tell people about your exciting journey," they said.

So here I was, just me, on my own in the fresh air, putting one foot in front of the other, mile after mile, not a care in the world, singing to myself, and I absolutely loved it.

After about ten miles I arrived at a small town called Berkeley. It had a castle. I remember approaching the place and thinking it looked very regal. There was a short steep uphill as I arrived into the village and I noticed a sign for a café. The Berkeley Tea Rooms, it sounded like the perfect place for a refreshing brew, so I went in.

I approached the counter to place my order and was made most welcome by Kim Lewis, the owner. The counter was filled with an array of home baked goodies, and I was spoilt for choice. Having placed my order I went to find a table. There were two cyclists seated at a table enjoying eggs on toast and coffee and we exchanged greetings. I looked around for a plug to charge my phone but the only free one was at the table occupied by the cyclists. I took the next table and they plugged in my phone for me as I explained how much I was relying on it for my maps. This led the conversation onto what I was doing and when they heard, they both jumped up and asked if they could take selfies with me. They took my twitter details and a few minutes later my phone was pinging with pictures and good luck messages.

My breakfast and coffee arrived and having finished their meal the cyclists left so I moved to the table they had vacated. Other diners came and went and with all the tables filled a lady came in on her own carrying a cycling helmet, but not clad in lycra. I was on my own at a table for four so, as there were no other seats available, I invited her to join me explaining I would be going shortly anyway. Just as soon as the phone was fully charged. She sat down and asked if I was cycling too. I explained about my run and about Andy's Man club. She worked for the NHS and said she knew what a problem the issue of men's mental health was. We talked about my run and some of the people I'd met. She told me I should write a book as it sounded really interesting.

Just then the owner brought me a second cafétiere of coffee and a piece of the caramel shortbread I'd been eyeing up when I'd ordered my meal. She said these were on the house because of what I was doing. It made me feel a bit like a celebrity. I thanked her and the lady who had joined me took our pictures on our respective phones and Kim put them on the Tea Room Facebook site. I sat back to enjoy my free fare and we continued our conversation with me asking her if she did a lot of cycling. It was at this point our conversation took an unexpected turn. She told me that she had only recently started cycling as her escape from day-to-day issues she was having. She told me that she had hoped it was something she could do with her eldest son, and said she was trying desperately to get him to come with her. She then said the strangest thing.

"I hope my children will forgive me."

She explained that just prior to the pandemic, her husband lost his job. It came with a big salary and the usual perks. Aged late forties he had been unable to find another suitable job, despite sending out a lot of applications. After six months he became more and more disillusioned. He started to drink, a little at first, but very soon a little had become a lot. He couldn't bring himself to go get help of any kind. She couldn't stand to see him like that and eventually felt compelled to ask him to leave the family home, which he reluctantly did. Holding back tears she told me that she couldn't bear to come down each morning and see him, or worse have the children see him, asleep on the sofa or sometimes the floor, next to an empty spirit bottle or in some cases a pile of vomit. Falling into arrears with the mortgage she had to sell the family home and move into a smaller house where the three teenage children now had to share one bedroom. Her husband was living in a hostel. She was struggling mentally with everything life was throwing at her. Cycling had become a release as it gave her two or three hours each week of escape from what she felt was the prison of her home and the worry that her children would never forgive her. It sounded tough. I really felt for her as it was a sad situation.

For most of the next few miles I reflected on situations in my own past employment. Being made redundant or not seeing eye to eye with bosses or company owners had left me unemployed from time to time. Ending up in a bad place could so easily have happened to me. I too sought comfort from the situation by seeking solace in my own addiction. Thankfully my addiction has always been running. Yes, I may like a pint from time to time but in all honesty, given the choice of a few pints in my own company or a five-mile run, the run will win every time. I genuinely believe that running has helped me through so many of life's difficult times. Some will read this and say you can't compare the two, running and drinking. Actually, I believe you can. After a bad day, going for a drink or two is seen by many as a good way to unwind, and it is. Chewing the fat with a work colleague or friend who can help you put things into perspective can be a lifesaver to a stressed, overworked, under-appreciated individual. I would argue that so too can running, and it has helped me enormously over the years. The bigger the issue, sometimes the further you run. There is also the social aspect of running. Heading out for a social run for two or three hours on Sunday morning with friends allows a lot of time to share problems and talk things through. I am a very lucky man and grateful for the free therapy sessions provided to me by my friends on numerous occasions that possibly saved me from turning to drink or other equally destructive forms of escape.

From the Berkeley tea rooms I continued to follow cycle route 41 along quiet lanes. Eventually it brought me to the Gloucester canal at a place called Slimbridge, a few miles southwest of Frampton on Severn. The sun was shining and it was a very pleasant afternoon.

There was an old couple sitting on a bench, perched on a small embankment overlooking the canal. They were holding hands. I waved to them as I ran past, and they waved back. We were all smiling. It was a nice moment. Silly that something so small and seemingly insignificant can cheer you up. The conversation with the lady in the tea rooms had upset me but now the mere sight of that old couple sitting on a bench in the sunshine had brought a smile to my face. Perhaps it was that they were holding hands that seemed to restore some kind of faith inside me. A belief that for every troubled soul, there are two people in love. I assured myself this must be true, as if it wasn't the case, the population would be decreasing.

I was now running along the canal towpath. The sky was blue, the sun was shining. I was eating up the miles and enjoying the journey. I was in a good place physically and mentally and could only put the latter down to chemicals in my brain being released by the running. Endorphins or adrenaline. I'm not sure which, but it makes you feel great. I was flying along. A few miles later as I approached Gloucester I saw a guy ahead of me out on a training run. I actually sped up to catch him, which I did but in doing so I tired myself. I had run four miles in under 28 minutes. That was way too fast. I had no idea why I had done that, stupidity perhaps. I just got carried away. Just before I caught him my watch said my pace was 6:40 per mile. Having run almost two hundred and eighty miles in the last eight days I knew it was the wrong thing to do but I was having fun. So, I had done the running equivalent of having that extra drink when I should have gone home to bed because I was having a good time. A few miles later I had to stop and rest, although sitting on a bench in the warm afternoon sunshine was no hardship. I spent forty-five minutes watching the world go by. I ate two brunch bars and some wine gums and washed it down with the last of my water. I then had a ten-minute nap after which I phoned Angela to give her an update. I told her that quite a few of the people I'd met in the last few days had asked me if I was going to write a book about this adventure. She said,

"Sat on a bench, ate wine gums and had a nap. Yes, I can see your book will be rolling off the shelves." We both laughed and I said. "You're right I'll never write a book."

I set off again at about 3.30 walking the first few hundred metres to get the blood flowing again before breaking into a slow jog. Nothing seemed to work properly, and my progress was definitely more of a shuffle than a run. My running style is not that good at the best of times but for that last hour along the Gloucester canal, it would have only been used by any running coach as an example of how NOT to run. In my excitement I'd overdone it, however I made it, arriving in Gloucester around 16:30, another day nearer my destination. I found my hotel, checked in, and then after a shower and change of clothes, made the following report on Facebook including a selfie.

8/4 End of day 8. Have you seen this man? He is calling himself a runner! but was seen shuffling along the Gloucester canal this afternoon. Clearly the term "Runner" is a broad description. He is in the Gloucester area, and we understand will be on the canal again tomorrow. Other users are advised not to approach unless you have a face mask and earmuffs. Seriously folks. Thanks for all the kind words and donations. So far, I have met six people in eight days who have lost a sibling to suicide, which is pretty sobering. – And before any of my mates say it…No the people I spoke to were not suicidal after a conversation with me.

After posting the message I discovered I'd made a little bit of a schoolboy error. Each evening after my shower I'd wash all my kit, this usually includes my running shoes if there's a hair dryer. I had washed everything on this occasion, only to discover there was no towel rail, radiator, heater or hair dryer in the place. Remembering something I read in a Jack Reacher novel, I wrapped my damp kit up in rolled up towels and slept with them. They were dry by morning, but I could do nothing about drying the wet running shoes, much to the confusion of the staff, who asked me if it was raining when I left wet footprints as I walked into the restaurant.

CHAPTER 13

No S.O.S. Today

Day 9 – Saturday 9th April 2022 – Gloucester to Worcester

It was another beautiful morning as I made my way from my hotel through Gloucester quays at around 7am. Two ladies were out early on their way to the gym, and I complimented them on their dedication, telling them I was only up because I'd a long way to go. Actually most of my route would be along the River Severn and looked flat all the way. With only twenty-eight miles to cover, I considered today was probably one of the easier days of the trip.

The area around the quays looked picturesque as the water reflected the bright blue sky. I stopped to photograph the scene. My route took me across the canal to pick up the national cycle route forty-five. I'd been going just over ten minutes when my phone rang. I was surprised someone was calling me before 07:15 on Saturday morning but it was a work colleague, Richard Smith, who had seen the tracker start and called me to see how I was feeling. It was nice to hear from him. Richard had circulated the news of my journey on our company twitter and Facebook pages and several of our customers had donated to the charity. I always feel it's a fine balance when a member of a commercial organisation asks for sponsorship from its clients. It really has to depend on the cause and the challenge being undertaken. Richard is the company sales director and having discussed the issue with the board they felt it was a worthwhile cause and certainly enough of a challenge to warrant telling customers about.

My employers had also kindly made a substantial donation to the charity. As I spoke to Richard, I emerged from woodland into an area of marshland at the side of the River Severn called Alney Island. Sun shone on the slightly frosty grass. It was beautiful and I tried to describe the scene to Richard, but sometimes you really have to be there to truly capture the beauty. We finished the call and I was running again, although I planned to walk a lot of today's route as the feet and stomach were feeling a bit battered from all the pounding. Maybe this was a hangover from the faster paced running the day before.

The cycle route rejoined the road A417 near the village of Maisemore where it crossed to the West side of the Severn. Immediately my route turned right onto a smaller road, heading directly North.

My phone pinged with a message from my friend Andrew Nicoll,

"Have you ripped the liners out of your shorts yet?" To which I replied,

"Yes. As soon as I bought them. I'm running in swimming trunks."

Immediately I sent a second message knowing how much he loved a TK Max bargain. "Actually, that's not true, They're not trunks but the bottom half of a ladies bikini, size fourteen. They're TK Max specials that Angela saw cheap for £1.00. Very comfortable." Andy replied

"I DO NOT need a picture!"

His message was a reference to a previous ultra run I'd done where I suffered really badly from chaffing. Actually, perhaps it would be more accurate to describe it as the S.O.S. 'Sanding (as in sandpapering) Of Scrotum' and leave the rest to your imagination. All I will add is that it was tremendously painful and was a lesson I didn't need to learn twice. It involved a new pair of running shorts which came with an inner lining sewn into the shorts to replace the need for underwear. This had rubbed the skin of my scrotum red raw, to the point where my 'personal possessions' looked like overripe plums about to burst forth from their skins. On the occasion in question, I was forced to stop high on a lonely moor above the Yorkshire village of Reeth, where I sat down and almost cried. I was miles from anywhere with no first aid kit and in excruciating pain.

To be fair to the manufacturers, that type of running shorts are really designed for athletic events. For running five or ten kilometres or at the most a marathon where you may be running for three or four hours at the most. On the trip in question, I was then into my second day in the same pair. The first day I had run sixty miles and at that point on the second day I'd covered another forty-five. but still had another twelve miles to go. I needed to take some drastic action or I was in trouble. I removed my shorts and began to rip the lining from inside, whilst the refreshing moorland breeze cooled my area of anguish. It was not a two minute job, but eventually once the lining was removed, I put my shorts back on and was able to continue, comfortably commando. Since then, whenever I buy a new pair of running shorts, I cut out the liners immediately and always run with swimming trunks under my shorts as my base layer. They don't move so there is no friction. I've not suffered the S.O.S. since. We live and learn.

Back in the present I followed the road for about two more miles before turning right onto a farm track. This took me down to a footpath through fields of dry grass to reach the banks of the Severn. I followed the river for several miles. It was very quiet and I only met one person, a man walking a dog just before the village at Ashleworth. I passed through a field of new lambs and took a photograph of them for a friend, Mary, a former international runner, and now a high-level cyclist, but also a sheep farmer. She was following my progress and had just finished the lambing season herself. I thought she would appreciate the photograph, although at that point I had no Wi-Fi or phone signal. As I emerged from the fields I arrived at a beautiful church, St Andrews and St Bartholomew's, which I also photographed. Next to the church was a small field with two piglets. The piglets came right up to the fence, so they were photographed too. As soon as I noticed I had a signal I sent Mary a picture of the lambs saying.

"Saw these and thought of You". She came back with a message.

"What are you trying to say?"

I was puzzled and didn't understand her message. It was a few days later I realised I'd sent her the picture of the piglets and not the lambs. I felt very embarrassed and immediately sent a message of apology with the correct picture and a comment that maybe I needed to visit Specsavers at some point.

I made my way across two fields, firstly passing in front of a small graveyard and eventually emerged on a lane which was where I reconnected with the cycle route. However, I had decided to stay off the roads today and where possible to keep to a network of public footpaths that crisscrossed the area. The cycle route followed the country lanes winding around the fields and I hoped my route would be a little bit shorter. I crossed the road and picked up a path straight ahead, leading me uphill and directly North. At the top of the hill I could see a large farm ahead. So far that morning I had seen just three people. It was now about 10am. As I arrived at the farm buildings suddenly there was a large crowd all chatting excitedly. There was also an ambulance and three paramedics stood around drinking coffee from a flask. It was clear I had dropped in on some kind of event. I passed the front of a large barn and a lady's voice called

"Are you here for the young farmer's do?" She was laying quarter pound hamburgers on a tray. I replied, "Not really but if there is a free cup of tea going I could be persuaded."

"Oh sorry, we don't have any hot drinks ready yet. It will be about half an hour until the boiler warms up, but if you stick around a bit longer you can have a burger with your tea" It seemed like a good offer but I politely declined explaining I was on my way to Worcester so needed to keep going. She smiled saying that was a long way and wished me luck.

I continued on the footpath, passing a row of around twenty Range Rovers. My route took me across a field of some kind of crop on a clear path. In the distance a few fields away was a large house that looked like some kind of grand home. I arrived at a gate on the other side of the field, only to find it was fastened up with orange twine. It looked like it hadn't been opened for years. On the other side it was surrounded by weeds and nettles. I checked the map app. I was right on the path so climbed over the gate and fought my way for ten metres or so, through the undergrowth into a field of horses.

A lady was grooming one of the horses. The field was sectioned off into smaller enclosures with a network of white tape. Within each enclosure was at least one horse happily chewing away at the grass. There was no sign of any path, but the map showed it continuing in a straight line from where I stood, going close to where the lady was grooming the horse. It turned diagonally at that point, going off to the far corner of the field. I continued and as I approached the lady said.

"Excuse me please. Could you tell me where the public footpath goes please?"

She stopped grooming the horse and looked around the field, then said she was sorry but didn't know. She added

"I didn't realise there was a footpath." I explained the route I believed it took. The horse started walking towards me and she followed it at the same time saying to me,

"That may be right as there is a stile in that corner of the field." As she spoke she turned and pointed in the direction the map had displayed. The horse had come right up to me and she said,

"Tom, leave the man alone."

"Is your horse called Tom?" I asked.

"Yes" she replied, "and he's very nosey" patting and stroking the horse as she said this. "Can I take a photograph of him please?" I asked. "My son's called Tom and I would like to send him a picture of his name's sake."

I sent my son the picture, chuckling as I added a message 'Tom, meet Tom.'

It's funny how we are amused by little things. Sixty-one years old and I still haven't grown up. I thanked the lady and made my way to the corner of the field where I climbed the stile she'd mentioned. This brought me in front of a wall that bordered the gardens of the large house I'd seen earlier. I looked at the map. It was called Great House Farm and really was an impressive building. Half of the front elevation was covered with Tudor style cladding. The surrounding land most probably all belonged to the house at some point and from its position at the top of the hill it had a wonderful view of the Severn valley.

For an hour I made my way without incident along various public footpaths, each crossing fields, boundary hedges, fences or walls. Eventually I arrived at a small lane, and looked for another public footpath that should be about twenty metres on the right. Sure enough there was a signpost at the end of a hawthorn hedge, almost lost in the branches and blooming blossom. I arrived at the footpath sign expecting there to be a gate into the field but there wasn't. Just a short stretch of wrought iron fencing about one metre long. The land at the other side of the hedge went steeply uphill so the bottom of the fence was about one foot higher than the road. There was no stile over the fence and I would have to climb up and over, using the narrow iron fence rungs as steps. The fence was actually leaning towards me at an angle which made it difficult to climb. I couldn't get my foot far enough over the bottom rung unless I pressed right up to the top rung of the fence. The top rung was pressing right into the area of my sternum, and it was not possible for me to move any further forward and yet I was only able to get the toe end of my shoe over the bottom rung. I gripped the top rung with both hands but it was really thin, not much thicker than a climbing rope so there was not much to hold on to when pressing down. I put my foot onto the second rung and I pushed down on the top rung, raising myself up but had to hang on tight. If you can picture the shape of my body at this point, it was kind of jack knifed, with my feet being almost two feet in front of my hips and my hands, both of which gripped the fence, whilst my head was a foot in front of my feet. I pushed the top half of my body forward over the top rung, which was now at waist height. Still, I could not get over the fence because when I let go with either hand I started to fall forwards over the fence. Also because of the position of my hands on the top rung, there was not a lot of room to get either of my feet past either arm. and I could move neither foot past my arms.

After moments of deliberation I decided to grasp the nettle and leant further forward. Because of the steep angle the fence was standing at, it was easier to walk my hands down the other side of the fence head first, which is what I eventually did. When my hands reached the floor and my twig-like arms were unable to support me, I fell the last few feet, uncerimoniously face planting on the grass, still wet with morning dew.

I know I'm not the most supple or flexible of people but I am far from unfit and yet climbing over that fence was a serious challenge. I doubt there are many sixty-year-olds who could have gotten over it easily. The fence was not loose or rocky, and it appeared to have been deliberately erected at this steep angle, making it almost impossible to scale without resorting to some form of acrobatics. Why wasn't there a stepping stile to aid walkers, or a post next to it for holding onto.

The path went uphill for thirty metres emerging onto a small lawn at the side of a driveway. The driveway was bordered at the other side by a wooden three bar fence. The route went directly across the driveway where I'd have to cross this next fence. Once again there was no gate or stile.

What I could see was a small section about two thirds of a metre where the fence stopped and restarted. In between these two points the wood had been painted black, whereas the rest of the fence was light oak in colour. Where it was painted black, the spaces between the three fence spars had been almost filled in with additional spars of the black painted pieces. When I got closer I saw that the black pieces were actually plastic, whereas the rest of the fence was timber, in building terms, good old fashioned three by two (inches) and could be vaulted or climbed in a breath. The plastic however was very thin, about one centimetre, and the plastic panels were placed so that the space in between was very narrow making it difficult to get my training shoe into the gaps. It would have been impossible for a hiking boot; however, I made it over although once again, I wouldn't have won any points for style.

Once over the fence the grass was a lot longer. Lush ankle-deep grass with no evidence of any path on the ground. I was now at the top of a small hill and looked down to the bottom corner where I believed my route should be. The area was full of small trees, all covered in blossom. I appeared to be in a small orchard. It was a sunny day and it looked beautiful. I reached for my phone to take a picture but as the phone was still on the map app, I checked the route first. This was to continue diagonally down to the bottom of the field and into what looked like a vicarage that would lead me to the road. I had wanted to stay off the road so traced my finger along a second path coming from the vicarage into the field I was in, but this second path ran right along the line of the boundary wall and headed off into the adjoining field at what appeared to be the wrong angle to the meet the road. I started off down the hill, trying to pinch the screen to enlarge the map, and trying to work out which of the two paths would be my best option.

Halfway down the field I was now only about twenty metres from a stile where the second footpath exited the field so I decided to walk over and see if I could see where it went. I moved off the line of the path but had gone no more than five metres when suddenly there was an angry shout from behind me.

"Oy! – That's not the path!"

I was no more than five metres from the line I'd been on, and no more than twenty from the field boundary where there was clearly a stile with a footpath symbol on it. Both paths were marked on the map as public rights of way but there was still no visible evidence of either path on the ground. I turned my head looking back up the hill and saw a man in jeans and a checked shirt, standing on the driveway with his hands on his hips. I looked and pointed in the direction of the wall saying,

"I'm just trying to work out where that path goes." The man shouted back angrily.

"It tells you on that thing you've got in your hand."

I looked back in his direction to see he was now in the field and marching down the hill in my direction. I was about to speak when he lambasted me with a tirade of abuse.

"You people think you can just come wandering onto other people's land and go where you want when you feel like it. Well, I'm not having it!"

He strode purposefully in my direction, a man on a mission, seemingly intent on making a point. I replied,

"Sorry but according to the map, I'm on a public right of way. I'm not wandering aimlessly. In fact I'm doing the exact opposite and trying to ensure I stay on the right of way. That's why I'm looking to see where that path goes."

He was incensed. I can't tell you what he actually said next because he came out with such a volatile verbal volley that I stopped listening. I thought through my actions of the last few minutes to try and see what I had done that could possibly warrant such a reaction. I looked at the map again and could see the little red arrow which indicated my position on the map was right next to the green line of the footpath.

If I had strayed from the correct line of the invisible footpath I'd done so by no more than a few metres, so said to the man.

"According to the map I am right on the path."

Either he didn't hear me over the sound of his abuse or chose to ignore what I said and carried on ranting. He was now about twenty metres away and still screaming. For the first time I turned to face him square on. I didn't like his aggressive behaviour. He wasn't trying to help me go the right way, he was trying to bully me to stay off his land even though it had a public right way running right through it. I put my phone back in the case and clipped it shut. Then with my arms down by my sides I looked him directly in the eye, and began walking silently towards him, fists firmly clenched.

What happened next was absolutely laughable. As soon as I had gone three paces he immediately stopped in his tracks, He also stopped shouting. I kept walking slowly towards him and then said firmly at a normal volume,

"I've done nothing wrong and you're completely out of order shouting at me like that." He began walking backwards and then in a voice bordering on panic said.

"You can't come near me, I've got covid." I stopped and stared at him, then let out a kind of fake laugh then smiled at him before saying more loudly.

"You are a pathetic lying bully! My dad died from covid. I watched him in his final hours and saw how it reduced a fifteen stone Judo instructor to a feeble bag of bones. If you really had covid you wouldn't be able to walk and bellow at the top of your voice at the same time, and you certainly wouldn't be marching down this hill because you would know that you were going to struggle to get back up again. You really are pathetic."

He stood there, spluttering and stammering, but was unable to say anything meaningful for a few seconds and I continued to chastise him.

"I've come all the way from Lands' End in the last nine days and you are without doubt the rudest most obnoxious individual I have met. How does it feel to be the rudest person in the whole South of England?" He stood there with his mouth open whilst I turned and walked calmly out of the field.

It's funny what goes through your mind in certain situations. Ten minutes later as I jogged along the road, I suddenly thought of the charity Andy's Man Club and how they were trying to get men to open up about their problems. It crossed my mind that I should go back and invite him to one of their meetings. I began chuckling to myself, wondering what his reaction would be if I went back and asked him if he needed to talk to someone about what was causing his aggression. His head would probably explode. I smiled at the thought and carried on running. Looking back it had been a very strange few minutes. It could have been upsetting until the point where he said he had covid. Either he had it, or more likely he didn't, but either way I felt sorry for him. Having lost my dad to covid, only a few weeks after the first lock down, and having suffered badly with it myself, I knew only too well how debilitating it could be. But if he didn't have it and had used that as an excuse, he needed a serious reality check.

I made my way along the road and a few miles later was grateful to an old couple who refilled my bottles for me. They were in their garden planting bedding plants. They told me they were excited as that afternoon they were going to watch their grandson playing hockey for the first time. I told them I was going to be a grandad in July and somehow this made the encounter with the angry apple farmer seem all the more futile. I felt a tinge of guilt that I had responded to his aggressive behaviour with a need to stand my ground. To what end? Life is really too short for quarrels and grudges. It only seems like last year that as a spotty spindly sixteen-year-old I went for my first job interview and now I'm in my sixty second year and going to be a Grandad. Where does the time go? Why waste a second of what's left by falling out with total strangers. I resolved to not let any more idiots get under my skin.

Thanking the old couple I was on my way again and a few miles later reached the village of Upton Upon Severn. This was a crucial point as it was one of the few places I could cross back to the East side of the River Severn before reaching Worcester. My decision to spend the majority of the day walking rather than running was reflected in the statistics so far. Eighteen miles in five hours and thirty-nine minutes. A pace of eighteen minutes and fifty-seven seconds per mile. That was definitely walking pace but I'd also been slowed a little by the map reading as none of this route had been loaded into my phone.

I had hoped to find some kind of café in Upton but there didn't seem to be one. Not even a shop, So I fuelled up on peanut M & M's I'd carried from Gloucester. They would have to sustain me all the way to Worcester which was still a further ten miles away. I crossed the bridge and the main road, heading for what looked like a show ground. A large flat manicured grassy area, taking up a sweeping bend in the river. I made my way across to pick up a bridleway and followed this for a few miles before eventually arriving at a church at the southern end of the village of Kempsey, five miles from Worcester.

Just before the church in Kempsey was a ford, at the side of which was a small footbridge. A family made up of three generations were making their way across the footbridge. I said "hello" as I passed and we exchanged a few words. They turned left into the church yard and I carried on the road which I'd failed to see went around the perimeter wall of the church in a big looping semi-circle and I arrived just as the same family were exiting the church yard. The grandfather said,

"Are you lost? We both laughed and I said, "No, I'm just making my way down to the river where I will pick up the Severn Way and I'll follow that all the way to Worcester."

This was true and if all went to plan the Severn way would take me right to my hotel, 'The Severn View Hotel' It was around 2 pm and I was looking forward to finishing at about 3pm. I waved to the family as I ran off, and a few hundred metres later arrived at the river. There was a large sign saying the footpath was closed due to flood defence work and a sign showing an alternative route. This was back the way I had just come, to the church and then along the road to a housing estate. I retraced my steps and rounded the corner to see all seven members of the family I'd passed sitting on two benches. They all started laughing as I approached.

"Now are you sure you're not lost?" The father said.

"You would think so wouldn't you," I replied, then laughed again adding. "Maybe we should define the meaning of lost. I know where I am now, and I know where I'm going, but at this moment I've no idea how to get there, so if I'm not lost yet, I soon will be" and we all laughed again as I left them for the third time, hoping it would be for the last time.

I ran along the road and the diversion took me up a snicket, dumping me on the A38. I asked a local lady if it was possible to get back down to the river at any point and follow it into Worcester. I was told it was closed all the way into the city and my only choice was to continue on the A38. I couldn't muster the energy to run and sauntered the last four miles into Worcester.

The map app said I was only half a mile from my hotel, when my phone ran out of battery. I knew the hotel was on the A38 so it shouldn't be that hard to find. Just then, I almost walked into a traffic warden. This was a stroke of luck, so I asked her if she knew where the hotel was. She did but said it was difficult to explain so I will blame her for the fact that I ended up down in the grounds around the Cathedral. An hour and a half after arriving in Worcester I still hadn't found my hotel. It was now after 5pm. I was tired, hungry and fed up but was sure it was close by. I asked several people, none of whom had ever heard of it. I had made the booking online but had also seen the place on google street view and google maps. Further, I hadn't paid any money at this point, so I was sure the place existed. I stopped a man who was out running, hoping that seeing me standing in my running kit he would be sympathetic but he wasn't really and said.

"I know I've seen it but I couldn't tell you where it is." He turned to carry on down the street. I watched him run off then above his head I saw a sign. 'Severn View Hotel'. We were literally ten metres from the hotel. A hotel that was covered from floor to roof in scaffolding. It also had a large builders skip right outside the front door. I called out to the runner, and as he turned. I pointed to the hotel and he said

"I told you I had seen it" and laughed as he ran off.

The hotel looked like a dump. I was apprehensive as I walked through the door. It was 17.30 on a Saturday night. I was tired and hungry, and I didn't want to have to start phoning around the city trying to find alternative accommodation. How bad could it be?

It was fifteen minutes before the start of the Grand National horse race and a big crowd was gathered in the bar to watch. Out of the crowd a man came up to me and asked if he could help me. I explained that I had a room booked and he said "Stephen Fry?" "Yes." I replied expecting the usual whimsical comment but instead he turned his head to face the crowded bar and held out his hand towards me but with his palm facing up. He then shouted an announcement over the noise of the TV and presented me to the entire room. "Stephen Fry."

Everyone looked at me. Some people laughed, some cheered and some clapped. He then said

"We weren't sure if it was a wind up, Stephen Fry and all that. Then when you hadn't arrived by 4pm we decided you weren't coming, and it was a wind up." I explained that I was definitely real, and I'd travelled on foot from Gloucester so was looking forward to a shower and some food. He asked me to pay in advance and I should have smelled a rat at that point, and maybe more so when he told me it was only thirty-seven pounds. I couldn't remember the price on booking. com but was sure it was higher. He gave me the key and directions to my room as he pointed to the staircase. I found the room, went in and surveyed the scene. It was long and narrow with a single bed running three quarters of the way along the right-hand wall. Beyond the bed was an opaque window that opened onto a rooftop. The window was dirty and didn't shut properly. Underneath it was a radiator which surprisingly was on. A good sign I thought. To the left of the radiator on the back wall was an old black dresser that should have been in the skip outside, and probably would be before too long. There was a plug socket above the dresser and I immediately plugged in my phone. Between the bed and the door was a small white bedside stand with a pink lamp on it. I tested the lamp and it worked. I pulled back the duvet to see crisp white freshly laundered sheets and a spotless pillowcase covering the one pillow. On the black dresser was a kettle and a small supply of tea, coffee and a packet of biscuits. I picked up the kettle and walked past the dresser to a door which opened to a tiny bathroom or more accurately a shower area. Less than one stride in front of me was the toilet. On the right there was a small wash basin with a mirror mounted on the wall above, and on the left was a shower. It all looked as if it would benefit from a really good clean. I shook my head and looked back at the bed. I filled the kettle and decided to have a cup of tea before making any hasty decisions.

I plugged in the kettle, reached for a tea bag and removed it from its wrapper. It was then I noticed there was no cup. I returned to the bar area and was given a mug. I went back to my room, made a cup of tea and ate the biscuits. I switched on the shower and stripped off my running kit, leaving this on the floor of the bathroom so I could wash it as soon as I had showered. There was one small sachet of shower gel. No soap, no shampoo. I washed myself and it was only then I looked round for a towel. No towel. I cursed and dried myself on my running tee shirt. I dressed and rinsed my kit in the wash basin, then put it over the radiator, shirt, shorts and running socks.

I could hear a lot of noise from downstairs and considered what sort of nights sleep I was going to get. I sat on the bed and drank what remained of the tea, weighing up my situation. Yes, the room was rubbish, but the bed was clean, it had heat, it had light, it had a kettle. I was clean and I'd washed my kit. There were people out there a lot worse off. I finished my tea, picked up my phone and went to find something to eat. Another day done and I was well and truly in the Midlands.

CHAPTER 14

Humble Pie

Day 10 – Sunday 10th April 2022 – Worcester to Wolverhampton

I was up and out of the hotel at just after 6:30 am. It was another cold morning and my breath was visible as I jogged along the A44 at the side of the river. Despite my disappointment with the hotel, the bed was extremely comfortable, and I slept soundly from around 11:30 pm through to 6am, without interruption for any midnight bathroom breaks. This had been preceded by a trip to the cinema that provided much needed relaxation and distraction from the run. When I had left the hotel the previous evening to get something to eat, I decided I really needed an early night. I was tired and irritated by the standard of the hotel. This affected my positivity and suddenly everything was an effort. To make things worse I couldn't find anywhere to eat. Everywhere was either full or very busy with a long wait for a table. Suddenly I was irritated by everything, the people I met, the noise, the fact I was hungry, the fact I was tired and probably that I still had over seven hundred miles to run. Cracks were appearing which was not a good sign.

Eventually I gave up trying to find a restaurant and joined the queue in Greggs. I fuelled myself on sandwiches, two pints of sweet tea and caramel custard doughnuts. Yes, there is an S on the end of doughnuts. One was just not enough but a pack of four did the trick. I was 'comfort' eating. The body gets what the body needs and at that moment I needed calories and rest. As I was leaving Greggs, a lady stopped me to ask for directions to the cinema, and although I couldn't help her, it did give me an idea. I took myself off to the 'pictures' and once I'd munched my way through my bucket of popcorn, I slept soundly for the remaining 90 minutes of the film. I woke as it was finishing, grateful for the much-needed rest. I walked back to my hotel via a Tesco Express for some breakfast items and as I got into bed noticed the dramatic improvement in my mood. I was excited for the next day's running. If I ever meet Eddie Redmayne, I will thank him for his part in my recovery, assuring him it was probably the script and not his acting talents that cured my insomnia.

The A44 turned to the right, moving away from the river and headed uphill. Immediately at the top, I turned left into a side street, then passed a Police station and a further two turns later I re-joined the main road which had morphed back into the A38. I covered the first few miles without seeing another pedestrian. There was the occasional passing car but by and large I had the world to myself. The road split again and the A38 went off to the right towards Birmingham. I stayed on the left as the road became the A449 heading for Wolverhampton and the Black Country.

A few miles further on, residential houses were replaced by frosty fields where morning mist mixed with spring sunlight. Mist and sunlight were each doing their best to fight for weather supremacy. My money was on the sun and a beautiful day looked to be in prospect. The A449 is a major road but with a good footpath, so for the moment I had no safety issues. The air was cool but pleasant. I had covered five miles and was back in the grove, enjoying myself. My positivity tank had been topped up. I said to myself ,

"Thanks Mr Redmayne," I will try and stay awake for your next film."

I reached a roundabout, or island as they call them in this part of England. At this point the road became dual carriageway but still with a footpath at the side. We were now well and truly out of Worcester and in the countryside, green fields and pleasant views all around. A few miles later I was forced to leave A449 as the footpath ran out, so for the next mile I ran through the village of Ombersley. It was here I saw the first pedestrian of the day, a man wearing pyjamas whilst walking his dog. They were on the path ahead, going in the same direction and therefore had their backs to me. The dog, some sort of medium sized mongrel must have heard me as I approached, because as I got closer he turned round, planted his feet and stared in my direction. Maybe my perfumed aroma from ten days on the run preceded me. Whatever had attracted his attention he was standing his ground and sending out a 'thou shalt not pass' message. Our eyes locked and he instantly cocked his leg as if transmitting a second unspoken message to tell me I was not welcome. In doing so he wrenched the arm of his unsuspecting owner who was lost in a world of his own. The owner was forced to a stop and he too turned, looking first at the dog and then at me. By this time I was within ten yards of the man so I bade him what I thought was a friendly greeting.

"Good Morning", but he just grunted as if to confirm the unspoken message I had already been sent by the dog. 'Piss Off. Runners are not welcome here.'

I have family and many friends who are dog owners. They all tell me they are part of a happy community, the dog walking community, and every day they have unplanned meetings with other like minded dog walking folk in all kinds of weather, early morning and in the late evening. They exchange pleasantries and chit chat with these fellow canine enthusiasts and generally all get along happily. I have been running for many years. Thirty years ago, when I ran at 7am I may see one or two dog walkers around my favourite thirty-minute run route, however since lockdown the numbers have increased dramatically. Unfortunately, I don't seem to usually encounter the same pleasant bonhomie when I meet members of the dog walking community as they take their daily exercise. I always try to make an effort by offering some greeting but usually the response is to look at me as if I am a piece of something soft and squelchy, swinging in one of the sacks they carry. Irrespective of the day, the hour or the weather, I seem to get the same response to my cheery

"Good morning" or "Hello," namely, "Grrrrrrrr" and that's just the owners. I know it's me that's somehow in the wrong and not them. It must be me as I am the odd one out. They are the normal ones; I am the one out of kilter with what is normal. After all, normal people just don't set off to run the length of the country.

A few miles later I was in the village of Hartlebury but there was no time to visit its thirteenth century castle, which was about a half mile off my route. I bought water from the village store and checked the map, looking out for an important junction I was sure I must be getting close to. There it was less than half a mile ahead where the A449 meets the A450 near the village of Torton. I arrived at a small but busy roundabout and continued on the A449 but it seemed as if I had gone the wrong way and left the main road, as the wide pedestrian friendly path of earlier had been replaced by a narrow, litter strewn obstacle course, with traffic much too close and travelling too fast for my liking. Luckily, I only had a mile to go to the village of Summerfield, and my next key navigation point, a right turn off the A449 onto a road marked on the OS map as Stanklyn Lane. It's not often road names are shown on the OS map. It's only usually if they have a historical significance. This was not evident as I made my way up the long straight road that climbed gently to reach an area of woodland and a lake called Stanklyn Pool. I turned left and in a further half mile I reached Bromsgrove Road in the village of Stone. I turned right, then left onto a quiet lane, and in a few hundred metres my route finally left the tarmac, as the lane became an unmade farm track, then a woodland path. It was now about 10am on Sunday morning, a time when many runners are out enjoying the off-road tracks and paths in their locality, and sure enough a few minutes later a figure emerged from the woodland heading in my direction.

As I made my way up the country it had been my intention to email local running clubs a few days before I reached their towns, to ask if members of their club were willing to run with me. Effectively guiding me whilst I was on their patch. In this way more people would get to learn of the charity I was running for. Alas I only noticed that there was a problem with my outgoing emails when I was on the train to Penzance. For whatever reason I couldn't reply to or send any emails at all. I was certain this was down to operator error, namely me, but try as I might, I couldn't get it to work. So I just accepted my failure and decided I'd speak to every runner I met whilst running and tell them what I was doing. So as this lady approached me I prepared my speech, waving my arm laterally to get her to slow down and she stopped about fifteen yards in front of me, looking a little nervous as I began saying,

"Hi. As a fellow runner, please can I tell you what I'm doing?

I'm running from Lands' End to John O'Groats, and I am stopping every runner I meet to ask them to spread the word around their own running community in the hope that some of you will be interested and possibly donate to the charity."

As soon as I finished my little sales pitch, she commented on my Yorkshire accent. She then said,

"I was at university in Leeds."

It was at this point that I demonstrated a trait inherited from my dad, namely how to pay someone a compliment but word it in such a way that it borders on being offensive, or comes out the wrong way and you end up digging a large hole trying to recover the situation.

The conversation went like this.

"I used to run for Leeds City Athletic Club".

"Really, I run for Bingley Harriers, what's your name?"

"Lucy Wright."

"Lucy Wright! Wow. I remember you. You used to be good! Er, I mean…. What I mean is, you used to be fast! Er, Mmm actually you may still be fast, err good or both, I don't know."

She stood across from me and put her hands on her hips. She began to smile.

I paused and looked at my feet for a second before saying,

"Shall I stop digging now?" Still smiling she said,

"In fairness to you, it was a few years ago. In fact, two children since."

"You were a GB cross country international, weren't you? Also, I believe you still hold the record for one of our local races. I bet we have loads of mutual friends," and I began reeling off names of friends and club mates, many of whom she had competed against and some she was still in contact with. We spent five minutes chatting before she gave me some useful directions to get me through the woods. It was a nice encounter and gave me a boost.

A few miles further on I latched on to more runners, a group of three ladies and a man enjoying the countryside and morning sunshine. It was a nice area to be running in, with lots of woodland paths and shaded trails, not really how I pictured the Black Country. From looking at the map the night before, I remembered that at some point I'd be running on the course of a Roman road, and now here it was, a wide straight track laid out in front of me and suddenly the running had become even easier.

Up ahead at a junction of tracks, a horse rider turned left on to my route, right at the point where the woodland track became a metalled road. It was a shaded tree lined avenue, as it passed some expensive looking houses. To avoid spooking the horse and protect the rider from being thrown, I stopped running about thirty metres behind the horse. Instead, I walked slowly and called out to the rider.

"Excuse me please. Will your horse be OK if I run past?" The rider turned and a young lady probably in her early twenties looked back at me. She smiled saying "Thank you but he will be fine. You're OK to come along."

"Thank You" I said and began to jog by. Just as I passed the horse she called after me.

"Are you lost? You're a long way from Yorkshire." I replied,

Yes but I am a lot closer than I was yesterday." "Why what are you doing?"

I allowed her horse to cover the distance between us, then I walked beside her.

"I'm running from Lands' End to John O' Groats."

"Wow, that's a long way," she said. "I would like to do that on a horse someday."

"You could and you should. Most of my route so far has been on bridleways, or quietish roads, so it will be possible. Anyway, it's good to have an ambition or dream to look forward to and work towards."

"Are you doing it for a charity?"

"Yes, I am doing it for Andy's Man Club."

"I've not heard of that. What is it?"

"It's a club that was set up to get men talking about things that are affecting their mental wellbeing. The club now has almost one hundred branches throughout the country. They meet once each week to get men talking about issues they have and to help each other get through tough times. It was set up by a lady six years ago after her son committed suicide."

"My Dad committed suicide in February."

It was as though the mystery man on the grassy knoll had shot me. I was floored by metaphorical bullets I never saw coming, and was so glad I wasn't the one on the horse. I would definitely have fallen off. My eyes filled with tears that mingled with the salty sticky sweat running down my face, and I fought for words that wouldn't come as our eyes met in a moment of appreciation and mutual discomfort. I managed a feeble apology mumbling,

"I'm ever so sorry." Looking sympathetically, she replied, "No please don't be. I think what you are doing is wonderful and if you can help just one person avoid what I've gone through in the last two months, you will have done something really special. Please let me have your details and I will send through a donation."

In that brief moment she must have relived a plethora of different emotions. Pain, sadness and loss, I'm certain, but also confusion as to why, pity possibly, maybe even hate. Perhaps understanding and acceptance of a situation she couldn't change, but hopefully forgiveness. It was strange but at that moment, in some small way, I shared those feelings with her. That moment was a turning point in my journey. Suddenly I was not just doing this for myself but for every father, every brother and every son in the country, especially if they were considering taking their own life and I was doing it for their wives, their mothers, and their daughters. If I could help just ONE person avoid the trauma and upset she'd gone through I would have changed that person's world forever and that must surely be one of the greatest achievements it's possible to accomplish. The words used by this young lady, mature beyond her years, went through my head for days after.

Over the next few miles I thought about the encounter with the dog walker who ignored me that morning and wondered if he too had a lot on his mind. I resolved to try and be less judgemental with people because who knows what troubles they're having. Somewhere in the fog of the next few miles I recall chatting with a man near Stourbridge. The back door of his car, a people carrier was open, and he was standing on the sill, desperately trying to put something in the roof box but he wasn't really tall enough. I noticed he was wearing Hoka running shoes which have a really thick sole and my first thought was to wonder if he bought these monster soled shoes just so he could reach the box?

"Nice Hokas. Do you run?" I asked.

"Yes, a little," he said.

"Can you tell me if I can get to the canal this way, please?"

He looked at me blankly. Then he looked up and down the street.

"Er I'm not sure."

He called his wife and she appeared at the door holding the hand of a young girl.

"Oh, it's OK" I said, "I will work it out. It's just that I've run from Worcester today and I'm heading for Wolverhampton. I don't want to run further than I have to, but this is the route I've put in the phone."

"Wow from Worcester" his wife said, and this led to the run, the charity, and me giving them details before I set off up the street.

At the top of the street was a snicket that took me to an area of grassland, and allotments, then eventually down to a canal. Rather than run along the waterway, which headed towards Birmingham, my route went straight over a foot bridge and up a hill opposite, continuing to head Northwards. Eventually I arrived in a village called Rushford Bridge arriving at 1pm so I stopped for a well-earned lunch of beef and onion sandwich, coke, tea and refilled my water bottles.

Half a mile further I crossed the A449, taking a quiet lane that led around a care home called St Anthony's, the name of my first school. I crossed a field containing horses, reminding me of my morning encounter with the girl. I emerged near a church where a family was getting out of a car. They were all dressed up with suits, ties, elegant frocks and perfectly styled hair, but it was the clean fragrant smell that I was really jealous of. Suddenly I longed for a long soak in a hot bath and that thought stayed with me all the way to my hotel.

Finally, I re-joined the A449 for one last time that day, in the Goldthorn district of Wolverhampton and before long I arrived at an enormous traffic island with subways and under passes and lots of road works that took a while to negotiate, but eventually I made it into the town centre.

There is a saying that goes 'it's not over until the fat lady sings. This summed up many of my days on this journey. Often the day would go brilliantly and then go pear shaped right at the end. I would get a few hundred yards from my destination only to take my eye off the prize and end up on the wrong side of an industrial estate or retail park with only one entrance and therefore required a detour. A detour that in a car would take only a few minutes, but on foot could add another mile. "It's only a mile" I hear you say, but if it happens every day for 29 days it's an extra day's worth of running. This day was one of those days.

From the town centre, I was less than five hundred metres from the hotel, but as I dropped down to another large roundabout with more under passes, I somehow ended up on the wrong side of a canal and railway line. Once you make this type of navigational error, you should turn around and go back to the last point where you knew you were right, but something in my head said,

"Come on son. Trust your judgement. It's definitely here somewhere. It must be that building there at the bottom of this road." Twenty minutes later I gave in, turned around and went back to the town centre and started again. Immediately I saw my error and five minutes later was in the reception of the Premier Inn, having wasted almost forty-five minutes. It was 1545 on Sunday. I had fifteen minutes to check in, jog the quarter of a mile to the Aldi and buy snacks for tomorrow before the store closed. My trainers were muddy so I took them off at the door and walked into the hotel in my socks.

As I checked in, I explained to the two ladies that I just wanted to dump my bags and run down to the Aldi before the store closed. One of the receptionists said,

"It's OK, you're on the ground floor so your room is just along this corridor."

I took my key card and walked fifty feet along the corridor and saw the door to my room, however between me and it was a short length of the corridor where the carpet was covered in standing water. There was a yellow sign standing in the middle of the flood. This warned me that the floor may be slippery. Directly above, ceiling tiles have been removed to reveal a leaking pipe that dripped large droplets of water at an alarming rate. Towels had been placed on the floor, but they too were now submerged.

I returned to reception in my stocking feet, bags in one hand, shoes in the other, possibly a little irritated. My wife says that when I'm hungry I can come across a little bit forthright. She calls it my 'hangry' phase. So my conversation with the reception team properly sounded unintentionally off hand. How shall I put it? Like a Yorkshire Basil Fawlty.

"Look ladies if you don't mind I am in a rush. I need food for tomorrow. I've just run thirty-four miles from Worcester so I need to eat, and tomorrow, I'll be running another thirty-two miles to Stoke, so I also need food for that journey. I should have been here forty-five minutes ago but now the Aldi is closing and all I want is a long soak in a hot bath, a hot drink and copious amounts of chocolate. It would help me if you could please hold on to my bags until I return so I don't have to wade across the river you have in the corridor and get my socks wet because I don't have time to be putting my shoes on and off, not that can reach my feet very easily anyway, because the Aldi will be closed."

Having completed my moaning monologue, I paused for breath, tried to give them my best smile, dumped my bags on the reception counter and jogged in my stocks to the door. I struggled to put my shoes on, much to the amusement of two smokers standing at the door. I made it to the store just as they announced something about closing which I totally ignored. I grabbed a large bar of fruit and nut chocolate, a pack of baby bell cheeses, a packet of chocolate fingers, some yoghurt, a bag of Werther's original sweets, Some peanut M&Ms a fruit cake and a packet of six muesli bars. Payment was made and I was trotting out of the door at exactly 4pm.

Munching on the chocolate I sauntered back to the hotel. I thought what a complete knob I must have sounded as I addressed the unfortunate reception staff. Never mind chocolate. I would be eating humble pie for the rest of the evening. I returned to reception where there was only one receptionist and an empty countertop. My bags had been moved, but before I could speak the lady stood up and pointed to a room opposite that said private.

"Your bags are in the room across" she said. I replied, "I'm sorry about earlier, It's been a long day and I was concerned about not getting any food. Sorry!" She didn't say anything, but half smiled as she continued to point to the door. I opened it and was met by three other staff members, all folding sheets and stacking them in a tall cupboard. They all stopped talking immediately then smiled simultaneously. One of the ladies who had been in the reception and witnessed my Fawlty impersonation, passed my bags over saying;

"Well done on your run."

"Oh. Yes, Thank you." I said sheepishly. "It's amazing how hungry it makes you," adding feebly. "Thanks for looking after my bags," and left the three of them still grinning like Cheshire cats. I walked slowly along the corridor to the wet area and removed my shoes and socks. As my feet squelched the two strides across the damp towels, I said to myself,

"You are a pillock sometimes Stephen." A minute later I entered my room to find a note on the corner of the bed.

"To Mr Fry. We hope your stay is peaceful and hope you can relax!

Congratulations on your marathon run. Enjoy your bath and have a drink on us."

Signed Chloe and Beth.

Underneath the card was a sachet of Epsom salts and a sachet of Hot Chocolate.

"Double helpings of humble pie are required." I said as I went to set the bath running.

CHAPTER 15

Pondering Perplexing Problems

Day 11 – Monday 11th April 2022 – Wolverhampton to Stoke

You may be wondering what I think about when I'm running for hours on end with no one to talk to? You would be amazed what goes through my head. Today I ended up preoccupied by what to many will seem trivial, but it kept me enthralled for a while.

Overnight the man in the Hoka shoes had kindly left a donation. The Just giving page stated clearly, 'Man in Hokas' and this made me think about how a family of four with two smallish adults one about 5ft 8" and and the other about 5ft 5" get a large roof box onto the top of a people carrier. Yes, I know you're properly bored by this, but it played over in my mind and with nothing better to think about I gave it my attention.

If the two people are of similar height but both smaller than the vehicle they want to lift their roof box on top of, how is done? A fully loaded roof box for a family of four probably weighs about fifty kilos and that is too heavy for an average couple to lift above their heads, even if they use a pair of step ladders. An empty roof box is difficult to manoeuvre. If you are attempting to lift one on your own you need to somehow work your way underneath the middle of it, but having managed that, it's still not going to be easy to lift it above your head. If your arms are stretching to grip the edges of the box, you have no ability to push the box upwards those extra all-important inches so you can slide the box on to the roof bars. It's at this point you need an assistant. Now I won't bore you with all the other pieces of the thought process that went through my mind like, does the person at the bonnet end of the vehicle need longer legs or arms, than the person at the back etc. I'm just giving you an example of the sort of important stuff that goes through my mind when I am running these distances each day.

One day when I was a boy, I was in the car with my dad when I asked him this question. If something happens that creates a sound, but it happens in a place where there is no person, animal or recording device to witness the event or hear the sound, does the sound actually occur? My dad thought about this for a few minutes then said "You should become a buddhist monk, that's the kind of thing they meditate on every day." Now it may be a rule of parenting to change the subject when your child asks a question you can't answer but, what it told me is that it's perfectly normal to ponder perplexing problems and that has kept me entertained over many a mile throughout my life. and I wrestled with this metaphorical roof box as I made my way along another canal for a few miles before rejoining our old friend the A449 just south of the M54.

Once under the motorway and a mile further on I parted company with her, the A449, for the last time, heading for the village of Cross Green. The A449 with its wide footpaths and purposely constructed cycle tracks had served me well. The local council have set the bar high in what other areas should be striving for. Thank you.

The now quiet country road led me through Cross Green, and I came to a bridge over the Stafford and Worcester Canal. This was to be my route for most of the morning but not quite yet. Thirty metres before the canal bridge I turned right under a railway bridge and joined a bridleway along a farm track leading to Larches farm. After going through the farmyard, the track headed out into fields, going continually uphill. This was a shortcut that went over a significant hill before descending to a road near a sewage works where I did join the canal. The waterway had taken a two-mile detour from the outskirts of Cross Green to avoid the gradient. I was pleased with myself for saving the extra distance and it was another example of a little thing adding to my positivity. In a way it's similar to how the Sky cycling team became the world leaders in their sport. Marginal gains. All those small seemingly insignificant savings of fractions, all adding up to monumental improvements. I was feeding off all these small wins. A message of support or Facebook posts, a new donation, or, a time saving shortcut, a stunning setting or pretty view, and the sunshine. I stored it all. It was all positive energy and fuel to be used when the journey became difficult. If the journey got really tough there was always singing. This had been used as a last resort on many occasions, getting me through the harder parts of many long races.

A few miles further on I phoned Angela. It was 9am and she was surprised to hear I'd already covered twelve miles. I love running along canals. For the most part they are really great places for running. Many of them have a tow path of hard packed mud or short cropped grass. Both surfaces do a lot less damage to the feet, ankles, shins and knees than road miles. Many of the canals are out in the countryside with clean fresh air and you truly get a feeling of solitude. I recognise that in and around the major cities that they can be litter strewn and neglected, but even in those areas, groups such as the Canal and River Authority, Sustrans and many local volunteer groups are working hard to restore them and make them pleasant spaces for all to enjoy.

The canal passed through the village of Penkridge, and I considered going in search of food but settled for a muesli bar and pressed on. The tow path took me all the way to the A34 at which point I joined the national cycle route number five. I chatted to a cyclist for a few minutes interrogating him for information. Cyclists usually know the best café's and he did, but none of them were nearby, so he directed me into Stafford town centre via the shortest route where I arrived at 10:30. With eighteen miles under my belt, I was in need of sustenance.

Another meal in another café and another encounter with someone who's life had been affected by suicide, thankfully this had a happier ending for the lady concerned, at least to a point. As I was finishing my meal one of the staff came up to me and said that my meal was on the house. I said no you don't have to do that, but she said the supervisor had agreed that because of the charity I was running for they would cover the meal. I was touched and obviously thanked them, making a note to put this amount on my just giving site myself. It was as I went out of the door that the lady in question came outside for a cigarette and began to tell me her story.

"I didn't want to say anything in there because the other staff don't know, but my fifteen year old daughter tried to take her own life a year ago. I came home and found she'd taken a bottle of pills. Luckily, I got to her just in time and forced her to be sick whilst the ambulance came. It was awful and very scary. She was hospitalised and is still having counselling. Thankfully she's in a much better place now but it's still a worry. Sometimes when I return home from work, I have flashbacks as I enter the house, or if she's late, it goes through my head again. I'm constantly on my guard, wondering if she's OK. It never really goes away."

At this point she finished her cigarette and reached for the door saying,

"Anyway it's nice to meet you and good luck with your run."

With that she went back inside. Once in the door she turned to face me and waved. She definitely seemed to be a lot happier after our conversation, appearing somehow unburdened, like she had needed to tell someone. I walked away feeling that I had helped her in a similar way a therapist would, and it made me wonder how many therapists are in need of their own therapists. As I tried to find my way back to my route a thought smacked me between the eyes. Perhaps it was the nicotine and not my careful counselling that improved her mood.

I'd entered the town from the south but wanted to leave it going north, so I tried to pick my way across the town centre but gave up after trying a few different streets. My route was blocked by a multi-story car park, a hospital and a prison, so in the end I walked back down the road I had come in on, arriving at the spot I had been at almost two hours earlier and re-joined the cycle route. I then looped around the north of the prison sticking with the cycle route as it twisted and turned between industrial units and small side streets eventually taking me to a ring road at the north of the town. This had a marked cycleway on the wide pavement as it went past a large industrial estate. Just after the estate the cycle route turned right and headed into the country on a small narrow lane towards a village called Marston. I wondered if this was the place the Marston Pedigree beer was named after.

I meandered over fields and country lanes for an hour before arriving back on the A34 just south of Aston by Stone. After half a mile I left the road before it entered the town, instead turning towards Aston Hall. Out of the corner of my eye I saw a face staring at me and looked up to see three faces carved into old tree stumps on top of a wall. They looked out along the road like guardians of the garden. I followed the road through the small village and over a bridge, arriving at my third canal of the day. This was the Trent and Mersey canal, another of those early water highways, built specifically to move freight from the workshops and factories of central England to the country's ports for shipment to the wider world. A few hundred metres along the towpath, a sign welcomed me to Stone. At the same time, it informed me Stone was the birthplace of the Trent and Mersey Canal. The sign included a hand drawn artist's impression of four of the town's key points of interest, one of which was a brewery. Maybe my Marston motivated musings were correct after all.

Once again progress along the canal was easy and it wasn't long before I passed a sign notifying me I was on the edge of the Wedgwood Estate. This was fixed to a gate on the side of the towpath informing passers-by that the estate was open daily from 10am to 5pm and proclaimed it to be 'A Great Day of Discovery,' although it made no mention of a cost, perhaps an empty wallet was the great discovery. It did however state that it was a twenty-minute walk from this point. Much less than twenty minutes further along I passed a field of llamas, and a family reaching over a hedge trying to feed them. It was not too long before I arrived in the outskirts of Stoke. My route left the canal at the southern end of the town and my day finished outside the railway station near the University.

My lodgings for the night were a big old hotel right opposite this railway station. The hotel looked to have been a grand place in days gone by with its impressive entrance and reception. I registered and made my way to my room, up a wide marble staircase. After negotiating a warren of corridors, I found the room but was thwarted as the key didn't work. It was a proper key, not a wannabe bank card but just wouldn't turn at all. I returned to the reception where the receptionist checked if it was the right key, and then sent for the maintenance man. I stood there in my socks holding my bags and training shoes and five minutes later a cheerful chap in a cap arrived. He took the key from me, and I followed him to my room. He tried the key and the door opened immediately. I felt like a complete fool until he tried to remove the key from the lock. He twisted one way and then the other. He pulled and pushed and suddenly the whole lock mechanism fell to pieces. 'Vindicated', I thought.

"That's fu<ked it" he said. "Right mate you need a new lock. I'll go and get one now and I'll be back in twenty minutes, in the meantime don't close the door." I explained I needed to take a shower and didn't want to sit around in my sweaty running kit.

"You will be alright," he said. "Your room is the last one on the row. No one's going to walk in on you, even if you wedge the door open. I'll see you in twenty minutes." and with that he was gone. I put the bathroom bin in the door jamb to ensure it wouldn't close and set the shower running. I threw my bags on the bed and filled the kettle. My room was long and at the front of the hotel. It had a big window facing west and the evening sunlight filled the room. I stripped off and showered and followed the usual routine of washing through my running kit as soon as I had finished. I dried myself and dressed then went to make a cup of tea, but the water was cold. I thought I mustn't have switched it on but discovered the plug wasn't working. I tried the light switch for the first time. Nothing. Just then the maintenance man arrived with the lock.

I told him about the electricity, or lack of it, and he went to check the fuse box. He came back saying there was a fault on the whole floor and I would need to go back to reception and ask them to arrange a different room, which I did and to be fair to the lady on reception, she sorted it out very quickly. Ten minutes later I was in a suite with a luxurious bath that would have been very welcome had I not showered already. Although I had an extra floor to climb, the new room was nearer to the grand staircase so probably a shorter journey from reception than the first room. Once I'd transferred all my belongings, including my dripping running kit, I went in search of food.

CHAPTER 16

500 HPS

Day 12 – Tuesday 12th April 2022 – Stoke to Heald Green Manchester

I checked social media before setting off and was amazed to find a picture of my niece was all over twitter. One of my sister Maureen's daughters, 'Emma Lloyd', was a part of the main cast in the stage show, 'Back to the Future'. Last night the show won the 'Olivier award' for the best new musical. That's the equivalent of being in the team that wins the premier league. I sent her a well done message saying " Well Done Superstar" as I was leaving the hotel.

I love the early mornings and being out and about as the world is waking up. I believe it's by far the best time of day to see a place, as it's coming to life, and as Stoke was coming to life I made my way past the University heading uphill to Hanley Park. I went a bit wrong here before correcting myself and eventually finding the town centre. The morning weather was like most of the days had been. It was cold, it was a bit grey and anything could happen, however the forecast was for rain . Of course it was! I was going to Manchester after all.

I made my way across the city, doing my best not to lose national cycle route five that was now my companion, but it wasn't easy. I constantly had to check the map, once again draining the battery. I passed a museum to the potter's art, the Moorcroft Heritage centre, marked by the seventy-foot-high brick-built bottle shaped chimney, and a reminder of the area's historic past.

After an hour I arrived at an area called Ford Green. Here I picked up national cycle route fifty-five, which would take me into Cheshire. The day's navigation to this point had been tricky but should be straight forward for the next ten miles to Congleton, after that it would need closer attention.

The way was broad, straight and flat and was flanked by houses on one side and a huge pond on the other. After half a mile the track began to climb gently, the houses and pond being replaced by open fields. The path kept rising and a sign told me I had entered the Whitfield Valley Nature Park. Here the land dropped away to my right down to a small lake. My route continued to climb and I rounded a bend to see a large whale shaped hill, probably about two hundred and fifty feet high, directly in front of me.

For a while my route climbed gently as it skirted to the left of the hill but eventually climbed steeply for the last thirty metres to the top. The steeper gradient forced me to walk as my legs instantly ached after days of flat running.

"Welcome back to the North" I said out loud with no one around to hear.

At the top I stopped, turning around to look in all directions. Behind me I could see little as the view was blocked by the hill I had rounded, but to my right was a large area of cleared earth and beyond that a disused coal mine. Although a rain mist was forming, you could still make out the silhouette of the tall chimney, the lift tower and the large wheel. All were further reminders of the area's industrial history. I stopped to take a picture and noticed small spots of drizzle on the phone and quickly stowed it away as I moved on. There was no need to put the rain jacket on as apart from the last climb, so far today I hadn't really warmed up so it was already on.

I now joined an old railway line and after a few hundred metres crossed the A527 and minutes later a sign welcomed me to Cheshire and the Biddulph Valley Way. I photographed the sign but later in the day as I looked through the pictures, it seemed insignificant. It was just a white sign with three words on 'Welcome to Cheshire'. It wasn't going to win any photography awards. It was just another signpost, but to me it was much more than that. Crossing into another county was a huge milestone, giving me a boost every time. More positive energy to be stored up for when I needed it. Cheshire. That was a long way from Lands' End. and I celebrated with a handful of peanut M&M's as the drizzle grew heavier.

The route was great for running and easy to follow. In no time I was on the outskirts of Congleton. As I neared the edge of the town I knew I needed to have a good long look at the map. In my planning I had looked at a few different options from Congleton, none of which were straightforward, and I would really need to use the map again until I reached the outer suburbs of Manchester. As this was going through my head the rain arrived with a vengeance and I was grateful for the leafy canopy that provided some shelter from the wilds of Cheshire. I stopped under a bridge and tried in vain to open up the screenshots I had taken of today's route, but even this proved impossible. I wasn't sure if it was because my hands were cold, or because I was unable to dry them properly but whatever the reason, the touch screen suddenly opened and closed pages in a flash, momentarily showing images on the screen, that then disappeared immediately, I likened it to the earlier days of dial up computer systems.

With the phone stuffed back in my bag I trotted on to the rhythmic rain wrapping on the leafy canopy. As the watery droplets got heavier so the noise increased. A drumming deluge drowning out other sounds and sending me into a trance like state as I ran on alone through the tunnel of trees. Leaving the railway line at the next opportunity I headed into Congleton in search of somewhere warm and dry to eat and shelter. I asked a local if there was a café nearby to which he answered

"No! but you can get a coffee at the co-op" and he pointed along the road towards a housing estate. I ran on recalling an early TV advert for the co-op where the message was sung and reached a crescendo at the end.

"It's all at the Co-op – Now!"

Sure enough, one hundred metres along the road was a Co-op and It had a large coffee machine. I arrived just as the rain stopped. Looking at the sky though, this was only temporary.

I bought a coffee, a pecan Danish pastry and one litre of water. After a few minutes with my hands wrapped around my coffee, I was able to open the maps. I spent five minutes checking the route ahead for the next ten miles, then after filling my bottles and dumping the empty bottle in a bin at the store's entrance. I set off to tackle the next stage of my adventure and the run to Manchester.

Thoughts of Manchester brought to mind words from the Gallagher brothers, and I began to sing one of their famous songs. I wondered if they would ever heal their rift and thought how sad it is when brothers fall out. My thoughts turned to my own brother who lives in Tain, a town forty miles north of Inverness, and one I would be running through near the end of my journey. I sang in my best Manchester accent as I ran up the street,

"And all the roads we have to walk are winding,"

"And all the lights that lead us there are blinding."

"There are many things that I would like to say to you, but I don't know how."

I made my way to Congleton Park, which was at the other end of the street from the Co-op. Once in the park a signpost for the cycle route pointed me through the park and brought me to a small industrial estate. I noticed a forty-four-ton articulated lorry parked outside one of the units. The truck was parked along the pavement and taking up all of the cycleway and yet was so far in the road, traffic could not pass both ways at the same time. The roads in the industrial estate, like so many other industrial estates around the country, were actually too small and narrow for the size of the trucks that deliver to them. I thought back to the towns I had visited already and at the number of times the cycleways had ended up in industrial estates. Clearly the route planners don't expect many cyclists to be using these routes at the same time as the country's transport industry.

The cycleway then crossed the A34 and headed out of the town on the wonderfully named Giantswood Lane, and into the Cheshire countryside. The rain started again, big drops of heavy rain and before long I was wet again. It continued for the rest of the morning, getting heavier and heavier. Eventually it became what a fell running friend of mine describes as 'Horse Pissing' rain. The first time I heard this colourful comparison, whilst being amused at this vernacular poetry, it did make me wonder if the force of rain was measurable in such terms. I mean to say, we know the engine capacity of a motorbike is say 500 HP (horsepower), why not say the rain will be as heavy as 500 HPS (horses pissing) and then you know how wet you're going to get.

Anyway, it felt like I was running under the entire field of the Grand National as they and their jockey's all relieved themselves simultaneously and I didn't see another person for the next hour, pedestrian or motorist. I was completely drenched. When I did finally see another motorist, the roads had streaming torrents running at the sides so as soon as a vehicle approached I had to get well out of the way to avoid getting caught by the bow wave they created. Although I couldn't have really been much wetter. At one point my phone rang but I was not able to answer it. Oh, I did try, swiping my finger sideways on the screen but nothing was registering and eventually John, my friend, rang off.

Eventually I arrived at a large junction with a Shell Petrol station and once again sought a hot drink, a sandwich and ten minutes to dry out. The staff there were very kind. They allowed me to shelter and willingly put my phone on charge whilst I ate and drank my snacks, standing in the shop, and generally getting in the way of the people purchasing petrol.

My ten-minute stop turned into half an hour and although it was still raining, I knew it was time to go. Despite being inside I was still wet and cold but decided the best way to generate heat was to run. The rain was now drizzling again and certainly not as heavy as an hour earlier.

It was lunchtime and up ahead the driver of a delivery truck was taking his break. He saw me running towards him and called to me through the window. He was from Essex and explained that both he and his girlfriend were runners. We had a brief discussion and he told me that he was running a race in the Welsh Mountains the following weekend. We wished each other good luck and after a fist pump, I was on my way again, wondering just how difficult it was to be a serious runner and a long-distance lorry driver. It must be nearly impossible to run after work when you were forced to park in a layby overnight at the side of a main road, or outside a customer's premises on an industrial estate.

The rain stopped as I arrived into Alderley Edge, then after a few quiet streets and snickets, across an area of parkland around the river Bollin at a place called the Carrs. The heavy morning rain had soaked the ground and unfortunately, I ended up in a short patch of swamp. Both shoes were submerged in thick, sticky mud and came out covered in this stinking, tar like black sludge. If that had happened two hours ago it wouldn't have mattered because the heavy rain would have washed it off in no time. Now, just when I needed the rain, the sun came out, and it was shining brightly as I ran up Style Lane. A sign offered me the opportunity to dine at a restaurant called 'The Clink', in the open prison nearby. I estimated I'd only three miles to go to my destination so decided to pass on the potential penal porridge and pressed on.

I arrived at my hotel early in the afternoon at around 2.30 pm and was grateful to them for letting me check in immediately. Once washed and changed, I set off to visit a couple of friends, Kelvin and Elliott, who worked in offices next to the Premier Inn at Manchester Airport. My hotel, the Premier Inn at Heald Green was only two miles away according to the Hotel website. This turned out to be true but two miles as the crow flies. What it didn't say was that the airport runways were between the hotels, so it was a twelve-mile round trip costing me fifteen pounds each way in a taxi.

I was on a high when I arrived at their offices, full of joy and feeling pleased with myself for making such good progress today, however once I got there, tiredness took over and I spent the next hour yawning, eyes watering and fighting to stay awake. It was understandable, although somewhat embarrassing and after an hour I gave up and returned to my hotel thirty pounds poorer. I went straight to bed for the next couple of hours before going for a meal at 7pm. After that, I wandered up the road for half a mile to buy chocolate and breakfast fare and was back in bed by 9pm with day twelve completed. The heavy rain had made it somewhat of an underwhelming day, but I was almost on some familiar ground and was excited about tomorrow's journey.

CHAPTER 17

All roads lead to Leigh

Day 13 – Wednesday 13th April 2022 – Heald Green to Whittle Le Woods

When I booked my accommodation, I didn't really pay too much attention to the local geography. The hotel, a Premier Inn, was right on the route of the cycleway, and at approximately thirty miles from Stoke, it was a suitable distance from the previous day's accommodation. So, when I was woken in what seemed like the middle of the night, by what sounded like a train pulling up in the corridor outside my room, I actually jumped out of bed and ran to the door to see what was going on. Nothing there. The noise stopped but a few minutes later started again as the train pulled away from the station. I looked at the map and saw that directly behind the hotel was Heald Green Railway Station, and it wasn't the middle of the night but actually only just after 11pm. Luckily I was back to sleep in minutes although other trains did disturb me through the night. It meant that I was awake early in the morning, and set off running at exactly 6am. I headed northwards along the B5166, towards the Sharston area of Manchester. However I was still tired so could have been forgiven for believing I was hallucinating.

In his book 'The rise of the ultra-runner,' author and Guardian journalist Adharanand Finn, describes how when running the UTMB, a one-hundred-mile race in the Alps, he began seeing buildings in the middle of a forest that were not there. Even after finishing the race, he describes how he was walking with his daughter from the shower block on the camp site and was steering her away from imaginary cows. Many other ultra runners will have their own tales of similar experiences, I know I do, of when they too have been visited by what we term as 'the sleep Monsters' due to pushing our sleep deprived bodies to extremes. So when, a few minutes after leaving my hotel I saw a five-foot-high pink frog in a garden, I questioned if it was really there or a figment from my under rested brain. I looked again. No this was definitely real because right behind the frog was a giraffe! Obviously. Maybe Manchester was wilder than I thought. I stopped to take a photograph because to be honest I wasn't really sure if I was dreaming or not.

A mile further on I crossed the M56, and was back to reality, or what we call civilization and after another mile or so I crossed the M60. My route now took me through woodland at the side of the M60 and then alongside a river as I looked at the map. I was inside the Manchester outer ring road, the M60 and yet the river next to me was the river Mersey. I thought about the bitter rivalry between the football teams from Manchester and Liverpool and wondered how many Liverpool or Everton fans were aware that the famous river their city stands on actually starts off in Manchester. I certainly wasn't.

The running was easy and I followed the riverbank for around three miles before entering a nature reserve near Sale. I met a few people out running or early morning dog walkers but generally I was on my own. Just before Stretford I crossed over, then dropped down onto the Bridgewater Canal. There were a few active commuters along the canal, either cycling or running to work, but again it was still largely quiet. I headed Northwards towards Manchester City Centre, as the canal ran parallel to the busy A56. Eventually the canal went under the road, at which point there was a fork in the waterway and the towpath. One way went left and up a spiral ramp before turning right and over a bridge to the other side of the canal where it joined another waterway that headed into the City and the old dock area around Salford Quays. My route was to stay on the main Bridgewater Canal and head west and through Trafford Park. A few miles later I passed a citadel to the retail industry, the Trafford Centre shopping area and was surprised by how much it resembled a church. It was still well before 9am so the car park was empty and for some reason I felt the urge to photograph it. I continued another mile to Barton upon Irwell, where the Bridgewater Canal met up with its big brother, the Manchester Ship Canal.

I'd spent most of my working life arranging the shipment of goods manufactured in Northern England to destinations around the World. One of the main places I was involved with was Canada. In my early career, to get freight there we used the services of a shipping line called Manchester Liners. They operated a small fleet of ships from Manchester to Montreal. I couldn't believe it when my boss told me that ships actually sailed from Manchester and recounted how on several occasions she had been invited to dinner at the captain's table to celebrate the launch of a new ship from Manchester.

The thirty-six-mile Manchester Ship Canal was opened in 1894 and at the time it was the largest river navigational canal in the world. Very soon Manchester became the third busiest port in Britain and was a profitable port for many years reaching its peak in 1958, but the growth in container shipping in 1960's and 1970's resulted in an increase in the size of ships being built. Now although some freight still moves along the canal, it is too small to accommodate the large vessel now operating on the main shipping lanes and so the service from Manchester to Canada was stopped.

It is difficult to comprehend just how large today's container carrying vessels really are. They are more akin to floating towns than what we may imagine a ship or sailing vessel to look like. Many people will have been on a cross channel ferry and arrived at Hull or Dover and driven their cars on and off the ship. Those are dwarfed in comparison to the large international container ships.

In 2021 international trade was severely disrupted when a ship became stuck in the Suez Canal. The vessel, the 'Ever Given' operated by a shipping line called Evergreen Marine, is typical of modern-day vessels and has a capacity to carry over twenty thousand containers. That is just a meaningless number to most of us, so I will try and put the size of these humongous hulks into layman's terms. On my run I'd just been within a few hundred metres of the Manchester United Football Stadium, the second biggest football ground in the country after Wembley, and apparently the eleventh largest in Europe.

Manchester United's pitch is one hundred and five metres long. The Ever Given is almost four times as long as the Old Trafford pitch. 399.9 metres in length. The maximum vessel length along the Manchester ship canal is only 130 metres so, the Ever Given, nor any of her sister ships are likely to be sailing along the Manchester Ship Canal any time soon.

My background in arranging these shipments meant that I was excited about my route today. Even passing Trafford Park resonated with me. I'd held many meetings with companies there, in an attempt to secure their business. Trafford Park was the world's first planned industrial estate and is said to be the largest industrial estate in Europe. I was also looking forward to leaving the ship canal at the Barton Swing Bridge which contains the world's only swing aqueduct, which I crossed twenty minutes after photographing the Trafford Centre.

There are many interesting and historical features along our canals if we take the time or are interested enough to look for them and I could have spent longer exploring but was conscious that I still had a long way to go to reach my destination on the Leeds to Liverpool canal near Chorley. I was still deep in the heart of Manchester, or more accurately in a City within the City, or so the sign said, Welcome to the City of Salford.

The Bridgewater Canal carried on at the other side of the ship canal and I continued to take advantage of this highway from the Victorian era, making my way past Patricroft railway station and under Salford's own motorway the M602. Soon after this I had open views into the country and as I approached Worsley, I was blessed with a fantastic photo opportunity.

As I rounded a bend, on the other side of the canal was a grand building with a black and white Tudor style frontage. I felt this warranted a photo so reached for my phone. I was about to take the shot when a swan floated majestically into the picture. I captured the moment but my photography skills are not the best, so it does not do justice to what was really a lovely moment, scene and setting.

I was curious as to what the building was but could see no reference to it on the OS map. So, I asked social media for the answer and posted a picture of the building. Some people came back to tell me it was Worsley Old Hall, whilst others suggested it was RHS Bridgewater, both of which are close by, however I believe neither are actually correct and now think the building I photographed is Worsley Court House which curiously isn't named on the OS map either.

Worsley Old Hall is certainly worth a mention as it has its own place in history. It is said to be where the founders of the Bridgewater Canal first discussed and planned its creation. A few miles further along the towpath stands a metal sculpture of each of the three founders, James Brindley, John Gilberth and Francis Edgerton, the Duke of Bridgewater.

It would have been possible for me to continue along this canal and meet up with the Leeds to Liverpool canal at the other side of Wigan, but this would mean I would then have to run up the famous Wigan Locks, or rather 21 locks, climbing over 200 ft in less than 2 miles to what is known as Wigan Top Lock. That route would effectively be two sides of a square. Instead, I was leaving the Bridgewater Canal just after Worsley and following a more direct route laid out by Royston Wood in his book.

The one downside to this plan turned out to be the underfoot terrain. So far, the day's route had been perfect as most of it had been along well-maintained canal towpaths with easy-to-follow marked paths. The next part though involved a network of paths and tracks which turned out to be neither marked or particularly well maintained but before that I needed breakfast as I'd been running for three hours, covering fifteen miles so the search for a café was on.

I left the Bridgewater Canal at 9am just after the Boothstown Marina and made my way to the main road, called Leigh Road. Less than five minutes later I was seated inside a wonderful little place called Mason's Café Bar, waiting for my bacon and poached eggs on toast. This was nicely washed down with a cup of tea. With my meal finished, I'd just stood up to leave but was distracted by an order being delivered to another table. This conjured up memories of days past and I couldn't resist the temptation so called the waitress over.

"Can I have a chocolate milkshake, and will you put an extra scoop of Ice cream in it please?" Thus, my departure was delayed by another fifteen minutes and I left feeling ready for a nap rather than fired up to tackle the twenty miles I still had to cover, but 'by eck' it was worth it.

The next ten minutes were spent walking so my milkshake could find a suitable resting place with the bacon and poached eggs, whilst I navigated my way to the A580. For those who don't know it, the A580 is a fast and furious thoroughfare, well known to long distance lorry drivers and travelling salespeople in the North of England as the East Lancs Road. My route took me along a wide cycle path at the side of this busy road for about half a mile, before crossing and heading along what appeared to be farm track but brought me to an industrial estate at Astley. Here I picked up a footpath that ran at the back of a housing estate. Navigation was tricking and luckily all this had been plotted into my phone weeks before. I'd also looked at as much of the route as was possible on google street view, so had seen some of the places, but where the route was not along a road or street it was all new territory. Many of the off-road sections along this stretch looked unused and certainly had become overgrown. In more than a few places it was clear they were used for fly tipping. Those sections offered untold hidden dangers and concentration was paramount. A rusty nail, or broken bottle through the side or bottom of a training shoe at this point would put paid to my chances of success and believe me, both have happened to me in the past. Now there is the added worry of discarded needles, so I kept my 'peepers' peeled.

A few minutes later I joined another road called Leigh Road, although the spelling on the map of this one was Ley Road, rather than the name of the nearby town Leigh. I followed Ley Road for a few hundred metres before turning northwest up a muddy bridleway called Meanley Road. This led me on to a disused railway track that was very muddy and overgrown. For the next few miles the going was a stop start affair. Because of the mud, various small alternative paths had been made, few of which were waymarked so I kept having to check and recheck the map. At one point I arrived at a section where the track was completely submerged under stagnant water. It was obvious other users had climbed a broken fence into a coppice, so I followed suit, but once in there, having gone only five metres the path vanished and I was left to fight my way through overgrown branches, tree roots and brambles. It took me over two minutes to go twenty-five metres and I emerged looking like I'd wrestled a lion.

After my water enforced workout the track brought me to another main road. I wasn't really surprised to see this was also called Leigh Road, my third different Leigh / Ley Road, in as many miles. It made me wonder if Leigh is a Lancashire way of spelling Rome. Being in and around the environs of Leigh, I hoped I may bump into one of the town's famous residents, namely superstar athlete and Olympic 800 metre medallist Keely Hodgkinson out on a training run but it never happened. At least I don't think it did, I was preoccupied with lion wrestling so perhaps I missed her.

The off-road route was marked on my map as a national cycle route 55 but it was getting muddier and more difficult to follow so I decided to change tack. For the most part this route had gone diagonally, heading northwest but in the last mile had turned and was now heading west. It was now running parallel to a busy main road going from Wigan to Manchester, the A577. Eventually I would have to cross this road anyway so I decided the going must surely be easier along there. I left the cycle route and joined the main road, just as a road sign announced I was at Hindley Green. Suddenly out of the shelter of the woods I became very cold. I was running directly into another head wind. The sky had grown darker and sure enough it started to rain. I was just passing a petrol station and decided a five-minute stop to buy a chocolate bar of some description seemed like a good call and hopefully the cloud would blow over. It was here I met Audrey Wilson.

Audrey was working in the kiosk in the petrol station and couldn't have been more welcoming. I just went in to buy a Snickers bar, but once inside I asked if they sold tea or coffee. Audrey said they didn't have a machine but she would gladly make me a cup of tea if I wanted, which she did, and even brought me a chair from behind the counter out into the customer area. She asked how far I had run and at first didn't believe that I'd run from the other side of Manchester Airport that morning. I explained about the run and the charity, telling her how long I had been running. Audrey insisted on giving me some money for the charity. The petrol station was fairly busy, but many of the customers were regulars and Audrey introduced them to me. "This is Stephen and he is running from Lands' End to John O'Groats." I was sitting on a high bar stool, drinking tea and shaking hands with complete strangers who appeared to be queuing up to meet me. It was completely surreal.

My tea and fifteen minutes of fame completed, I set off again but not before getting some directions from Audrey and both of us sending each other a friend request on Facebook. It was really nice of her to take the trouble to help me. She brightened the day and as soon as I was back on the road the sun came out. I followed her directions, heading along the main road for a mile, straight on at the traffic lights, then taking a side road that led me to some playfields. Here a public footpath ran between the playing fields and a small wood. This path led me up and over a foot bridge to negotiate a railway line, emerging at the side of a golf course and fifty minutes later I arrived at Wigan Top Lock and the Leeds to Liverpool Canal.

This was a welcome sight. I knew this stretch of the canal from here to my lodgings very well. After an obligatory photograph, I set off in pleasant sunshine and 'fine fettle' for the last nine miles that equated to almost a quarter of today's journey and recalled memories of a past visit.

CHAPTER 18

There's always Someone Worse off than You

I thought back to the last time I'd run along here. It was a time when I was to learn another valuable lesson in life which was, it doesn't matter how bad things are for you, there's always someone worse off.

At 6pm on 11th May 2018. I set off from Liverpool to run to Leeds along the Leeds/Liverpool canal. It was Friday night, the aim was to run the whole route of one hundred and twenty-seven miles inside twenty-four hours.

The idea came about after a conversation with my brother-in-law Steven Howley. He asked if I fancied cycling the route saying "I bet we could do it in a day." He planted a seed in my mind and I wondered if I could run it within twenty-four hours and so a new challenge was born.

I spent months reading about the canal, discovering the first meeting about creating it took place in Bradford, at a public house called the Sun Inn. I read that much of the early finance was put up by the textile merchants in the city. The first section built was from Shipley to Bingley. Bingley being the hometown of my running club, Bingley Harriers, and I'd run along sections of it many times.

I thought about the significance the canal had played in my life. Unbeknown to me this historical highway had helped build the industry, freight forwarding, I had been employed in for the last forty odd years and it had created a platform allowing me to enjoy my favourite pastime. I felt I owed it something and I definitely had to take on this challenge. I told Steven that I wasn't going to cycle it but was going to try and run its entire length in a day, and would he be willing to cycle the route at the same time to support me? He agreed and we set a date.

2018 was also the one hundred and twenty fifth anniversary of Bingley Harriers and the club were looking for an event to mark the occasion. So, twenty-five of my club colleagues agreed to support me in a kind of relay, by running sections of it with me.

A few months before this, one of my close friends, Dave Stephenson, lost his wife to multiple myeloma. This was just six weeks before the run so I decided to raise funds for the Myeloma charity. Dave was set to be one of my pacers. He and I had run and supported each other on all sorts of events over many years, including the Bob Graham Challenge, races at the UTMB, The Joss Naylor Challenge and we had run the Pennine Way together in 6 days in 2015. Suddenly the run took on even greater significance so I arranged to have tee shirts made for all the runners to mark this special occasion. Our club colours are blue and white hoops but the Myeloma colours are orange so I asked the shop to make the shirts up with orange and white hoops.

"Very striking", the shopkeeper, Tim Agar, commented when I went to collect them.

"You're going to look like a prison chain gang." he said grinning. "We certainly shouldn't be missed," I said as I paid the bill.

The date was set for 11th May and after months of training I went to bed the night before full of confidence. I was in really good shape and believed I would come close to achieving my goal. I had even been filmed by BBC Look North and received a personal video message from the legend that was Harry Gration, what could possibly go wrong. Well at 2:48 the next morning I found out when I was woken by my neighbour's car alarm. This continued intermittently for the next few hours, and I never got back to sleep. It proved to be my undoing. I even tried to have an afternoon nap, unfortunately to no avail, so not exactly refreshed, I arrived at the Liverpool end of the canal at 5.30 pm to prepare for the off. My family, friends and supporters gathered and there was a real buzz of anticipation. A group of two or more runners would accompany me for a section of around twelve miles and timings had been worked out so they all knew where they had to be and when.

As the route was a linear route this meant that the support runners were going to finish miles away from their starting point, so my wife Angela and daughter Vicky had agreed to collect groups of support runners from where they had parked their cars, and then drive them to the starting point of their particular stage. This was going to be crucial to the success of this event. Steven was going to follow me on his bike and he was going to be accompanied by my friends Dave Weatherhead, Barbara Carney and Kerry Gilchrist. They had all supported me in the past and were long serving members of our running club. David would cycle with Steve through the night, Kerry would take over in the morning and Barbara would do the thirty-mile glory leg from Skipton to Leeds in the afternoon. The four of them would act as 'first responders' in the event of problems or accidents in the more remote sections.

We were all going to need food and drink as you can't run or cycle that sort of distance on fresh air alone. So, our road support crew were going to be vital, and this important role was in the hands of my old school friend and mentor John Crowley and his wife Catherine, my biscuit monitor from my first day at school. As we prepared for the off John, Catherine, Angela and Vicky went through the various meeting points so they were all clear on where they needed to be and when. Angela would be driving and Vicky navigating. John had been to every meeting point in advance and knew some of them were a bit out of the way, and would be tricky to find, especially in the early hours of the morning. He teased Angela and Vicky that they would not find them all. He also asked.

"And have you brought your spare car key?"

"No" replied Angela "Why am I going to need a spare car key?"

"What if you lose it?" replied John.

"I'm not going to lose it though am I John?"

"How do you know? Anything could happen. It's going to be a long day," replied John.

I set off at 6pm on what began as a pleasant sunny May evening but at 10pm dark clouds had gathered and it started to rain. The temperature dropped and by midnight it was a cold wet miserable night. I was moving at around 6 miles per hour so I was reasonably OK, but the poor cyclists were freezing, so cycled on ahead, going hard up the 200 ft climb of the 21 canal locks at Wigan in an attempt to warm up. Here we would all meet up with John and the support crew at the Top Lock for a welcome cuppa.

When I arrived, Steve was sitting down enjoying his tea whilst John and Dave Weatherhead repaired a puncture. My support runners and I left them behind in the rain and pressed on. About an hour later, approximately 1.20am I had covered a total of forty miles. My two support runners, Andy 'Gibbo' Gibbons and ultra running coach, Kate Farley did their best to keep me motivated and on pace but I was starting to flag. We were now several miles from the nearest town. It was dark as we passed fields of cows and deserted woodland, the only light was from our head torches and it reflected back at us from the mist or our breath and the drizzle driving into our faces. This gave the appearance that we were running through a tunnel. It was a real low point and I began feeling a bit sorry for myself. I was wet through, cold, tired, hungry and still had well over eighty-five miles to run.

"Woopy doo, who's bloody idea was this?" I remember saying out loud to no one in particular, but it transpired I was the lucky one.

It had taken Steven and David longer than expected to properly repair the puncture. The first time they got going again the tyre immediately went flat and they had to start all over again. By the time it was all sorted, Kate, Gibbo and I were miles in front. Once back in the saddle the powerful pedalling pair really put the hammer down to warm up and catch up. The towpath was shrouded by tall trees and was very dark in places, The added drizzle made visibility difficult. It was somewhere along this stretch that Steve hit some kind of pothole and went over the handlebars, 'face planting' on the towpath. It transpired that what he actually hit was a channel in the path where slurry was running off one of the surrounding fields and he landed headlong in a quagmire of sticky smelling slurry. Any farmer will tell you, slurry is basically liquid cow shit. It covered his bike and bike light to the extent that he had to dip the entire bike in the canal several times to wash it. The shitty sticky sludge covered his clothes, it covered his face, it went up his nose and in his mouth. He was effectively chewing cow shit. I was just a bit cold. There is always someone worse off than you.

At about this time John and the support team were setting up at the next checkpoint, when Angela and Vicky arrived with the next set of runners. One of these was John Parkin. John is a renowned ultra distance runner and is, or was at one time, sponsored by Montane. I believe they made a short film about him after he won a seven-day stage race from Scotland to Wales. He is affectionately known as 'Arctic John.' a nickname I'd given him, as he always seemed to wear at least one layer of clothing more than the rest of us when we were out training or racing. He was always well prepared and tonight he was in the right place at exactly the wrong time as he witnessed with my wife and the support team, one of those slow-motion moments when time seems to standstill as Angela dropped the car key and everyone stood statuesque, watching as it disappeared down a grate in the road.

I was not there so I can only go by what I was told, which was that Catherine made a dive for the key as it disappeared into the abyss below and then grabbed the grating and lifted it up. John Crowley brought a bucket, and Arctic John, after feeling around for it with his hands, began ladling bucket after bucket of the slimy sludge out of the hole whilst Angela silently sifted the stinking sediment, to try and locate the key. Bucket upon bucket was brought out of the drain and poor Angela did a fingertip search of the contents before the key was eventually found. At the time, all three of us were probably wishing we could swap places with someone, or at least be somewhere else. However, two days later, my sister told me what she was doing at this exact moment in time.

Maureen had planned to drive out to meet me at 6am in the morning at the halfway point but didn't arrive. She did however come to Leeds to see me finish with her husband, Iwan and family. Although I had missed out on finishing in twenty-four hours, I did manage to complete the run, but in twenty-six hours and thirty-five minutes. Having twice fallen asleep standing up, I took the decision to stop and sleep. Running along at the side of a canal is a dangerous place when you're out on your feet and I needed two sleep breaks to conquer the tiredness. As I got nearer to home, more and more people came to support me and the time just slipped further back. To be honest the finish was all a bit of a blur and I didn't really get time to talk to anyone properly.

The following Monday morning, Maureen told me why she'd missed our early morning rendevous, saying that in the early hours of Saturday she was in an ambulance with blue lights flashing on the way to A & E after one of her children, who at that point was hooked up to a drip with wires to various places, had become ill in the night. The paramedics were concerned and one turned to Maureen and informed her,

"I need to tell you this is really serious."

So, whilst I felt pretty shit, Steven was eating shit and Angela was rummaging around in something very similar, none of us were hooked up to an IV line or going through the helpless feeling of looking at one of our children in what was a life-threatening situation. Thanks to the work of the paramedics and hospital staff her offspring was none the worse for the journey, but it is a stark reminder of just how precious life is and that no matter how bad you think things are, there is always someone worse off than you.

These were the thoughts going through my head four years later as I ran that stretch of canal again and was counting my blessings when I received a message from a friend who had come out to meet me. Nicola Jones, another Bingley Harrier, was visiting family in Wigan. She met me at the hotel I was staying at which has a David Lloyd leisure centre and Spa next to it. As luck would have it, Nicola's brother Rob was a member of the gym there and kindly signed me in as a guest. Thus, I was treated to a spa and sauna which was very welcome after my thirty-five miles that day. I had now covered a total of four hundred and forty-two miles in thirteen days. My plan was to try and finish in twenty-eight days so by the end of tomorrow I would be halfway.

CHAPTER 19

Words of Wisdom

Day 14 – Thursday 14th April 2022 – Whittle Le Woods to Lancaster

I was up bright and early again and left at first light on another cold morning. A mist hung over the water as I made my way along the canal towpath at exactly 6am. I had only been going a few hundred metres when the canal turned eastwards just before a place called Johnson Hillock, this is the highest point on the Leeds to Liverpool Canal and if I'd been heading home, it would have been all downhill from here, however my route was North, into the wilder parts of Lancashire, Cumbria and beyond. This point did have a significance though, as I estimated I'd exactly 500 miles to reach John O'Groats.

Leaving the canal meant I would again have to pay closer attention to route finding, at least until later in the day, when I would join another canal for the run into Lancaster. A few hundred metres after leaving the canal I reached a road taking me under the M61 motorway before bringing me to the A6 and the old road north at Whittle le Woods.

I headed straight across and up a small lane. Unfortunately, at the top of the lane the public right away had been blocked off by builders fencing. This was fastened together with a heavy chain and securely padlocked. Attached to the fence was a sign instructing me to retrace my steps back down the lane and use a footpath around a cricket field. It wasn't far adding about a quarter of a mile, but it was just frustrating. It was made more so when the grass in the cricket field was very wet, and in no time my shoes, socks and feet were wet so this wasn't the start I wanted.

The path crossed a small wetland nature reserve at the side of the river Lostock. So far, I had largely managed to keep my feet dry and not had a single blister. That's how I wanted to keep it. The biggest danger to this was if the feet got wet for long periods so despite the scenic setting I hoped I would soon be on dryer ground.

The route followed the river but the path became gravelled or properly surfaced in places, and my wet shoes began to get heavier as the pieces of gravel stuck to them. I arrived at a road and spent a minute stamping my feet and scrubbing the shoes against the kerb edge to remove the gravel. A sign informed me I was at Clayton Le Woods and another one pointed me right, along the road. A short distance further on, another sign directed me left and into the Cuerden Valley Park. The route finding was easy when it was signed and saved the aggravation of trying to open up the mapping app. This was a pleasant area of traffic free parkland, perfect for an early morning run.

After a small climb I arrived at an impressive view that could have been a film set. In the foreground was a mist shrouded field of rich pastureland. In the middle of the field was a big old spooky looking tree. The field was bordered by a wrought iron fence. The scene was completed by the backdrop of what the map said was Cuerden Hall, an impressive building that wouldn't have looked out of place in a production of Downton Abbey.

A few hundred metres further on I arrived at a footbridge over the M6. As I looked up the motorway I saw a sign showing left for Preston and right for Blackburn and decided to photograph this, to send to friends and family as an easy way of showing them my location. It was only after I had taken the photograph that I noticed a series of posters fixed to the fence running across the bridge with information about a charity and provided a phone number. They all had a slightly different message but ultimately they were all placed there for the same reason, to stop people killing themselves.

It was a sobering moment. To think that people had probably jumped off that bridge to their deaths. How low must they have been, how desperate their situation must have seemed if they felt their best or only option was to throw themselves from a bridge. Even If the fall hadn't killed them, the traffic surely would. It certainly seemed like a definite decision to end it all, rather than a cry for help. I hoped they had now found peace. Was it the cold wind or emotion that made my eyes water? I had difficulty reading the map momentarily.

The footbridge and pathway brought me to the A49 near Bamber Bridge, and after a few wrong turns I finally found the right route, which was on another former railway line. This brought me to a pathway known as 'The old tram road' that would take me across the river Ribble and into Preston town centre. At least it should have done, if someone hadn't closed the old bridge. Little did I know that the route had been changed. Instead of joining the old tram road, I should instead have continued on the former railway line to a new bridge. The annoying thing is, I did, at first, then realising I was off the course of my plotted route, I retraced my steps to the junction and the right route only to find when I reached the old bridge, it was fenced off and I was diverted to the new bridge, effectively running up and back down one side of a V shape, then up the other side, then running from the top of the V in a directly line to the top of the other side. I hope that description makes sense to you but if it doesn't and you find it a bit frustrating, just think, it took me a lot longer to run it, than it did for you to read it, so imagine how frustrated I was.

This was my second diversion of the day, and once again it was not that long, but added another needles mile to the route. These little add-ons were becoming like the drips of Chinese water torture. Instead of just accepting them as necessary, a kind of occupational hazard so to speak, I let them frustrate me and dampen my spirit for a period. So just before 8am I stopped running and stomped my way past the railway station. I turned right onto a shopping precinct in the centre of Preston to find a café for comfort food.

Food and good company usually lift my spirits, and the bacon sandwich and coffee did the job. They were just what I needed and although there was not really anyone to talk to, a massive sign, painted mural style, on the wall of the café made me smile as it seemed to sum up my journey. Well maybe not the second line but the other three lines certainly did.

'This is your life. Do what you love and do it often.

Enjoy the power and beauty of youth.

Travel often, getting lost will help you find yourself.

When you eat, appreciate every last bite.'

I left the café after half an hour, ready for my next challenge which proved to be some major road works in the Town Centre. These hampered my progress for several frustrating minutes but eventually, I made it across the road and found my way to the University. Here a network of small side streets led me to my second canal of the day, The Lancaster Canal in an area called Maulands. It would have been possible to follow this all the way to Lancaster, my next sleeping place, but that would have added a good number of miles to my journey, as the canal wanders around the countryside trying to avoid every hill. I planned a few shortcuts so left the canal after about three miles and made my way through a housing estate to join the A6 at Broughton. This was another area I had researched extensively, trying to find a safe route, and whilst I didn't really want to run up the A6, this section did seem to have a good footpath. It would also take me north on the most direct route for the rest of the morning. At one point I received a text from my pal Andy Nicoll who earlier had teased me saying that all that road running must be very boring. In his latest text he challenged me to bring into conversation the word 'dandelion' with the next person I met.

As luck would have it, at that exact moment there was a long row of dandelions bordering the roadside. I photographed them and sent him the picture immediately.

A short while later I arrived in Garstang and the sign welcoming visitors informed me that Garstang was the World's first Fairtrade town, so I resolved to give it my lunch business. This proved to be easier said than done. It was Thursday, market day and everywhere was very busy. The main street was lined with stalls and packed with people either buying or browsing, and progress through the small town was very slow. I meandered along the busy streets trying several eating establishments without success as they were all full. Eventually I found a wonderful oasis in the form of Bella's Coffee House. Bella's is owned by a mother and daughter team, Mother, Carol and Daughter Edmae who'a middle name is Isabella, after her Gran who says she loves the idea of having a coffee shop named after her.

I had arrived on a sunny spring morning just before lunch and was won over immediately by the setting. Bella's is located in a quiet courtyard away from the hustle and bustle of the main street and busy market stalls. The outdoor tables were all taken as people enjoyed their lunch in the spring sunshine, so I headed inside. I chose one of several homemade soups and a sandwich. The food was perfectly cooked and nicely presented, the cake choices excellent and the coffee magnificent. I enjoyed the visit so much that I vowed to return at some point with my wife, who will love browsing the market whilst I enjoy cake and coffee, and people watch. It is now on my bucket list as one of the things I must do before I move on to that great cake shop in the sky.

After a forty-five-minute phone and caffeine charge I was on my way again. I headed through the town, crossed the A6 then continued on the B5272. This was reasonably quiet but just occasionally I had to give way to vehicles. Eventually I re-joined the canal but just as I was about to do so, a car pulled up and a family climbed out. The driver called out saying hello as if he knew me. I said hello and we looked at each other, trying to work out where we knew each other from. We fired a series of questions at each other before realising that there were no connections and we didn't really know each other at all. As we were chatting I noticed some writing on the training shoes of one of the children in the family, a boy called Joseph. It said on his shoes. "Go Run" so I insisted on a photograph of these words of inspiration before waving them farewell.

I was back on a canal and back in the mood to run. Bella's caffeine was still energising me and the endorphins were really kicking in. The afternoon was sunny and having left the road I was charging along again. Walking towards me on the canal towpath were two ladies each pushing an identical pram. Actually, a double buggy would be a more accurate description. This made me think of my own mum pushing our pram along with my two younger sisters laid side by side and me trotting along out in front. If she could see me now.

As I approached Lancaster, I worked out that I'd reached the halfway point about 6 miles before the town. At the start of the day I had run 442 miles and estimated I had exactly 501 miles to reach John O' Groats, so a total of 943 miles. At this point I had covered 30 miles in the day so far, meaning a total of 472 miles and so had passed the halfway point.

This was a significant moment so it was quite apt that here I passed a barge with musical notes painted on the side. Between the notes was the title of one of my favourite songs by the Beatles. 'Let it Be' I pondered if these were words of wisdom or a wish for me for the second half of the run. It gave me another lift and I began to sing. With this tune firmly in my head, I ran into Lancaster in search of my hotel, spurred on by the fact that tomorrow was Good Friday when I would be meeting up with my wife and friends.

CHAPTER 20

A Little Help From My Friends

Day 15 – Friday 15th April 2022 – Lancaster to Shap

This was going to be a long day. I was set to run almost thirty-eight miles, but the day also had a projected three thousand feet of ascent, the most climbing in one day along the entire journey. My plight was not helped when I looked at my plotted route as I sat in my hotel room the previous evening. I'd messed up again and forgot to change my route which was plotted from a different hotel. I had originally planned to stay at the Premier Inn which was at the Northern end of the City, but when I tried to book, the price had gone up to £120 per night, probably because it was the start of the Easter holiday weekend. So I found a much better deal in a grand hotel near the castle in the city centre. The only downside was that I had plotted the route for day fifteen starting from the Premier Inn and had forgotten to change it. This added at least an extra mile to my route for day fifteen before I had even started, So I scoured the map to see if there was a possible short cut and found what looked like an excellent route. This would take me over a brand-new footbridge crossing the river Lune, after which I could rejoin my route, the canal again, half a mile further on. However, interrogating the map again revealed the possibility of an even more direct route.

I left the hotel at just after 5.00am and within minutes reached the new bridge, an impressive brightly polished, stainless-steel structure. I was guided over by lighting set into the walkway that created an impressive sight. Once across the bridge I saw signs for national cycle route six, which I was to follow later in the morning. For now I was planning to try this more direct route. I turned right at the end of the bridge heading up a sleepy side street at the end of which I crossed the A6. I carried on straight ahead as my route now ran northwards and hugged the river for a short while.

It then entered a small estate for a few hundred metres, then headed out into open country. After another fifty metres, the road crossed over a small canal, at one end of what was described on the OS map as 'The Lune Aqueduct.' I left the road to pick up a muddy footpath heading west for about fifty metres. This led me into a field and I continued heading west for another fifty metres where I arrived at a broad farm track.

This track was a real find and headed directly north cutting out lots of twists and turns from my original route which had been basically to follow the cycleway which joined the canal earlier but headed off in a big loop. The farm track used a bridge to cross high above the A683, the Lancaster bypass. My revised route was wonderful, easy running with excellent views. It was still well before 6am and it felt like the world was all mine. Eventually the track came to a crossroads and my route took me straight ahead on a quiet lane. There were steep hills to my left and right, both of which were topped with a tower or mast. The lane went slightly downhill with fields of young lambs on one side and young cattle on the other. I must have spooked the cattle as they suddenly charged along the edge of the field running with me until the field boundary.

I passed through a sleepy village with an historic church and arrived at the Lancaster Canal. A tiny gap in the wall led down to the towpath and momentarily I became wedged in. I was forced to take off my bum bags to extricate myself. Although it was still only 6am I sent a message to Angela, and to John and Catherine AKA the Flying Crowleys, telling them I had covered my first six miles. Many years ago, John started to refer to himself and family as 'The Flying Crowleys' after he discovered one of his family was a gymnast in the Olympics. After the Games I believe they joined a circus as a trapeze artist. Angela had now joined the Crowley 'circus' for the day as they were all travelling together to meet me in Kendal.

I had the canal to myself and followed this for two miles to a hump backed bridge where I left the canal for the moment. I turned right, heading up a steep hill on a metalled lane for one hundred metres where I was forced to walk. This reminded me to drink. It was vital I remember to drink early in the day. It was easy to forget to do this, particularly when I was running well, but that would create big problems later so I tried to ensure I drank at 330ml every hour, in addition to café stops. The lane became a farm track and contoured along a terrace in the hillside, emerging at another bridge and back to the canal. I crossed the bridge ignoring the canal and joined the A6 for a few hundred metres, heading towards the small town of Carnforth. Just before the town I turned slightly left. At the end of this road I came to a T junction and right in front of me was a Co-op. Even though it was not yet 7am, it was open and I took the opportunity of buying water and a croissant. As Jack Reacher says, 'Eat when You can' – Excellent advice if you ever decide to follow in my footsteps and take on this Lands' End to John O' Groats challenge.

I left the co-op and headed west over a railway line, and then north following cycle route six. The road went under another railway bridge and led me out into the small villages of, firstly Millhead and then to Walton. As I approached Walton I was impressed by the view beyond the village. A giant wall of a sheer rock overlooked the village. This would have many of my climbing friends reaching for the skimpy shoes and chalk bag to go and tackle the dramatic looking climb. I was not sure if this was a natural feature or if it had been made by man, but either way, it was an impressive sight.

I followed the flat road through to the far end of the village where it began to climb steeply. Here I passed a really old church dedicated to St Oswald. The sign read 'St Oswald, King and Martyr.' I thought about recent publicity surrounding Prince Andrew and it led me to wonder if any other of our country's monarchs have been granted sainthood over the last one thousand years or are ever likely to be again. I took a photo as the church clock chimed 7am.

After Walton, the road climbed a long hill, surrounded on both sides by dense woodland. This would be a challenging climb on a bike and I was determined to keep running. It was a very quiet place and I tried my best to ensure my feet hit the road's surface with as little noise as possible. Any noise seemed to echo off the walls. The gentle tap tap tap of my feet and the rhythm of my breathing seemed deafening in the calm and quiet of the shaded woodland as I worked hard to ascend the hill. Suddenly the noise of my exertions was drowned out by the engine of a high performance car following me up the hill, and a Jaguar saloon glided past me. It disappeared in the distance and vanished as quickly as it had appeared. I passed the gateway to a convent. It struck me as exactly the right setting for those who had decided to place themselves in such an establishment having taken a vow of silence because it did seem to be an intrusion to make any sound at all.

At the top of the hill a splendid view opened up to my right as I looked Eastwards. The morning sun behind the silhouetted skyline showed 'Ingleborough', one of Yorkshire's highest and possibly its' most easily recognised mountain. A friend who is himself an Alpine Mountain guide, refers to Ingleborough as 'The Mighty Inglehorn' . I think the slightly made up name perfectly sums up this iconic mountain. Well, here she was in all her glory, brightening my morning and reminding me I was close to home and God's own country.

This definitely warranted a photograph and I sent the picture to Angela and the Flying Crowleys. Knowing that they would recognise the view I also sent it to my pals, Dave Stephenson and Andy Nicoll on a WhatsApp group we have and included the caption, "my early morning view" To which they both sent pictures of four feet sticking out at the bottom of their respective duvet's as they enjoyed a bank holiday lie in.

A little further on, I ran through the wonderfully named village of 'Yealand Conyers'. I spend a lot of time looking at maps and often ponder on how places got their names. Sometimes it's easy to work out, but 'Yealand Conyers' had me scratching my head. It must surely be based on some local dialect words for which the meaning is probably long forgotten except to a handful of locals. At 7.30 on Good Friday morning, no one was around to ask so I was forced to leave the village none the wiser. At the other side of the village I turned right onto a small lane and after a few hundred metres took a footpath diagonally across two large fields to emerge at a gate onto the A6. Thankfully I was on this road for less than one hundred metres before turning onto what I hoped would be a quieter road. At this point I had a choice. I could pick up the Lancaster canal again or stay on the road for about two miles which I estimated would be one mile shorter than the canal route. It was not yet 8am so I chose the road option.

The road was indeed quiet and for fifteen minutes I didn't encounter a single car travelling in either direction. However, it only takes one car to kill you, and as I got near to the point I would be leaving the road I heard a car speeding towards me. As well as being a quiet road, it was also a lot narrower with no footpath on either side. It was also bordered by a hawthorn hedge on each side and they were right up to the road. As I heard the car approaching I looked up and down the road, it wasn't really possible to see very far in either direction so it was clear to me that the driver was not going to see me until the last moment. I crossed over the road to ensure I was on the other side, to that of the car. It whizzed by, less than two feet from me. I don't think the driver even saw me and had I stayed on the correct side according to the highway code, I think we would all have been visiting the hospital or worse.

I was glad to get off that road and join the canal. I made my way along the towpath, but a mile further on was surprised that the way ahead was barred by the M6. I thought there would be some kind of tunnel for the towpath but instead the route was blocked and diverted along the side of two fields where it ran parallel to the road. A beech hedge, ten feet high and a half the width, was all that stood between me and England's longest motorway. With the fields negotiated, I arrived onto a narrow farm road, where a right turn and a bridge took me over the motorway to re-join the canal. The going was once again easy and pleasant. After a short while the towpath went under the A65. This is the main route from West Yorkshire to the M6 and the Lake District. I had driven along the A65 many times and never knew the road went over this canal. It was nice to see the area from a different and more relaxed angle. As I entered the tunnel under the road I met a man walking two Labradors and I realised he was the first person I had seen all morning. I had been running for just less than four hours and had covered almost nineteen miles.

At around 9.20 the canal came to an end and I picked up cycle route six again. Heading northwards my route once again climbed steeply, slowing my progress. I would like to say the view at the top was worth it but that would be a lie. Actually, what I saw was the road descending the thirty or so metres I had just climbed, followed by an even higher and steeper climb directly in front of me. This time I was forced to walk briefly on the climb but once at the top, Kendal and the fells of the Lake district came into view. Stunning. What goes up must come down and I enjoyed a long descent into Nantland. As I was nearing the bottom of the hill a large group of cyclists all dressed in white cycling tops, turned onto the road and started the long ascent. Each one had to step up out of the saddle and really stand on the pedals as their work rate increased. I was glad I only had to push myself up the hill. To me the uphill always feels significantly harder on a bike.

I had arranged to meet Angela at 11am at the Morrisons in Kendal. At 9:45 am she sent me a message to say they had arrived, just as a timely placed road sign told me I had only two miles to reach the town. My watch told me I had covered twenty-two miles so far that day and it dawned on me that I had just completed mile number five hundred since leaving Lands' End. I messaged her back to share the news adding that I should arrive at about 10:15. I had given myself about ten extra minutes for any navigation errors, which was just as well as it seemed to take forever to get through the town. In the end I arrived at 10:10 having covered the twenty-four miles in five hours and seven minutes. After two weeks away it was nice to give Angela a long hug. Nice for me, that is. I am sure it wasn't very nice for her as I dripped sweat everywhere after my morning exertion, thankfully she had brought me clean clothes for the second half of my journey. After a quick wash and change, we descended on Morrisons café for a breakfast party, just as her brother Steven arrived and we both tackled the large full English whilst Angela just had a bacon bap and tea.

We returned to John's camper van for another cup of tea. Steve and John can both tell a good tale and I enjoyed being in their company whilst Angela held my hand and we all relaxed before the afternoon section. So far that day I had climbed around one thousand feet in the twenty-four miles, however in the afternoon I was set to climb twice that height in less than half the distance and suspected I would be walking much of the way. I had been concerned by this section as the 'Safe' cycling route, by Royston Wood in his book, is to go directly up the A6. He writes that most of the traffic is heading up and down the M6. There is a lot of truth in what he says but I still didn't fancy running up this busy A road with no pavement on the afternoon of a bank holiday. I had looked at every possible side road, bridleway and footpath nearby to take me northwards. Thankfully I was joined by two friends, both stellar athletes, to escort me over parts of this tricky and demanding section.

First was Sarah Tunstal who arrived at Morrisons on her bike and cycled the first and lower sections of this famous climb as I ran along. We took the side roads and bridleways where possible, adding distance to the more direct A6 route but meaning we were much safer. At one point the bridleway became too rough and muddy for Sarah's road bike, so she cycled back to the main road, then cycled up the road to meet me higher up this monster climb. Sarah is a former international runner, winning medals in European and World Mountain running championships as well as being runner up in the National Cross-Country championships. She made the steep climb look incredibly easy as I chugged along like an overworked steam engine. It was nice to have her company, to hear about how she was doing and the plans for her forthcoming wedding which was to take place a month later in probably my favourite town, Chamonix.

After a few hours Sarah had to head home but said,

"I can't leave without giving you this" and with a beaming smile she produced a Mars bar from her pocket. The significance was not lost on me although it won't mean anything to anyone else it brought a big smile to my face and memories of another epic run. It was a nice moment as she photographed me holding the Mars bar.

In 2008 I ran across England on my version of a coast-to-coast run. I set out from St Bees in Cumbria but finished at Ravenscar instead of Wainwright's traditional route to Robin Hood's Bay. The route took me through the town of Kirkby Stephen, Sarah's hometown. She had run up from the town and placed two mars bars in a clear plastic bag with a note that read;

'For Stephen Fry's coast to coast run'

The bag was fastened to the last gate on the road that runs to the foot of the fell and the route up Nine Standards Rigg. I knew nothing of this and as I ran up the road, I met several walkers who asked me if I was Stephen Fry? They wished me luck and yet not one of them mentioned the note or bag. I was puzzled until I saw it then blown away by her kindness. It still makes me smile fifteen years later.

I wished Sarah good luck with the wedding and she left to cycle home. I crossed over the A6 and headed across a muddy field. As I have said before sometimes little things make you smile and a wooden waymarker sign at a gate did exactly that. The sign informed me that this part of the route was 'Old Shap Road' and carved into the signpost were the figures of a person walking, a person on horseback, a bicycle and a person sitting on the seat of a horse and cart. The route itself was across pastureland with sheep grazing all around, so there was no evidence of a road and it just made me feel part of a lifestyle long forgotten.

At the top of the field a figure running down the hill came into view and I was joined by Victoria Wilkinson, another legendary runner. Victoria has represented England at four different disciplines. As a junior runner she was World Mountain Running Champion. Later she was part of the GB Elite cycling squad then represented England in the Commonwealth games at mountain biking, before being selected for England at Cross country. She is the current ladies record holder for the three peaks mountain race with a time of three hours and nine minutes. Vic ran down the hillside and greeted me with a beaming smile and cheerful "Aye up". She then produced a small backpack with a whole host of snacks and goodies including a pot of Devon custard. Dreamland.

I wolfed it down. That's the good thing about ultra running. You can eat what you want, when you want, in whatever quantities you want. If you are burning over four thousand calories every day, you are likely to be in a calorie deficit and Vic remarked that I had lost weight since she last saw me at our club Christmas meal. All true. I had run five hundred miles in the first three months of the year training for this run, and now in two weeks I'd covered another five hundred more. As we reached the top of the climb we could see Vics car next to a red campervan parked in a layby on the main road. Angela, John and Cath stood waving to us. Our path crossed the main road about half a mile further up the road from the layby. At this point Vic returned to her car and I thanked her for her company and the food she had brought and asked her to tell Angela to meet me about two miles further up the road at a layby on the right. She wished me well and told me to keep her updated on my progress and with that I was on my own again.

I was now right at the top of the climb, and lucky enough to be there on a clear day, with extensive views in all directions. I headed along a gravel track which was totally different from the grassy carpet of the pasture I'd enjoyed earlier. The trail now passed a series of old quarry workings, and at this point the track was all large lumps of limestone chippings, perfect for large trucks carrying stone, but not too good for the feet, ankles, knees or hips of a sixty-one-year-old runner. Even though the route was flat, I was forced to walk along that section until the rocky track became more pedestrian friendly. A look at the map told me I was less than half a mile from the layby so sent John a message saying,

'Put the kettle on' He replied saying 'It's never off' then signed off as 'Betty's on wheels'.

Less than ten minutes later I climbed into the van and enjoyed afternoon tea, and in particular a custard filled caramel doughnut. Angela informed me she had bought four but her brother had eaten two of them before heading for home.

So far that day I had covered thirty-five miles and was right at the top of the hill. I had about three miles to go to reach our destination, the Hermitage Bed and Breakfast in Shap. This is run by a lovely lady called Jean Jackson and is a wonderfully atmospheric place. Angela was staying with me, whilst John and Cath were staying in their campervan at a site about ten miles away. I left the three of them to pack everything away, but not before telling them I should be finished in twenty-five minutes and set off along the small grass verge. After two hundred metres I joined another bridleway. This broad grassy track led across open moorland and five minutes later I arrived at an oversized corral. On the left was the gable end of a large shed, open at one end. To the right of the open end was the corral which was crisscrossed with a series of fences and gates. These had been erected across the track. My route lay on the other side of this corral but to get to it I had to go through three gates where the sheep had been gathered. It was impossible to avoid the carpet of sheep droppings that covered the area and I would certainly have to remove my shoes before entering Jean's pristine premises.

Once I had negotiated 'sheep shit sea' I was on a nice grassy carpet for another half mile before descending to a granite works. Here a concrete road led me to a worker's walkway and out to the A6, which now had a pavement and this would be my route for the last mile and a half. I sent Angela a message saying I would be there in fifteen minutes, then stowed my phone away as I would no longer need it. The road was straight and flat, there was no headwind, and the running was easy. I was looking forward to finishing and relaxing in a hot bath and began to savour the moment.

I would sink into a warm bath with a mug of sweet tea and a packet of chocolate covered biscuits. As the warmth of the bath eased my aching limbs I would dip the chocolate biscuits into the steaming tea, just long enough to melt the chocolate, which would take on a luxuriously silky texture and as it coated my taste buds with sticky sweetness. The beautiful brew would wash those much needed calories on their way as I lay cocooned by the bubbles of some luxuriant muscle soak. I had lost myself in this comforting world when I heard a lady scream.

Up ahead three ladies were standing at the side of the road. They were looking into a narrow field where two horses darted from one side of the field to the other. Something had startled them all, ladies and horses. One of the ladies wore a bright pink coat and I guessed she was the one who had screamed because she had both hands clutching her heart. The other two were holding the handles of large wheeled suitcases. The kind you pack to fly somewhere exotic. Not the sort of thing I would have expected to see being wheeled along the A6.

The horses seemed to calm down after a few seconds and the ladies began walking down the road again. It was then I heard what sounded like muffled machine gun fire being created by the suitcases. The path was littered with stone chippings and the noise from the wheels as they ran across the tiny stones startled the poor horses again. Suddenly one horse jumped the fence, escaping onto the main road. Then taking one look at the ladies it turned and began galloping down the road in my direction.

About a dozen swear words went through my mind, none of which I will repeat here, but will leave those to your imagination. Suffice to say, I didn't think it was a good idea to have a loose horse charging down the white lines of a major road on a bank holiday, which meant, with no one else around I was going to have to try to catch it. I would have much preferred to have ignored the situation and made a direct route to the bath I was telling you about, but realised I had a duty to try and prevent an accident, so with this in mind I stepped into the middle of the road and tried to make myself look as big as possible.

I recaptured the horse and then, after removing my shirt, rode it bareback, up the road to the applause of the three ladies who all called out "my hero" before reuniting it with its' equine acquaintance in the field and we all lived happily ever after…Hold on! I was in Cumbria not California. No sorry it was not exactly like that.

I did manage to capture the horse and gripping onto its mane, walked it back to the area of the fence it had jumped over, There was no gate into the field and on closer inspection I realised it wasn't even really a field. It was more a long narrow triangular piece of grassland where someone had erected what could have just been a makeshift fence around two horses they had left to graze. I really tried my best to get the horse back into the field, makeshift or otherwise, but it just would not go back over the fence. All this time the three ladies had been standing watching from the pavement but after probably twenty minutes, they had seen enough and set off walking again. They tried to move around the horse I clung to, but as soon as they moved they startled both horses again as their suitcases trundled noisily over the chippings. At this point the other horse jumped the fence and causing the first horse to rear up, tearing its head from my grip, and leaving me with nothing more than a few strands of horse hair to show for my efforts. I soothed my frustration by uttering a few more unrepeatable words as with hands on hips, I watched helplessly as the horses hurtled headlong in the direction of Kendal. I dialled 999 to make the police aware of the situation and then ran up the road, flagging down every motorist I met for the next five minutes to inform them of the potential danger. Most of them thanked me but It amazed me that there were those special few who having been given the information that may prevent them from having an accident, failed to even muster up a thank you or any comment at all, and drove off looking as though I had just left a rather unsavoury 'gift' in their swimming pool.

As I entered Shap village two police vans came flying in the other direction with their lights flashing and I hoped this was in response to my 999 call and not to an actual accident. A few minutes after seeing the police vans disappear down the A6, I arrived at the B and B and Angela greeted me on the driveway. She informed me she had started a bath running and that the kettle was on too. The bad news was the pub was booked up for meals but there was a fish and chips shop just across the road. That seemed a good option as the Hermitage doesn't serve evening meals. After I was restored by the hot bath, we dined alfresco, catching the last rays of evening sunshine with John and Cath in the garden of the B & B. Fish Chips, mushy peas, bread and butter, washed down with lashings of tea, brewed by John in his camper van. They laughed as I recounted the incidents with the horses. It was a perfect end to an eventful day.

CHAPTER 21

My Geordie Carer

Day 16 – Saturday 16th April 2022 – Shap to Carlisle

I ate a hotel breakfast for only the third time on the trip but obviously I'd wanted to share as much time with Angela as possible. This meant I made my latest start of the journey so far, setting off at 9am, leaving Angela to enjoy a leisurely hour whilst she waited for the Flying Crowleys to collect her, then meet me in Penrith. I was hoping today would be one of the easier days, as the ten miles to Penrith were nearly all downhill.

My original plan was to use a network of side roads and bridleways rather than running along the A6, but I was assured the road would be quiet on Saturday morning, and informed there was either a footpath or large verge for most of the route anyway. This turned out to be the case and just under an hour later I reached the small village of Clifton. As I ran through the village I noticed a memorial at the side of the road and stopped to read a metal plaque screwed to the wall. This informed me that Clifton was the site of the last battle to take place on English soil. The Battle of Clifton Moor took place in 1745 between the Scots, led by Bonnie Prince Charlie, and the English led, by the Duke of Cumberland.

After taking an obligatory photograph I was on my way again and wondered if the mining communities of South Yorkshire and North Nottinghamshire would consider this to be the last battle on English soil or should it be something closer to home called Orgreave? As I was pondering this, a horn sounded and I looked up to see John's campervan on his way to collect Angela. I waved and pushed on to Penrith, and our meeting point at Morrisons. I would also meet up with Meryl Levington, another member of my running club who was travelling across from Newcastle with husband Martin. She was going to run with me from Penrith to Carlisle.

I arrived first and made my way to the café. I was in the queue when another pal and Bingley club mate turned up. Robin Lawrence and his partner Jacquie had been up in the Lake District the previous day, running over part of the Bob Graham route in preparation for Robin's BG attempt in the summer.

As we were eating I received a dressing down from one of the catering staff for using an electric socket within the restaurant to charge up my phone. I was told this was against company Health and Safety policy as the device had not been pat tested. I explained that I had eaten in six or seven different Morrisons so far on this journey and had been allowed to charge my phone in all of them. This counted for nothing and the manager arrived. It was explained to me that if my phone had any kind of fault and blew their power supply they may have to close the restaurant, so whilst he was sorry, he unfortunately couldn't let me charge my phone in that store. I thanked him for his explanation and sheepishly unplugged the phone, deciding that as it was a straight road to Carlisle I was unlikely to get lost, and anyway I had Meryl to look after me.

Angela arrived and we had another drink together before she had to head home. As she hugged me, she said.

"You have come this far, you must go on and finish it, even if you need to rest for a few days. What an achievement it will be. I'm so proud of you, good luck."

Angela isn't easily impressed and is not usually given to displays of false praise, so this meant a lot to me. I set off with a lump in my throat as I trotted along the road with Meryl who'd arrived as I was having my second coffee. The sun had come out and it was again a pleasant day. In fact it was getting quite warm and unbeknown to me the back of my neck was starting to burn.

Meryl had supported me in the past, running a fifteen-mile stretch on the aforementioned canal run. It was nice to catch up again. Our route was straight forward and every so often Martin met us, resupplying us with refreshment. The road was straight with gentle rolling hills enabling us to cover the first ten miles in one hour and forty minutes. Maybe this was a bit too quick, as with just two miles to go my right knee decided enough was enough. I had not noticed any pain but suddenly the knee joint had stiffened up. As we stopped to cross a road at a roundabout just on the outskirts of the town, I struggled to start running again. I looked at the knee and noticed it was badly swollen. I was forced to walk down the road into Carlisle.

Meryl was no longer pacing me; she had become more of a carer looking after an invalid. My Geordie carer saw me safely to the front door of the hotel and gave me a plastic phone cover having read about my earlier problems with the wet screen. Martin, who had been and bought a bag of ice for me, photographed us outside the hotel and they wished me good luck before setting off for the drive back to Newcastle. I was grateful to them for the company and for giving up their Easter Saturday.

I rang the doorbell of the Abbey Court Guest House and after explaining that I wouldn't require the breakfast that was served from 8am, I settled my bill and was shown to my room. It was a twin room and I was blown away by how fresh, clean and well laid out it was. The room was small, but it was so ergonomically perfect, it could have been designed specifically for me, an inflexible long-distance runner who just wanted to sit down and have everything to hand. I sat with some of the ice on my knee and washed down two ibuprofen with half a litre of water. I then took a shower and washed my kit before hobbling fifty metres to a nearby retail park we'd passed just before reaching the hotel. I bought a tube of Ibuprofen gel, a packet of chocolate biscuits and a few other snacks for the next day. I then headed up the road for a further two hundred metres to a McDonalds. This wouldn't have been the first choice for my evening meal normally, but I needed to stay off the knee as much as possible. The McDonald's was nearby and here I could eat between fifteen hundred and two thousand calories quickly. This way I could get back to the hotel and spend more time resting and trying to get the swelling down. I ordered a large Big Mac meal, a milkshake and an Ice cream and ate the whole lot in less than ten minutes. I returned to the hotel and once safely ensconced in my room put the ice into a hand towel and began the process of trying to get the swelling down on my grapefruit sized knee. I lay on the bed with the towel full of ice balanced on it and updated social media. The last line of my post lifted my spirits.

"Tomorrow I will cross the border into Scotland."

CHAPTER 22

Hitching to Gretna

Day 17 – Sunday 17th April 2022 – Carlisle to Johnstonbridge

Another day and another early start. I had woken at around 5.15am and was really pleased to see the swelling had gone down. After icing the knee for thirty minutes the night before, I'd then taken two naproxen tablets and washed them down with almost two litres of water in three hours. I then covered the knee in Ibuprofen gel just before going to bed. I woke drenched in sweat but surprisingly refreshed despite three nocturnal bathroom visits. The drugs had done their work and the swelling was gone. Nevertheless, I decided I was going to walk this morning, at least for the first hour and then I'd see how the knee felt. I was on the road at exactly 6am.

My route took me through the centre of Carlisle which at that time was deserted except for two men setting up a market stall. I photographed the castle and a wonderful floral display in front of the town hall. A few hundred metres further on, I arrived at a traffic free dual carriageway which was fenced off to pedestrians. As I looked up and down the road for a crossing point or subway I noticed a large metal object lent against a wall. At first I couldn't tell what it was because I was too near the wall but as I moved away I could see it was the side door of a large van, just leaning against the wall. I wondered if the van was hired and tried to imagine the conversation when it was returned. Somehow I don't think they would be getting any deposit back.

After scaling crash barriers at either side of the road, I continued onto a bridge above the river Eden. I turned off the road and onto a tarmac footpath between some houses and a cricket ground. Here, national cycle route number seven skirted the cricket field. The intention was to follow this for much of the next few hours which would take me across the border into Scotland. However, a few hundred yards ahead a possible short cut presented itself and I left the cycle route and re-joined a road. This went past a nature reserve before rejoining the cycle route about three miles further on. I had now been going for one hour and the knee seemed fine. I began running, alternating one minute of running with one minute of walking. This part of the route was long and straight with open fields on both sides. Unfortunately, it was not what I would call scenic as it passed several industrial units and a smelly sewage farm. The scenery improved when I arrived in the small village of Rockcliffe where the route turned west, to the side of the river. A chilly breeze persuaded me to put on my windproof jacket then almost immediately the route turned north, away from the river and headed into a forest. It was a degree or two warmer in the trees so the windproof came off again. Fragrant forest scents filled my nostrils and small patches of sunlight pierced the woodland canopy, giving some indication of the pleasant weather that was to come later in the day. I continued along the road for another mile and came to a crossroads where a finger signpost offered different route options.   Directly ahead the road turned into a small lane, whilst the route that pointed right said cycle route seven and to Gretna four miles. I remembered that the cycle route did a large loop at this point and I had noticed a possible short cut. I checked the map again and could see that after a half a mile the lane turned into a forest track for another half mile to a farm where it turned into a footpath. About a quarter of a mile further on it crossed a footbridge over a railway line. This would lead me right to a collection of buildings where I would rejoin the cycleway at the Southern end of the bridge over the river Esk, the North end of which would see me on Scottish soil. This route would save me almost two miles. What could possibly go wrong?

Well, nothing did, at least not at first. The tarmac lane went for half a mile where it turned into a forest track and then a farm. Here the right of way continued as a farm track to a fence next to the railway line. A small stile and narrow footpath led to a flight of wooden steps that, although a bit slippery, went up and over a footbridge, and back down at the other side. The route then continued as a small footpath leading me to the river. It then followed the riverbank for three hundred metres to a caravan site at the side of the road where I would be reunited with the cycle way. A good result and I turned left along the road and expected to be heading across the bridge but the road just went to a small club serving the caravan site, on the southern bank of the river and underneath the bridge. I was about thirty feet below the bridge. The road carrying the cycle route was less than twenty metres in front of me, but between me and it was a steep bramble-filled banking around thirty feet high, on top of which was a solid barrier another five or six feet high.

I looked at the map again and with my eyes followed the cycle route from where I was now, to a mile down the road and noticed it crossed a thin brown line on the map, a contour line. Where the contour line met the road it disappeared. The road was also shown in brown and it appeared to me that the contour line ran along the road.

"Bugger." I said under my breath.

I had two choices. One was to turn right and run about one mile towards Carlisle, to the point where the road met the cycle route again. Then a mile back again to a point about twenty metres from where I was standing. Or see if I could scramble up the banking and scale the barrier. I settled on option two and began to tiptoe through the brambles. I used my bags to push back the worst of them and after a few minutes made it to the top. After clipping my bags around my waist, I reached up to the top of the barrier. I used my stringlike arms to pull myself off the ground, then managed to lift one leg onto the top of the barrier. Twinges of cramp began to make themselves known in my quad muscles and in trying to shake them out almost fell off. I lay along the top of the barrier clinging for dear life. It was like trying to lay on a gymnastic beam. I threw one leg over and twisted my body to face the barrier, then brought my other leg to join its twin, bracing my feet into the barrier as I held the top. Then I effectively walked my feet down the face of the structure until I felt near enough to drop down to the ground. I breathed a long slow sigh of relief as I inspected several severe looking scratches across my quads and forearms, Scared but I would live.

I started running across the bridge. Half a mile and I would be in Scotland. I had come the whole length of England in less than seventeen days and suddenly felt elated. I took a screenshot of the map showing my location and sent it in a WhatsApp message to my family. I received a concerned reply in seconds. Why Are you running along the M74?

'Welcome to Scotland' the sign read. I photographed it, along with the Gretna sign, the old toll house., and a finger post informed me it was four hundred and seventy-eight miles to Lands' End.

"Not the way I have come, it isn't." I said out loud and calculated I'd come five hundred and fifty-three miles to Gretna. In fairness this did include a few detours and wrong turns but even allowing for those, it didn't equate to an extra seventy-five miles. The sign also told me it was three hundred and sixty miles to John O' Groats but I estimated it was more and calculated it as three hundred and ninety miles. Whichever was correct, I still had an entire country to run. One down, one to go.

I sat on a bench in Gretna town square, munching purchases bought from a small shop. A saucer sized chicken and ham pie, two snickers' bars, a bottle of coke and two bottles of water. The pie tasted absolutely fantastic. I was also enjoying the spring sunshine and thinking how much better the weather was, than it had been on my only other visit to Greta, a very brief stop of about 15 seconds at around 1.30 on 2nd September 1985.

Angela and I got married on 31st August 1985 and after a two-night stay at a posh hotel in the Yorkshire Dales, we set off on our honeymoon proper. Foreign travel was not common in those days and the furthest I'd ever travelled was Cornwall. However, neither of us had ever been to Scotland so we loosely planned a six-day tour of the country. We didn't have any specific destination but would head up the west side of the country and then cut across to Inverness and then come back down the East coast.

On the way we stopped for lunch in Carlisle and as we were heading back to the car, the heavens opened. The rain was coming down like arrows at Agincourt. Large droplets that got faster and faster. They forced me to turn the windscreen wipers to full speed as we drove towards the motorway.

I remember stopping just before a roundabout near to the on ramp as the windscreen was all misted up. We each wiped the screen with the back of our hand, revealing the youthful face of a hooded hitch hiker peering in at us. Despite wearing waterproofs from head to toe he was absolutely sodden. Angela and I looked at each other. We knew we couldn't leave him standing at the side of the road so she stuck her head out and shouted to the soaking soul as she opened the back door. He climbed in the back and pulled down his hood revealing strands of wet ginger hair, plastered to his young head. I asked him where he was going but couldn't understand his reply, so repeated the question.

One thing that has certainly changed in the last thirty-eight years, is our nation's ability to better understand regional accents. Back in 1985 it was not so easy. I remember one of my work colleagues telling me the story of a driver that visited the warehouse one morning about that time. None of the warehouse team could understand the driver, so they sent for members of the office staff who spoke French and German. They too were unable to understand the poor driver either. Brian, the man describing the incident was himself a broad speaking Yorkshireman who had worked on the railways for almost fifty years and he was howling with laughter as he puffed on his pipe leading up to the punch line of the story:

"It turns out he was a bloody Geordie! " He chuckled, and almost choked during the coughing fit that followed.

But it's true. We're now accustomed to regularly hearing accents from all over the country, from Europe, even the world, that my parents and those parents of my generation never or rarely heard. Back in that car in 1985 our wet and weary wanderer repeated his destination three times, each one louder than the last but they all came out as

"Gruntna,"

"Sorry, what was that?"

"Gruntna!"

"Where?"

"GRUNTNA!"

It was only when I saw the sign that read 'Gretna One Mile', that I got the message.

We drove him into the town and pulled up to let him out. It was at that point he asked us where we were going. I told him our sketchy plan, up one side of the country and back down the other and then added. "We're on our honeymoon."

His face lit up in a big smile and he looked at each of us in turn then said.

"Honeymoon! Well use shud ne be here 'talkin' to me. Use shud be Shaggin!"

With that, he slammed the door and disappeared into the monsoon. He had been in the car for not much more than five minutes, but the back seat was soaking, however we felt we had helped him and in turn he had left us smiling at each other.

After my tasty breakfast, I left 'Grutna' at 9:30 and started my second run of the morning. Having left the town I picked my way along quiet lanes to emerge onto the A74 which is also a national cycle route that runs parallel to M74. It was long, straight and largely traffic free. I still had a long way to go so I increased the running periods from one minute to two minutes with a one-minute walk in between. The knee seemed to be holding up well, but the back of my neck was getting increasingly sore. Eventually I realised that I was getting sunburned so stopped just before the wonderfully named Ecclefechan to apply suncream.

Because I'd heard the name many times, I had imagined Ecclefechan to be a much larger place. I'd travelled hopefully, dreaming of tea and cake but there was no café to be found, just another small shop. As I entered a customer asked me which club I ran for. She had a distinctly Lancashire accent and told me she used to be a fell runner with Horwich. When I told her I ran for Bingley Harriers she, Linda, mentioned a few names of people she had run against including Barbara Carney. I took a selfie of the two of us in the shop as the shopkeeper was putting her purchases in two carrier bags. Linda paid and I held the door for her as she left the shop.

After buying another pie and more water I too left the shop. Linda was still outside, at the kerbside looking up and down the road. The poor lady was struggling to walk and was using a stick. It looked as if at some point she'd had a stroke or an accident. I asked if I could help with the shopping. She pointed to a house about thirty metres up the road with its front door slightly ajar. Taking the shopping from her, I carried it across the road. The bags were heavier than I expected, and I could hear the tinkling of glass bottles. On arrival at the cottage I pushed the door open a little more, just enough to allow me to leave the two carriers on the doormat inside the door. The house was dark and dingy with no paint or paper on the wall and from the small bit of floor I could see no carpeting or floor covering either. One of the carrier bags dropped slightly revealing two bottles of spirit and 4 cans of special brew. I was once again stuck for words and really felt for the lady. I have no idea if Linda had fallen on hard times, if she had turned to drink and done so due to an accident or if drinking had led in some way to her mobility difficulties, or indeed if the drink was for someone else. It just all seemed a bit sad and yet Linda seemed cheerful and happy enough. I tried not to be judgemental as I had no way of knowing what problems or issues had brought her to this place or stage in life. I was reminded of the red Indian proverb, don't judge a person until you have walked a mile in their moccasins. I turned to Linda and said I would pass on her best wishes to Barbara. She wished me good luck for my journey and with that I was on my way.

The sun was bright and my short shadow pointed the way North. A few hundred metres further up the road was a playing field with a bench underneath a cedar tree. I sat on the bench enjoying the shade and ate the pie, whilst I watched a father and two sons playing football. The smaller of the two boys kept saying he was not playing anymore. He was clearly tired but then when the ball came near him he would suddenly spring into life and try to score past his dad. I would have liked to join in as it reminded me of my own childhood and playing football with my dad and brother. Happy times. I suddenly wished I could turn back the clock.

Pie consumed and washed down with a bottle of water I was on my way again to Lockerbie and the next stage of the so far fruitless Scottish café hunt. Three miles south of Lockerbie I met a cyclist with heavily loaded panniers. We introduced ourselves and he turned out to be from a small place called Steeton which is less than fifteen miles from where I live. He was called Dave and had cycled from the north of Scotland. He was heading for Carlisle and the train home. We chatted for a few minutes, each took the obligatory selfie before wishing each other good luck and heading our separate ways.

Shortly before 2pm I reached Lockerbie and found caffeine salvation and other culinary delights in Greggs. A large coffee, a tuna crunch baguette and a caramel custard donut fuelled my machinery. Not your typical Easter Sunday lunch but it hit all the right places, and because I am healthy I drank more water. My watch informed me I'd covered almost twenty-eight miles in seven and a half hours so far that day. I still had about eight miles to my hotel at Johnstonebridge. So, with this premium fuel consumed I began the last leg of the day.

So far the knee had stood up to alternating the running and walking but I now planned to run the rest of the way. I wanted to get back to five miles per hour if possible and set off at that pace. The day had hotted up and I wanted to get out of the sun as quickly as I could. In the end I arrived at Johnstonebridge in a shade under ninety minutes from Lockerbie. It was ten minutes to four. I was looking forward to a bath followed by an afternoon nap, particularly as I was staying in a motel at a motorway services, where there would be really nothing to see, so catching up on my sleep seemed a good idea. I was sure it would not be wasted.

CHAPTER 23

A Mentor and A Nemesis

I looked at the map for the next days route There were no town, village, pub, restaurant, café or shop selling food between Johnstonbridge and Abington. According to Royston Wood's book I would have to go off my route to the town of Moffat if I wanted refreshment of any kind, a diversion of two and a half miles each way. The mention of Moffat reminded me of a race two of my friends had done. This brought back memories of my days in the St Bedes Cross Country team, and the day I met John Crowley.

In September of 1974 I started at St Bede's Grammar School. On our first day the whole school year gathered together for a welcome assembly. We were told of the school's history, its academic prowess and its sporting achievements. We were given the names of old boys who'd gone on to achieve fame and fortune. We were also informed that on one of the corridors photographs of all the school teams and lists of their achievements were displayed, including the school's athletics records and how it was considered an honour to have your picture or name on that wall. The headmaster added that earlier that summer, one boy had won a race at the English Schools Athletics championships, winning the under seventeen steeplechase in a record time. This boy was a member of the school cross country team and he had now been picked to run for England.

His name was John Crowley.

I listened intently and as soon as the assembly was finished, I almost ran to read what the record time was for 1500 metres for an under fourteen-year-old. I found the place but couldn't believe what it said. It's funny what sticks in your mind from school. Almost fifty years later I can see those numbers in front of me like a beacon. Hand printed on large white cards that were mounted onto the corridor wall then covered by a glass protection screen. Bright red lettering that still stands out to me like a flashing neon sign outside a shop.

1500 metres – under 14. – John CROWLEY. 4:17.1

1500 metres – under 15. – John CROWLEY. 4:01.2

Before the age of fifteen John Crowley had run 4 minutes and 1.2 seconds for 1500 metres, and I had just broken his record at our previous school, I couldn't wait to meet him.

John was three years older than me and now in the sixth form, so coming into contact with him during a normal school day was unlikely, however I had learned that the senior cross-country team trained every evening after school. Other members of the team were Jack Verity, whose brother David was in my year and would become a good friend and my main training partner for the next year, Stephen and Chris Walker, John Kennedy, Ted Zarkanko, Raymond Rogers, and Eric Walsh.

What I didn't realise was just how good these guys were and later in the year were to win second place at the Northern Clubs Championships, the first school ever to win medals at the regional championships in its one-hundred-year history. I was in awe of the incredible times John had run.

The day came for our first training session and I went along with my new school running vest and a few of the other boys from my year. I walked into the changing rooms, a cocky thirteen year old, full of enthusiasm and excitement at the prospect of meeting this English champion. A group of older boys were already gathered at the far end of the room chatting and laughing. I put my bag down and announced,

"Excuse me, is one of you John Crowley?"

Heads turned towards a long-haired youth dressed in a lemon-yellow heavy cotton rugby shirt, a pair of blue and white hooped shorts and blue suede running shoes with three white stripes down the side. He was tying his laces and seemed a bit smaller and stockier than I expected. How did he get over the steeplechase barriers? I walked across to him and he stood up saying,

"I'm John, who are you?

I stepped forward and held out my hand announcing,

"My name's Stephen Fry and I broke your record at Edmund Campion last year."

A hush descended on the gathered group. It was like the show down from the film, 'GunFight at the O.K. Coral' as momentarily we stood there face to face in a kind of unintended standoff. A couple of the senior boys started laughing. One boy, Eric Walsh said,

"Oh was that the time when all the stopwatches went dingy." To be fair to John, he didn't seem offended. He didn't laugh or challenge me but said,

"Well if that's right I will have to keep an eye on you."

John did keep an eye on me and in years to come I was to spend many hours training with him and Jack Verity, the founder of Saltaire Striders running club who was also a county champion at 1500 metres. Ten years later the three of us set off to Horton in Ribblesdale in Jack's car to run our first Three Peaks race. At the time this was one of my life's ambitions having watched the race for the first time in 1975. To run the three peaks race you had to have completed certain other races to demonstrate your experience. One of the races that John and Jack ran was at Moffat. John tells a good tale about how he misread the start time and they both arrived fifteen minutes after everyone else had started but the abiding memory is of how steep the hills were and how high the heather was. He left me thinking Moffat was not a place I really wanted to visit.

Over the years we did many races together and at some point, along with Jack's brother David, made up the raft racing quartet I alluded to in an earlier chapter when I met the man canoeing down the Thames. I should point out that there is a bit of poetic licence when I use the words 'raft racing quartet.' There were four of us so that bit is correct, but to describe our performance as 'racing' is pushing it. In fact, that is exactly what we were doing, pushing it. Also to describe our craft as a 'raft' is definitely stretching the imagination. 'Sitting on a sinking submarine' would be a far more accurate description. We started first and finished last and it's fair to say it was far from our finest hour. The problem was the rules, or at least our interpretation of them.

"Design and build your own raft using barrels, kegs, or floating containers not exceeding 50 litres. So we did and made a raft consisting of two plywood boards, sandwiched between which were 10 x 5 litre empty plastic orange squash containers, then the whole thing was covered in heavy duty polythene and it floated like a dream. Until we sat on it. I will never forget John's immortal words the night we tested our home made craft.

" Well I don't think it's a winner but I think it will get us round."

Master of the understatement is Mr Crowley. It was a complete and utter disaster.

My wife still howls with laughter when we recall the day, as a team was entered from her work, a high street bank. Their team was crewed by four of her colleagues, all non sporty, female bank cashiers. This was in the days of 'Charlie's Angels' and Farrah Fawcett hairstyles and the carefully coiffed cashiers set off about fifteen minutes after us. They paddled effortlessly past us and finished thirty minutes before us in full makeup beautifully manicured nails and not a hair out of place.

We on the other hand finished looking like the survivors of a disaster movie, and collapsed on the ground all suffering from exhaustion and early stages of hyperthermia, having been up to our midriffs in freezing river water for over two hours. It appeared that every other competitor remained dry, as every other raft had been built using 4 x 50 litre drums. Lesson of the day was to always read the small print and check for understanding.

At St Bede's I trained regularly and improved but it was three years before I bettered my time of five minutes and seven seconds, so perhaps the stopwatches did have a meltdown that afternoon at Edmund Campion. Not so for John. His time for the 1500 metre steeplechase set in 1974 still ranks almost fifty years later as third fastest by an under seventeen in the U.K. ever.

However, there was no error or mistake when I won the 1500m at the Bradford Inter Grammar School championship in 1977. On the day, although I won, I was a little disappointed because of who I didn't beat. I was in really good form and had convinced myself this would be the day I finally beat my B.G.S. nemesis, Andrew Jonathan Quentin Suddards. 'Sudds' to his friends, was the only member of the six Bradford Grammar School runners I'd followed across the line three years earlier that I still hadn't beaten. I had tried many times but just didn't seem to have the measure of him.

I'd trained hard, focusing on this race for months and had improved dramatically. I chatted with Sudds about ten minutes before the start and was surprised to learn he wasn't running in my race. He told me he was disappointed too as he wanted to run the longer event, but his teachers had asked him to run in the eight hundred metres instead and we were only allowed to run one race.

Unfortunately I never got the opportunity to race him again. To be fair he was a much better runner than I ever was, and if he had taken up the sport seriously, who knows what he would have achieved in later years. As a junior he would regularly beat several athletes who ran at a much higher level as seniors, including future Olympians. In later life I understand he was Squadron Leader A.J.Q. Suddards flying Harrier jump jets. A real life 'Top Gun' who was to retire from the R.A.F. in a very senior position. A high flyer indeed if you will pardon the pun.

If Sudds was my nemesis, John was to become my mentor, a really good friend, and the big brother I never had. He has more tales to tell than either I or Hans Christian Anderson. He has lots of interests, running, cycling, bee keeping, silversmith, folk music and morris dancing to name a few. He can entertain you for hours on any number of subjects and I never tire of being in his company. He is a devoted husband and father and although he wears shorts for about three hundred and sixty days a year, I look on him as the finest role model I could have. He married Catherine, the biscuit monitor from my first day at school. Without their support and friendship over the years I wouldn't have attempted many of the things I have done.

CHAPTER 24

No Cause For Alarm
But it's Going To Cock

Day 18 – Monday 18th April 2022 – Johnstonebridge to Abington

I went to bed on Sunday night deciding that I would have a lie in the next morning and enjoy a cooked breakfast. Monday would be a relatively easy day as the distance was only twenty-six and a half miles, just slightly over the distance of a marathon. I don't mean to be showing off or implying that running a marathon is easy, it's certainly not, especially if you are racing or going for a specific time. On the contrary, there is no hiding place if you are racing a marathon. It will find every crack or chink in your armour. Your armour is your training. If you try to race or achieve a tight time when you haven't done enough training it will find you out. However, on this trip I'd already had numerous days when I'd run much further than a marathon, so this was set to be a much shorter day, or so I thought.

There were two reasons for the proposed later start, yes there was the lack of catering on route, but it was also bank holiday Monday and for this reason I doubted it would be possible for me to check in to my room before 2pm. Thus, there was no reason at all to set off before 9am. So, when the fire alarm went off at 4:15 am, I didn't really see it as the same good opportunity for an early start that I may have done on some of the longer days. Quite the contrary, it was a right royal pain in the posterior.

Be honest, how many times have you entered the room of your hotel or accommodation and seen those fire safety notices on the back of your door, only to completely ignore them. I always read them now. Let me tell you, nothing wakes you faster than a fire alarm going off in the middle of the night. Definitely squeaky bum time. The only other experience I have had that was equally scary, apart from the Volvo car crash test dummy experience, was on a flight back from Florence.

Angela and I were flying to Manchester airport after a holiday. We were over Nottingham, and everything seemed perfectly normal when a voice came from the flight deck saying,

"Cabin Crew. Prepare for Emergency Landing!" Just as suddenly, oxygen masks dropped from a compartment next to the reading lights and the plane began to descend. One of the cabin crew went through the door onto the flight deck. She reappeared two minutes later, whipping smudged mascara from around her eyes. Maybe this was more serious than I'd first thought. Squeaky bum time. The plane had lost cabin pressure too quickly, but thankfully we landed safely twenty minutes later, in the cargo section of the airport where we were met by six fire engines. Once this has happened to you, you will never ever ignore the cabin crew as they go through the in-flight safety briefing again, no matter how many times you've seen it.

On the flight in question, two out of every three passengers didn't know how to put on their masks. Some were shouting at the flight attendants saying 'The oxygen isn't working' even though at that point they hadn't put their masks on. I really wanted to scream at them.

"You weren't watching, were you? There are few things I'm more frustrated by than seeing people ignore the safety briefing. I feel like saying to them.

"Oy! Pay attention. Play with your own safety but don't mess with mine."

Sorry, none of that has anything to do with my journey to John O' Groats only to emphasise that accidents do happen and when the time comes you have to be ready as you may not have much time, and luckily for me when the fire alarm went off at 4:15am I was prepared.

One of the advantages of travelling light is that you don't really have many belongings to worry about. My running kit was laid out on one chair with my shoes directly underneath. Everything else, apart from my toothbrush, was packed away into my two bum bags which were laid on top of the duvet on the other side of the bed. Chair and bags were between me and the door, so as soon as the alarm went off, I dived to the chair, pulled on my running shorts and tee shirt, picked up my running shoes in one hand, the two bags in the other and made my way to the service area, arriving before nearly everyone else.

It was starting to rain so we were moved into a staff restaurant whilst the building was checked out and a register taken, then after about twenty minutes it was decided by a staff member that it had been a false alarm and we were let back to our rooms. I was wide awake by this time and had the next stage of my run been further, I would have set off immediately but instead I made a cup of tea. Well, I am British. By the time 7am came I was still wide awake so after a shower and customary morning ablutions, I headed off to see if there was any possibility of breakfast. Alas I knew the answer No, the restaurant wasn't yet open for another hour.

I had enough snacks to last me to Abington so decided to forgo the Scottish Square Sausage for another day and set off running, but not before asking the receptionist if they would call ahead to their sister motel at Abingdon and ask them if they could arrange an early check in for me as I was likely to be there before 1pm. With that I was up and running. It was 7.30. I was quite excited about today because my sister Maureen and her husband Iwan were driving up to meet me in the evening and I was looking forward to seeing them.

The forecast was for a mix of sunshine and showers and luckily I managed to avoid both. The morning was damp from earlier rain but cool and perfect running conditions. I did have two very short spells of drizzle, each lasting about five minutes. The first part of the route was a gentle climb going up around four hundred metres in the first fifteen miles. It was along a straight road running parallel to the M74 and was lined with trees on either side. The motorway was behind the trees to the right. The trees meant that views for much of the way were limited but they did provide some shelter against the breeze I was running into. However, nothing could protect me from the down draft created by the trucks that periodically hurtled along the road. Eddie Stobart spotters would have been in their element as every hour or so two articulated lorries would shatter the relatively quiet road and fly past me, followed by a downdraft that would almost knock me off my feet. Thankfully on every occasion the trucks moved a few metres away from me. Although there was a footpath, it was less than one metre wide and I dread to think what would have happened if they had not been able to move across the white lines.

It was a bit dull during the first part of the morning, both the weather and the scenery. One bright spot was the numerous small white flowers in the grass at the side of the road. Actually, when I looked more closely they were not white but more accurately light pink. I know I have used this analogy before but my wife would still be referring to one of her colour charts and calling them something like 'maiden's blush' or 'winter sunrise." Basically, they were light pink. However, I can't deny they were quite pretty and broke the monotony of the drab grey road and equally drab grey hedgerow. Of course, neither were grey, they were 'morning mushroom.'

Further on the trees gave way to open fields on my left and a small church came into view. It was probably because up to now, the day had been so drab that I stopped to take a photograph of it. I wouldn't normally photograph a graveyard so it does say how dull the day was. Another few miles further on and I did actually come to something worth photographing but I still can't work out what it is or why it was there. Just before Beattock I joined a specifically created cycle path and breathed a sigh of relief to be off the road. It was around here that I came across what was a large spherical object that stood incongruously at the side of the cycleway. It was about two metres in diameter and was made of a series of square aluminium tiles. Most of the tiles were the colour of aluminium with a black bicycle printed on them, however there were a series of dark blue tiles each with a white letter on. These tiles were arranged around the middle of the sphere in the way you would put a ribbon around an Easter egg. The lettered tiles spelt the name of the French City, Toulouse across the middle of the sphere. I would love to be able to enlighten you why this was there and did look online but there were several different explanations.

The first explanation says it is a monument to the French painter Toulouse Lautrec, who, it says whilst on a cycling holiday in Scotland, married a barmaid in Gretna Green. It doesn't mention anything about having taken marital advice from a local hitchhiker. Another explanation says that it is a sculpture of a hot air balloon by Breton artist Stefanie Bourne and is classified as one of the 'Sustrans artworks'. A third suggestion is that the sphere is some kind of shelter on the Glasgow to Toulouse cycle route put there when the main road was upgraded to a motorway. I have no idea if any of these explanations are correct. All I will say is, it just seemed odd and out of place.

The village of Beattock is at an altitude of around one hundred metres, that's three hundred and thirty feet in old money, and after this point the route climbed steadily for the next three miles, going up another two hundred and ten metres to Beattock Summit. On the way up the climb a sign informed me I was crossing the border into South Lanarkshire and thanked me for driving safely.

"You're Welcome."

The traffic noise grew louder as I neared the summit. I arrived at a visible plateau where there were no trees between the cycleway and the motorway, and even though the road was over one hundred metres away the noise was deafening. The plateau is home to the Clyde wind farm, and windmills were dotted liberally across the skyline. Despite being humongous structures, they were dwarfed by the surrounding hills, the Southern Uplands. Although significantly smaller than their Highland cousins, the are still strikingly wild and remote.

As I took in the scenery, I was startled by a cyclist coming from behind who stopped when he noticed my shirt said 'Yorkshire runner.' He introduced himself as Mark from Huddersfield. He'd set off from Lands' End with a support crew a week before but one by one, the support crew got bored and returned home. He was now on his own but determined to finish and weather permitting, hoped to do so in another two or three days. I thought about the retreating support crew. Clearly even driving in a van from Lands' End to John O' Groats is too much for some.

The next twelve miles were all downhill and suddenly I was flying along. I made one more stop to take a photo that I couldn't resist about four miles before Abingdon. The surrounding hills were now largely clear of trees and dedicated to pasture for sheep and cattle. However, on the northeast side of the motorway, a small forest had been planted in what I would say is an unusual shape for a forest. At this point I don't want to lower the tone of the book, if that's possible, but I want you to understand what I saw clearly that April day so you can be as shocked as I was. There on the hillside was a forest that appeared to have been planted in the shape of the 'Crown Jewels. 'Hundreds of trees planted in the shape of the largest cock and balls you're ever likely to see.

With the phallic forest photographed I was on my way again and forty minutes later arrived at Abingdon Village where I was overjoyed to find the village bakery open. I bought a giant sausage roll, and a packet of oat biscuits then decided there was nothing to be gained from running at this point. I had only one mile to go, so spent twenty minutes eating my purchases as I strolled that last mile into Abingdon arriving at 12:25pm. I made my way to reception and was extremely pleased to find they had indeed received the message from the team at Johnstonebridge. I was in my room, number 007, enjoying tea and biscuits in the bath again by 12:35.

With the runner and running kit scrubbed clean, I went in search of food and paid a King's ransom for a sandwich and assorted snacks from the shop in the service area, before returning to my room. Once I had finished my second lunch I tried to let daytime T.V. cure my insomnia. That was a mistake. It was the world snooker championships and I was enthralled by the standard of play. Eventually I did fall asleep but only after the afternoon snooker session had finished.

Maureen and Iwan arrived and she presented me with a carrier bag full of assorted goodies including a stack of homemade oat biscuits, made to our mum's secret recipe which has been handed down from mother to daughter. Sadly, I don't qualify. Yum. All for me, they contain a bit of coconut so you can still enjoy them hours after you've eaten one. The bag also included an electronic tracking device that my club mate Kate Farley, a qualified mountain leader and endurance running coach, had kindly agreed to lend me for the rest of the trip. Using the phone as a tracker had been killing the battery so I'd switched the tracker off during the first week and done without it. I'd really wanted people to be able to track my progress because I felt it was important for my family, friends and those sponsoring me to know where I was. But I also know how exciting it can become when you are tracking the progress of a friend in an endurance race or similar challenge. In the world of ultra running we call it 'dot watching' and it can become compelling, with people sometimes setting alarm clocks to wake up in the night to see the progress. However, I felt it was also vital for safety. Once

I got into the more remote areas of Scotland, I wasn't sure if I'd have a phone signal. The tracker Kate was lending me was competition standard and pretty much bomb proof. It would give out my location to within five metres, so If I got badly injured someone would know where I was. It weighed about three hundred grams, was three centimetres square and one centimetre deep, so didn't take up much room in the bag.

Maureen and Iwan had booked a room at the hotel but we drove to the nearby town of Biggar to have a meal. This was beneficial for me as with a slight diversion it would allow me to have a look at the first ten miles of my next day's route. I was a bit apprehensive about it because it was along an A road and whilst the book described it as relatively quiet, it was an A road leading to a major Motorway Junction so I suspected it could be busy in the morning.

The ten-mile drive took us a fraction over ten minutes. Tomorrow at my normal pace it would take me two hours and unfortunately the recce didn't really do anything to allay my fears.There was no path at all, no verge for at least eight miles, a few tight bends where drivers would have no advanced view of my approach and all in all not where I wanted to be if there was much traffic or any freight traffic. Still, I had a choice to go earlier, or later and this occupied my thoughts as we ate our meal. I didn't want to be on that road when the morning traffic was at its busiest, which would probably be between 7.30am and 9am. I went to bed a little apprehensive but knowing that with only ten days to go, the countdown really had begun.

18 days completed. 10 days to go.

CHAPTER 25

As Easy as Apple Pie, If Only

Day 19 – Tuesday 19th April 2022 – Abingdon to Livingston

I woke to find my phone had not charged fully, showing fifty six percent. It had been plugged in all night and I concluded the connection must be faulty. It wasn't a great start. Maureen and Iwan met me in reception at 6.00 am and waved me off. I was grateful to them for coming all this way, and it had given me a lift. It also allowed me to send home bits of kit I decided I didn't need, after all, I now had the tracker to accommodate. This ultra running thing is like precision engineering you know. It's down to fine margins.

I set out running northeast along the A73 on another cold morning. Frost coated fields and ribbons of mist hanging eerily above the river confirmed this, I learned later the river was in fact the river Clyde. Thankfully there was not much traffic on the road this early, but five or six large trucks in the first quarter of an hour, all travelling west towards the M74 were a foretaste of what was to come. I decided to quicken the pace a little to try and warm up as the temperature seemed to have dropped a few degrees when the road got closer to the river. More pockets of mist punctuating the route, where the road crossed a stream. Each patch made me more eager to be off this road and my pace quickened every time I ran through one. I wasn't surprised to find that I'd covered the first five miles in under forty minutes. The road was mainly flat, having only climbed ten metres in those five miles. It was bordered by a low wall and wire fence on either side, surrounded by fields. There was no wind so the running was easy, provided there was no traffic. Apart from the odd small pocket of mist there was good visibility along the road for most of those five miles but I did decide to step up on top of the wall or wait in a farm driveway on a couple of occasions, when traffic was coming in both directions at the same time. This happened a few times. If one of those vehicles was a truck, I would move to the opposite side of the road. So, on those occasions, I was running with my back to the traffic. I could have kept running, in the hope that any driver behind me would slow down, and not try to pass until the road was completely clear. However, I can recount too many stories of drivers I've witnessed doing things other than driving.

For a short while I drove a furniture delivery van, and driving such a vehicle enables you to see things you would miss by driving a car, and it's frightening. This was demonstrated to me one day after witnessing the aftermath of a major accident. The accident was on the M1 and involved a BMW salon driving into the back of a truck. I was driving north through a contraflow. I could see a long queue of traffic ahead coming south heading into a contraflow, but nothing was coming through the cones on the other side. As I passed, I saw the first vehicle at the front of the queue was a large truck which was stopped, seemingly for no reason. However, behind the truck was a BMW saloon whose roof was touching the back of the truck. The front of the car was right under the truck and it looked like the back of the truck was sitting on the windscreen. Either the truck had reversed at speed into the car, or the car had hit the truck at such a speed the engine had pushed the truck's rear crash bar underneath. It didn't look good for anyone in the front seats of the car.

The following day on another motorway, driving through another set of cones, an almost identical BMW saloon drew up alongside to my right and I glanced down. The driver had a lap top open on their knee and was typing away with their right hand whilst holding the steering wheel with their left.

I've seen people texting, writing emails, peeling an orange, applying makeup, having a shave, doing a crossword. I have even witnessed one gentleman driving along at seventy miles per hour in the middle lane of the M62 at 7am eating a bowl of cereal. Why? I suspect any one of those people if playing a video game wouldn't play whilst texting or peeling an orange and yet when they step from the virtual world to the real thing, where real life is at stake they actually concentrate less. Astounding. So I'm not confident every driver following will be concentrating on what they are supposed to be doing.

After an hour the road did get busier. Luckily this coincided with me reaching an area of unfenced woodland that offered places I could step off the road more easily if I needed to. After eight miles I reached a junction where the A72 went into Biggar. At this point there was a large grass verge and I was able to get off the road completely. However, it was badly rutted and I was forced to slow my pace a little. Two miles later I arrived at the turn off to the small village of Thankerton which I renamed Thankfully as I left the busy A road for the last time. Breathing a sigh of relief I celebrated with a bottle of water as I leaned against a bus stop, and sent a message to Maureen who after viewing the road the night before had shared my concerns.

Studying the map as I drank I memorised the route. Over the railway line, right along 'boat' road, right at the bridge and over the river Clyde then left up the side of a big hill with the fort on it. It was a stiff climb and I was forced to slow down but kept running albeit at a snail's pace. I couldn't complain as the route I was following was taking me through a gap between the Pentland Hills and the Tinto Hills. Just over an hour later I arrived at a crossroads at the centre of the village of Carnwath having covered over sixteen miles. It was 9am.

This was another significant place because Carnwath lies almost midway between the westside and east side of Scotland and once I was properly on the east side, it felt like my ultimate destination was just up the road, albeit 300 miles up the road. A driver was delivering to the co-op and the manager was signing the paperwork. I asked if there was a café in the village or if they sold tea. The co-op man answered no to both parts of the question but pointed to a white building I had just ran past. I retraced my steps and entered the 'Apple Pie Bakery', the bread and pastry equivalent of Charlie's chocolate factory.

I was greeted warmly by the staff who were all hard at work setting up for the day. I ordered a turkey salad sandwich, a cup of tea and a strawberry cream tart. This is a bakery, not a café and the food is really to be taken away but I noticed a chair tucked away in the corner, next to a freezer, so asked if I could sit in whilst I ate my sandwich. They told me that I would have to be out of the chair by 1pm, as one of their regular customers, whose name, sadly I can't remember, but let's call him Harry for the purposes of the story. Harry would be coming in about that time after his bike ride and he likes to sit down whilst he has his tea and a cake. I said,

"He sounds like someone who knows what's important in life" They all laughed and said he is eighty-four and every day he cycles out into the hills, then finishes at the bakery for his tea and cake. I promised to vacate the chair by then, but threw in a caveat that if he was early he would have to wait as I am excited by all this lovely food on display and I may still be eating! They pointed me to some of the awards they had won which were displayed on the wall at the back of the open plan baking area.

The banter and bonhomie between the group was refreshing. They allowed me to recharge my phone and I spent a very happy forty-five minutes, eating, drinking, laughing and chatting with them before taking a photo and thanking them for their warm and welcoming hospitality. The (award winning) Apple Pie Bakery Carnwath gets five stars from me.

After leaving the bakery, my route took me past a small industrial estate and then a place on the map named 'Stanemuir

Toll' When I looked at the map whilst at the bakery I was curious as to what I would see. When I arrived it was clear where the toll was. There was a perfectly round house on the edge of a forest and I wondered what the charge would have been in days gone by.

A few hundred metres further on a left turn took me up a slight climb and past the wonderfully named farm of Calla Doone conjuring up images of Private Frazer from Dad's army.

"We're doomed"! …Well, I sincerely hope we're not because I still have a way to go.

The next ten miles were the best bit of Scotland so far. A pleasant sunny morning, a gentle breeze, excellent views all around, empty roads, a good running surface and fresh air. I enjoyed this stage immensely and arrived in West Calder at 12.30. Now I am not sure what you call your midday meal, Lunch? Dinner? Whatever. I am sure you have spotted a theme by now that If food was available, basically I was happy to join in and as luck would have it, right at the road junction was a café. I had only five miles to go but decided once again to follow the advice of Jack Reacher, 'Eat when you can.'

I enjoyed another sandwich and more tea but no cake as one has to watch one's figure at my age. I refilled my water bottles and made use of the facilities before setting off after forty five minutes, hoping to be finished around one hour later. It was 1.15 and I was looking forward to watching the snooker again. The route was straightforward, or at least it should have been, but I had made another error by plotting my route to the wrong hotel arriving at 'Livingston Lodge', instead of the Livingston Travelodge. Annoyingly I'd passed close to the correct place as I arrived in town but went another mile and a quarter uphill, only to have to retrace my steps once I had discovered the error. Still, I arrived safely and in good spirits. Tomorrow I'd pass Edinburgh and the Forth Bridge, a proper landmark moment.

19 days done. 9 days to go.

CHAPTER 26

Forth Bridge

Day 20 – Wednesday 20th April 2022 – Livingston to Kinross

I was a bit grumpy when I set off. Maybe it was because it was only 6.15 but more likely it was the fact that my route was planned from a different hotel, so the first mile seemed somehow unnecessary. I retraced my steps of the previous afternoon passing Livingston Hospital. The day started brightly, but I found getting through Livingston tedious and dull. All the roads seemed to lead from one roundabout to another, the Scottish equivalent of Milton Keynes and I didn't seem to be making progress. Thankfully the town was blessed with lots of cycle routes. These went in all directions, but it was easy to take the wrong one, a fact I'd discovered the night before when I gone out to eat.

I followed the road from the hospital to another roundabout. From there I headed over a footbridge and joined one of the cycle routes. This was lined with blossom trees and daffodils proving springtime had arrived in Scotland. I was moved to take my first photograph of the day. The floral scene was short lived as the cycle route dumped me in an industrial estate, and even though it was not yet 7am, it was suddenly busy with trucks and cars heading to the various offices and units. This demanded a high level of concentration as people arrived at work, turning into the units. For a few hundred metres it was all a little bit stop and start as very few people in a car arriving at work want to give way to a pedestrian trying to cross the entrance to their workplace.

It seemed to take an age to escape the industrial area but eventually I did and passed the railway station at Uphall. The road went under the Motorway emerging with open fields on both sides. Suddenly I was in the countryside but this too was short lived as half a mile further on I arrived at the A89. This is one of the major routes into Edinburgh from the west of the city, thankfully there was a wide footpath alongside it.

I was now heading Eastwards towards the morning sunshine. The road was busy but I was happy and in the zone again. All these people were going to work, I was on holiday so what was there to complain about. Eventually the road brought me to a large roundabout that went over the M9 at Newbridge. I estimated this was halfway to my first stop of the day at South Queensferry. With all the roads and turn offs at this roundabout I became a bit disorientated but eventually found my way over a footbridge to the other side of the motorway. Here I was supposed to join another cycle route but the start of it didn't seem to be correct as it went through a small gap in the fence causing me to waste minutes walking back and forth, probably to the amusement of the morning commuters. However, the way through the fence was correct and led to a gravel footpath that widened a short time later.

I followed this for about one and half miles, before opting for a more direct route through the village of Kirkliston. I was spurred on by the need to eat and in no time at all was on the outskirts of South Queensferry. I stopped the first person I met to ask for directions to a café. This person turned out to be a lady from Burnley, and after we'd discussed the strange decision of Burnley Football Club to sack their then manager Sean Dyce, she told me,

"There's a nice place at the bottom of the hill."

My route North should have had me turning left at this point and going straight meant I would have to retrace my steps so I wasn't happy when the road descended a steep hill. This got steeper and I began to question the wisdom of my decision. It was 8:30am and I suddenly wondered if it would be open. Half a mile later I arrived to see the café in darkness. On closer inspection staff were inside just setting up so I went in. A lady called to me apologising that they weren't open until 9.30. She must have seen the disappointment in my face or maybe it was the way my tears were landing on the nice clean floor, either way she asked what I wanted. I think my response of,

"Anything, as I have run from the far side of Edinburgh" may have given away my desperation. Thankfully she took my order for tea and two rounds of toast with butter and jam. She let me charge my phone and questioned where I was from. When I replied,

"Bradford" she said she recognised the accent as she was originally from Huddersfield. I am pretty good at accents and instantly knew the previous lady was from Burnley, before she told me, but this lady gave no hint of her Yorkshire roots. I thanked her for allowing me in early, saying I couldn't face trekking up that steep hill without having eaten.

Forty minutes later I was on my way again. I should have taken the trouble to look around South Queensferry but didn't. The town is also known as 'The Ferry'. The prefix of South was added to distinguish it from its neighbour on the North side of the Firth. It is said that a ferry service was first established here in the 11th Century by Queen Margaret. Apparently, the ferry service ran until the opening of the first road bridge in 1964. It never crossed my mind to go explore the town as I was focussed on the journey and to be honest quite excited by the prospect of crossing the iconic bridge.

Although it was less than an hour since I had come down the hill, I was surprised by the steepness of the climb back up. It brought back memories of Cornwall, but it was over within five minutes. I turned right where I had met the Burnley fan, happy to be back on flatter ground. A few minutes later I arrived at the road leading over the bridge, the old road bridge, the middle bridge of the three, It provided a great view of the new bridge on my left and the railway bridge to my right. The views were spectacular and I decided to video the occasion. I'd just begun recording when a train came over the railway bridge right on cue. I was able to capture the moment. There was a stiff breeze blowing and the bridge wasn't a place to be standing about for long. With the video completed, I stowed the phone and began running, grateful my crossing was in good weather.

At the north end of the bridge the road went uphill, passing North Queensferry and almost immediately entered the town of Inverkeithing. I was now following cycle route one, and this took me through the town where I stopped to photograph the ancient Kirk of St Peter. There has been a church on the site dating back to before the Norman conquest and although the present church has been rebuilt several times the foundations date back to Norman times. The site was bequeathed in 1139 by the monks of Dunfermline Abbey.

Once out of the town the route left the main road going over the M90. It was another steep climb and as the day had warmed up significantly, I removed my tee shirt. The map informed me I was running past Pitreavie, a small district of Dunfermline. This resonated with me as being the birthplace of Linsey McDonald, who aged just sixteen, won a bronze medal at the 1980 Moscow Olympics as a member of the GB relay team.

The route here was fairly dull and followed a road through a residential area with few people around and nothing of interest. It eventually brought me to a large road junction. After this it joined a track and went under a railway bridge but one hundred metres later re-joined the main road. This went uphill and I passed my second hospital of the day. After the hospital the cycle path left the road and joined a disused railway line that skirted the area called Townhill, going between a recreation park and a power station. I passed several lunchtime dog walkers before the cycle path returned to the road on the northside of Townhill. I passed an entrance to the recreation area and noticed a large sign informing me that I was at the Billy Liddle Sports Complex.

Billy Liddle was a professional footballer with Liverpool in the 1940's, 1950's and 1960's. Although an old-fashioned winger for much of his career, he was a prolific goal scorer and is still ranked as Liverpool's forth top goal scorer of all time, with two hundred and twenty-eight goals from five hundred and thirty-four appearances. One of my old bosses often told me that in his opion, Liddle was far better than George Best.

From here my route continued on quiet country lanes for three miles, then entered a large forest for the next three miles. Sadly, much of the forest had been felled, leaving the landscape looking like a war zone and providing no shade at all. My ears had started to itch and without thinking I reached to the back of one ear to scratch the itch and popped a blister. They were blistered from the sun. Stupidly I had neglected to put sunscreen on my ears, despite warnings from my wife. I recalled her conversation with a skin specialist at the hospital who'd told her that he regularly had to amputate people's ears who had skin cancer on them adding, it's the place people always forget about. I had been running Northwards for twenty consecutive days and although I wore a cap, this did nothing to keep the sun off my ears. That's potentially two huge problems if like mine, your ears are the size of Mr Spock's.

After a stop to coat them in suncream I was off again. My route went uphill for the next twenty minutes but it was gradual rather than steep. Eventually I was rewarded with a stunning view. It looked like I could see the whole of Perthshire in front of me. It was breath-taking. After pausing momentarily to take in the panorama I began a two-mile descent. Suddenly my quads started to twinge a bit and by the time I got to the bottom of the hill I was in a bit of mild discomfort. I had two miles of flattish country lanes to my lodgings and decided I should walk some of this to save the legs. I was suddenly feeling travel weary and lacking in energy. Forty minutes later I passed the sign welcoming me to Kinross. I was staying at another Travelodge and had taken extra care to know exactly where this one was. I arrived having covered thirty-three miles, grateful that there was no repeat of the navigation fiasco of the day before.

20 days done and 8 to go.

CHAPTER 27

Hope Can Change The World

Day 21 – Thursday 21st April 2022. Kinross to Dunkeld
It was another cold morning, but unlike the day before, today was grey, uninviting and downright miserable. I left the hotel at 6:10 and made my way over the motorway bridge. Today was another day exceeding fifty kilometres or thirty-one miles. On days like this you just have to go out and get it done. So, I set off optimistically, knowing that by the end of the day I'd be well on the way to the Highlands. Surprisingly today's route profile showed significantly more downhill than up. Five hundred and fifty metres of descent against four hundred of ascent, so I hoped for an easier day.

After passing through Kinross along the A91 I turned onto the B996 for a short way before turning left on a country lane and climbing over the M90. The cycle route was well signed and showed the distance to Perth as nine miles. Excellent.

As I trotted up the country lane suddenly a bird of prey took off from the top of a telegraph post as I approached. I watched it fly to a second post in a field to my left. I immediately stopped and photographed it. This was the first bird of prey I had seen on the whole trip and I watched it for a few minutes. It was still too cold for standing about though so after the brief interval I was off again.

Despite the promise of downhill, there wasn't much of it for the first hour. The route was quite undulating but mostly uphill. The surrounding fields were dotted with bright patches of golden gorse which thankfully added some colour to the grey. Let's call it 'shade of morning mushroom,' in deference to my wife.

I passed another of the signs for the cycle route. This showed the distance to Perth as eight miles but was at least twenty minutes after the first one that showed the distance as nine miles. I checked the map to ensure I was going the right way. according to the map on my phone I certainly seemed to be as the distance remaining on there was definitely decreasing. A bit further on another sign appeared showing it was nine miles to Perth. At first I found this really frustrating until the next sign read Perth eleven miles! I laughed and questioned if Perth town council were providing free eye tests for their workers.

The route crossed over the M90 again. I had covered just over ten miles in under ninety minutes and was running well as the route reached the highest point of the day. I now felt relaxed as the road descended. I had been going down for no more than a minute when my right quad locked up. I came to an abrupt halt. Several swear words somehow squeezed through my clenched teeth as I struggled to move. This was much worse than the day before. I stopped under a railway bridge and rubbed my quad vigorously, then started walking down the hill. Each step was really painful as the muscle was really tense, making it difficult to bend the leg at all. I stopped again and looked at the map. The bottom of the hill was less than three hundred metres away so I resolved to get there and see if I could run on the flat.

I limped to the bottom of the hill where I rested for a few minutes more before trying to jog, but soon realised there was no chance. I just couldn't bend the knee and at that moment, running was now impossible for this sixty one year old crock. I continued to walk with my leg at an angle trying to keep it as straight as possible. This too became painful as after another half mile my right calf began to tighten up. I stopped, leaning against a wall at the side of the road, thinking of what I should do. I ate a muesli bar, washed it down with some water, then rubbed the quad muscle with 'voltarol' cream to try and warm it. I had been running in shorts up to that moment so spent almost five minutes trying to put my leggings on. This was so difficult. I struggled then began to laugh at what I must look like to anyone watching and came up with the analogy of a man in a straitjacket trying to tie his shoelaces.

As I struggled to get my feet into the pants. twinges of cramp hit every muscle but eventually the pants were on and the energy expelled from the body popping and breakdancing display had actually warmed me and I was able to walk a little bit easier, not pain free, just easier. Progress was slow and it took me just under two hours to cover the remaining four miles to the outskirts of Perth. I became very dejected because I didn't think I was going to be able to continue. I stopped and looked up the road and saw a Tesco's so resolved to see if there was a café where I could lick my wounds.

It was 9:15 and I phoned Angela explaining what had happened and the fact that I still had a further eighteen miles to get to my accommodation in Dunkeld. She immediately said she would start searching for a physiotherapist around Dunkeld and told me to go get something to eat. She would call me back. At that moment I wasn't confident of even reaching Dunkeld, and as I switched off the phone said to myself,

"I have a better chance of winning the lottery," which was a long shot as I hadn't bought a ticket for at least ten years. I continued hobbling along the road towards the Tesco store that I could see on the far side of the road on the crown of a bend less than one hundred metres away. As I rounded the bend on my side of the road there in front of me was a large sign on the front of a building. I was aghast and stood open mouthed. The sign was over the window of a chiropractor and was advertising sports massages. Someone somewhere was looking after me. I sent Angela a message informing her not to start searching just yet. I went inside and explained my plight and was told they could fit me in at 11:30 that morning. My guardian Angel had done it again. I needed help and there it was. I headed over the road to Tesco's and enjoyed a leisurely breakfast as I counted my good fortune.

I returned to the chiropractors at 11am and was straight in for a consultation with Daniel. After he'd assed me, he began to work on my leg. In my head I gave him the nickname of Desperate Dan the massage man. He was a muscular guy, around six feet tall with the forearms of a wrestler. He had long dark hair tied back, a bushy black beard and reminded me of Desperate Dan from the Beano comics of my youth. He also had fingers that must have been made of steel and spent an hour working them into my right leg. Half an hour on the quad and the same on the lower calf. It's no exaggeration to say he made me weep with pain. It certainly made me weep when I parted with the cash. Fifty-three pounds.

As Desperate Dan was inflicting this much needed torture, we discussed my chances of reaching John O' Groats. He was reluctant to give me an opinion saying that really I should have been on the train home but we both knew that I was not going to do that. He said to me,

"You shouldn't really have gotten this far, but you have, so just keep doing what you've been doing, but if you can, try and get another massage in a few days."

When he'd finished and I'd paid the bill I said,

"Thanks for what you've done for me Daniel, You have given me hope that I have a chance of getting to the end. Two hours ago that seemed impossible." He gave me a friendly punch on the shoulder saying,

" Hey. You've Got this. Just keep doing what you've been doing. Good Luck."

I shook his hand and as I did so filled up with the emotion of the moment. I had been in a bad way, convinced it was all over. Now I may have a chance. As I walked to the door I said to him,

"Sorry about the emotion but that's what happens when a Yorkshire man is parted from his money. No seriously. Thank you. It's worth every penny. Hope is a priceless commodity."

I walked out of the door ready to take on the rest of the country and recalled a speech I had seen on YouTube by an American Admiral, William McRaven on graduation day at the University of Texas in 2014. He says

"If you want to change the world, give a person hope." Daniel had changed my world, at least for the rest of the day. I sent Angela a message

'Feel like I've got new legs.' I laughed as I walked towards the town centre because of the difference in the way I had walked into Perth and the way I was going to walk out at the other end of the town. The walking was easy and pain free. I decided that if I finished I would write to Dan with a picture of me at the famous signpost and thank him for making it possible. A thought crossed my mind that physiotherapists are not medical people but actually magicians or miracle workers and I was not going to destroy the newly named Dynamo Dan's good work by running this afternoon so decided to walk the remaining eighteen miles.

I told myself it was just an easy afternoon riverside stroll and as I went, I enjoyed the spring sunshine and pleasant surroundings of the River Tay. I re-joined the cycle route and made my way under a bridge to a park at North Inch. This was adjacent to the river and was busy with people spending their lunch time either strolling, cycling or running along in the sun.

The route followed the river for a few miles, eventually going under the A9 where a bridge took the road over the Tay. My arrival coincided with that of a lady jogger who stopped a few paces ahead of me in the shade of the bridge. She was admiring a series of street art in chalks that had been skilfully sketched onto the bridge supports, six images, one on each of the supports. Three were cartoons but one was a picture of a stag, another a goldfinch and another a kingfisher. I was blown away by them, each one must have taken an age to complete. I chatted to the lady about how good they were. Our conversation then turned to running and she informed me she was running from Lands' End to John O' Groats but on one of the virtual challenges where you upload your daily mileages.

"Be careful! That's how I got into this situation," I said laughing. "Let me know if you want the train times to Penzance."

I decided to leave the cycleway again at this point to follow a footpath at the side of the A9. It seemed like a good idea and definitely saved me both time and distance. However, for ten minutes was a very noisy experience. I was able to leave the busy route half a mile further on and join a farm track that turned into a lane passing through the village of Luncarty. This brought me to a large roundabout over the A9. At this point my map app got confused, or I did.

It was obvious there had been some recent alterations done to the road with what looked like a new slip road being built that went around in a big sweeping bend. The map app told me to ignore the road on the right which was the slip road on to the A9 northbound. It told me to go straight ahead and make a right turn further on, So I continued down a hill above the busy road but fifty yards further on the App showed the route as continuing along the side of the A9 indicating that I should have turned right earlier going down the on ramp. I was reluctant to walk back up the road to come back down again so headed directly across an area of grassy wasteland that led to a new concrete pathway at the side of the busy route. After a short distance of no more than a half mile the path left the main road and bearing left, went into a village at a place called Bankfoot.

Here I passed a hotel and I should have asked to use their bathroom but didn't. This was a decision I regretted twenty minutes later, and was relieved to be allowed to use the facilities of a Tennis club at the far end of the village. As I passed the club, I saw two men playing tennis so headed to the main door but it was locked. A lady from a house overlooking the club saw me as she put it "acting a little suspiciously" as I tried various doors. She came out of her house to see what I was doing. I explained my predicament and it turned out that she was a key holder for the club and she took pity on me.

The next place was called Waterloo and I chuckled to myself as I photographed the sign, glad that I hadn't passed the place in the morning when I'd been struggling. I'd have said it was a sign that I should be going home. With my fresh legs I was filled with renewed hope and shouted at the inanimate harmless metal two legged notification board.

"Ha! Up yours you spectre of Flanders. Dynamo Dan has given me fresh legs so I've had my metaphorical Weetabix," and I set off jogging for one minute just to prove I could.

Arriving in Dunkeld at around 5.30 I rang the hotel for directions. Annoyingly, once again I had walked right past the place one mile earlier in a village called Birnham. I was staying at the Birnam Hotel, a big grand affair with two gothic looking towers that I had booked via Booking dot com. I retraced my steps and was just about to moan at having to cover the extra distance when my positive side kicked in and I actually said the following out loud.

"Have a word with yourself, you couldn't walk this morning and you have just come eighteen miles." Hope had certainly changed my afternoon.

21 days done, 7 to go.

CHAPTER 28

The Good, The Bad and The Awkward

Day 22 – Friday 22nd April 2022. Dunkeld to Blair Atholl

A beautiful day welcomed me as having overslept I woke from my slumber. However with 704 miles covered , I think I was due a lie in. I left at 8am with the sun shining and the birds singing. My route took me along the banks of the river Tay. Two red squirrels were too quick for me to photograph, but having got the phone out I made a short video of the stunning surroundings. This was some of the best scenery so far.

My quad felt stiff when I woke so I'd made the decision to walk the whole day. As I ate breakfast I thought about the conversion with Dynamo Dan the day before.

"Well my professional advice should be to tell you to get the next train home, but actually, you shouldn't have really made it this far, so you're not likely to do that." Thanks to his skill I'd been able to continue and was about to start another day. By coincidence, because I had not been able to get accommodation in the place I wanted, I had been forced to have a shorter journey today. The distance between Dunkeld and Blair Atholl was only twenty-two miles so it seemed pointless to risk damaging the quad and calf by running as if I ran I would be there by noon and I couldn't check in until 3pm anyway. Far better to walk and take eight hours and have an easy day.

If all went well, after today I would still have another two hundred and twenty miles to reach John O Groats. The remaining journey would include three really long days, so today was about resting the legs as much as possible, enjoying the views and trying to absorb as much positivity from the surroundings as I could. I had to get my head into a positive mindset because at that moment, just thinking I was going to cover a further two hundred and twenty miles in only six days seemed madness in itself, but adding in the fact that I had already covered over seven hundred miles, seemed ridiculous. Even as I write this after the event, it does seem a tough ask.

So spurred on by the squirrels, I strode on soaking up the scenic Scottish surroundings. Nature is wonderful and really does have healing powers but sometimes we are too busy to notice. I was delighted by the trees, the wildflowers, the birds singing and the sounds of the river. Walking was easy and really relaxing after running for twenty-one consecutive days. After the first hour though I had only covered three miles on a flat woodland path but totally pain free, so slow and steady was the order of the day.

I was still on a cycle route, route seventy-seven and this crossed to the west side of the river using a bridge on the A9. It then joined a B road, running parallel to the railway line. A few hundred metres along the B road, I met an elderly couple out walking. The old man advised me to take care saying that courier vans used the quiet road as a shortcut and drove along very fast indeed. I didn't have to wait too long for his prophecy to play out.

I heard the sound of a diesel-powered vehicle coming along the road at speed from behind me. At this point there were several bends in the road and I stopped walking and moved off the road into the edge of the surrounding woodland. A courier van came around the corner. Once again the driver was looking down at a digital device in his hand. It may have been a phone or the gadget used to scan the parcels that also provide delivery information. Whatever it was, his eyes certainly were not on the road and his hands were not on the wheel. It was a cause for concern and was repeated again and again on the journey. Thankfully it was the only courier van I saw on that stretch of road.

I was surprised by how flat the road was as it made its way up the valley. I hadn't gone up a single contour for several miles and because of all the trees there wasn't much of a view to take in, so it had suddenly become a little bit dull. Not the weather, but the journey. To break the monotony, I was tempted to break into a run and had to force myself not to. Maybe towards the end of the day if there were no setbacks, just to test the legs. Like an alcoholic longing for a drink, I needed the endorphins.

The road did start to climb after I passed a farmstead called Glenalbert, gaining fifty metres of height in just over a mile. I wondered who Albert had been, to have a glen named after him. He didn't sound Scottish. The valley and road had been gradually turning northwest for the last few miles. Suddenly it broke clear of the trees, and a spectacular vista of snow-covered mountains opened out ahead of me. It really looked like painted scenery from a theatre. I was going in that direction the next day so I made a mental note to check the weather forecast when I stopped for lunch. The route descended for the first time that morning, only about thirty metres but enough for me to feel a few twinges in my quad. Like a child on a long car journey, it had done the muscular equivalent of saying "Are we nearly there yet?." Unfortunately, we had only just made it to the morning's halfway point, and still had several miles to Pitlochry where I was planning to stop for lunch.

I arrived at an old toll house and my route left cycle route seventy-seven and joined cycle route seven. This would now be my partner for almost the remainder of the journey. I crossed the river Tay for the last time, using an old toll bridge at Logierait. I stopped to take photographs realising that this wonderful old structure was the reason for the toll house back at the road.

Once across the bridge I turned along a main road for a few hundred metres before turning off again and heading up a steep road that looked as if it had just been constructed. After fifty metres the gradient eased and the road undulated wonderfully as it made its way through a forest. Again I was tempted to run as the setting was just perfect. As I crested one of the short sharp rises, I heard the gears of a bicycle click behind me. I turned to see an extremely lean and fit looking lycra clad cyclist almost grind to a halt a few metres behind me. He stopped for a brief chat. He was an Australian who had flown to Edinburgh the day before, and set off cycling earlier that morning. The plan was to have two weeks cycling around Scotland and then fly home again. I quickly calculated that Edinburgh was about sixty-five miles away and applauded his effort, adding that it had taken me two days to cover that distance. I think he was a bit taken aback and asked me what I was doing. When I told him about my journey he unclipped from his pedals and walked over shaking my hand vigorously. I can't deny that I felt a bit like a celebrity but tried to play it down saying that actually I haven't achieved anything yet as there was still a long way to go. However I wanted to draw every bit of the feel good factor he had created by his praise, and hold it in reserve until I needed to give myself a kick in the pants further up the road.

We wished each other well and then he was on his way, disappearing down the hill and around the next bend. What an adventure he was to have and it made me realise what an adventure I was having.

On entering Pitlochry, I passed a cardboard cut-out of a policeman strapped to a lamp post to fool motorists. I couldn't resist taking a selfie and I put my arm around the cardboard constable. A few moments later as I looked at the picture, I wondered if I was somehow guilty of preventing a policeman from carrying out his duty, albeit momentarily. Whenever I interact with the police now I can't help but think of the time when the police stopped me one evening whilst I was on my way home.

At the time I lived about one mile from Angela and was running home at around 10:30 pm one night to try and be home in time to watch the start of the 1984 Olympic Marathon, live from Los Angeles. Now when I say I was running home, that is exactly what I mean. I wasn't jogging but was trying to cover the route of almost one mile in under five minutes and with the start time fast approaching, I was racing hard along the pavement when a car suddenly screeched to a halt. Two men jumped out. One stood on the pavement about five metres in front of me whilst the other rushed around the back of the car. I had no idea who these guys were. They wore Jeans, tee shirts and leather jackets. I stopped running and stared at the one in front of me. He scrutinised me saying.

"Police! Where are you going?"

"Home" I replied.

"Why are you running?"

"Because I want to get there quickly."

He looked annoyed and started to say something, just as his partner arrived. The partner cut him short by saying

"Oh it's OK. I know this guy. He went to my school. He runs everywhere."

The first policeman said.

"Oh! OK mate, Sorry. There have been a lot of thefts from cars in the area and when we saw you running, we thought you were a thief. On you go." I continued my run home and watched Britain's Charlie Spedding, and Ireland's John Tracey win Olympic marathon medals whilst I wondered what would have happened to me if the policeman who recognised me had been on a different shift?

I arrived in Pitlochry diving into the first café I came to. Having covered fourteen miles that day I was pleased with the morning's work. It was 12.30 and I had around eight miles to go to Blair Atholl. I ordered a pot of tea, Beans on toast with two rashers of bacon.

"Sorry sir. You can't have bacon with beans on toast as the breakfast menu stopped at 12."

"Oh right, I see."

"So do you want beans on toast?"

"I thought I couldn't have beans on toast?"

"No, you can have beans on toast as they are also on the lunch menu."

"Ahh, So I can have beans on toast but you can't cook bacon?"

"No, we can cook bacon and you can have it, but only in a panini with brie as that's on the lunch menu."

"So can't you take the bacon out of the panini, cook it then add it to my meal?"

"Only if you order and pay for the panini as well."

I confess to being more than a little irked by this. If beans on toast had also been on the 12.00 curfew list, I could have understood. After all, beans and toast are accepted as breakfast items. So once both hands of the clock had ticked past twelve and the afternoon session had begun I would have happily accepted that beans were barred because we had moved on to a whole new set of choices. However, we hadn't. Beans on toast were still being freshly cooked and served. So was bacon but only in a panini. Beans on toast were priced £6.00 and I had expected to pay around £9.00 for my original order. If I had ordered before 12.00, I could have bought a full breakfast with toast for £8.50, but now if I wanted bacon with my beans on toast I had to shell out an additional £7.00. On another day I would have tried to persuade them to sell me the bacon but decided to supplement my nutritional needs with cake afterwards so opted for the veggie option ordering the beans on toast without the bacon but somehow felt both deflated and defeated.

As I walked away from the counter it struck me that there

may be rules about only ordering cake on an afternoon tea menu, so I called to the server from the middle of the room.

"Can I have a side order of Carrot Cake please, or do I have to wait for the teatime menu?"

I didn't think I had said anything wrong but realised I could have phrased it a little better when the three people behind the counter all stopped what they were doing and gave me what seemed like a death stare. Their eyes fixed on mine and seemed to be piercing holes into me, as a deafening silence filled the room. The whole café seemed to have stopped eating and suddenly it was like a saloon scene from a Scottish styled spaghetti western, The Good, The Bad and The Awkward Englishman.

Eventually one of the servers said quietly but firmly

"No, you can have cake at any time."

Did everyone in the café breathe a sigh of relief or did I imagine it? Was I really that argumentative and awkward? Is it so wrong to want two pieces of bacon in a café?

After finishing my meal I headed across the road and into one of the many stores selling outdoor clothing. I had reviewed the weather forecast for the next three days. Tomorrow was likely to be cold but clear with a twenty miles per hour wind blowing from the North. The following day was cold, cloudy but with no rain, but the day after that rain was forecast for much of the day. My route was heading into some exposed areas for the next three days and whilst I was confident I had everything I needed, I decided to buy another buff to use as face covering. At £2.99 it seemed like a wise investment. As I tell my wife frequently,

"You never know when you may need to use your emergency buff."

I walked up the road through the tourist thronged town, treating myself to an ice cream. I was still following the same cycle route. One mile out of town this joined the B8019 which was not really very inspiring. I took the decision to test the legs, giving in to my addiction and began to alternate one minute of walking with one minute of running. As I approached the wonderfully named 'Pass of Killiecrankie' I noticed a footpath sign pointing over a wooden footbridge crossing above the railway. Scanning the map, this seemed a better option than the road so I turned left and once over the bridge, descended a flight of steep wooden steps that took me down through the trees to where a woodland track ran beside the river Garry.

The forest track was perfect for running and exactly the sort of terrain I love so I continued my running / walking routine for another mile. The path led back to the road at the village of Killiecrankie. Here residents have done their best to create a series of short footpaths not marked on the map, which take pedestrians off the narrow road. I was grateful because at this point there were two blind bends. After Killiecrankie I was back on the road again, and I realised that for most of my journey through Scotland I had been running on tarmac, whereas in England, most of my journey had been on softer ground such as canal towpaths and old railways which surprised me. I had expected to be on more forest trails in Scotland.

One of the things I love about Scotland are the wonderful place names. I had just arrived at 'Bridge of Tilt' and this conjured up pictures in my head of a bridge built at a precarious angle with all who crossed having to fight against the camber in order to negotiate it safely. Images of General Wade's army marching across but tumbling off the bridge into the river percolated through my brain. Strong stuff these running endorphins.

Bridge of Tilt is just before Blair Atholl and this was one of the places Angela and I stayed on our honeymoon. A prevailing recollection of the place was of a meal we ate in the restaurant that included a portion of small silver onions as one of the vegetables. These were not shallots but the onions that were sometimes served with a cocktail. As we left the restaurant, I thanked the waiter saying how much I enjoyed the 'Silvikrin' onions. He looked at me with a puzzled expression. When we got to our room Angela pointed out that Silvikrin was in fact a hair spray and we giggled like the newlyweds we were.

When I arrived in Blair Atholl I was saddened to see that the grand old building we'd stayed at all those years ago was in the process of being demolished. At least it explained why I'd been unable to find it to make a booking and it had nothing to do with my technical skills. I made my way to the guest house I had booked a little disappointed, like I had lost an old friend. Still I'd now covered seven hundred and twenty five miles and tomorrow I would enter the Highlands. The last lap.

22 days done, 6 to go.

CHAPTER 29

Seeing Stars

Day 23 – Saturday 23rd April 2022 – Blair Atholl to Newtonmore

When planning this journey, there were only a small number of days I was really concerned about. Today was one of those. Most days were pretty straight forward but if things went wrong I would have ample opportunity to get help from someone. Today was not like that. I was heading over the Drumochter Pass, which at a height of four hundred and sixty-two metres, (over fifteen hundred feet) above sea level, was a wild and exposed place. It wasn't really somewhere you'd want to be if the weather turned bad, especially if you're not able to run. So, I wanted to try and break the journey across this exposed pass by staying in a B and B at the top of the pass. This way if the weather deteriorated significantly I would not be traversing the whole way in one go. From there I would have gone to Aviemore. However, when I tried to book the only place I could find for 22nd of April, it was full. The law of 'SOD' had come into play. The place had vacancies for the two weeks before and the two after the 22nd, but not the date itself. This meant I'd had to alter my schedule, hence the shorter day yesterday ending in Blair Atholl. So my journey today from Blair Atholl to Newtonmore, was a distance of 35 miles.

This was split into two distinct parts. Eighteen miles up to the top of the pass and seventeen miles down to Newtonmore. The route up the pass climbed over three hundred and fifty metres. Then there would be a long gradual descent, dropping two hundred and twenty metres in altitude over seventeen miles. Normally this wouldn't be too taxing on healthy muscles, but we would have to see how my bruised battered body held up to what I was putting it through. At least the scenery should be good and with these two conflicting thoughts in my head I set off at 6:15am for another day, forgoing the B & B breakfast once again.

The day was clear, bright and sunny but with a gentle headwind. This meant I kept a long-sleeved top on as well as my tee shirt. at least for the start of the day. The road was flat, straight and empty and my legs worked as if there had never been an issue. Despite the headwind I was able to cover the first two miles at my target pace of 5 mph easily. After four miles I arrived at the entrance to a museum and some kind of retail park that was clearly designed for coach parties, judging by the overly large entrance. The road went under the A9 and I realised that not one car had passed me going in either direction in the hour it had taken me. This changed a mile further on as I approached the village of Calvine in what may have been a close call had I not been vigilant.

As I climbed the hill, a sweeping bend in the road led underneath a railway bridge. I heard the groaning of a hard-working diesel engine amplified by the stone arch of the bridge and stepped to the side of the road just as a supermarket home delivery van shot under the bridge. I had a split second to look into the face of the driver who turned the wheel and lifted the palm of his hand, which I took to be an apology. He had been far too close for comfort. I stopped for a few minutes, taking a drink and a handful of Peanut M & M's, my snack of choice for the morning and was on my way again.

Once through Calvine I joined a cycle path with trees on both sides, sheltering me from the breeze that was to get stronger the higher I climbed. The cycle way is supposed to be for bikes only, no cars yet up ahead I saw a parked car. As I got nearer, I could see it was a silver-coloured Aston Martin.

I was thinking it may have been stolen and hidden there, but then the lights came on.

As I got closer I could see the driver, a man, was on his phone. As I drew close to the car I had a clear view of the driver as he was no more than ten feet away. Now at this point you're not going to believe me. You'll say my imagination was working overtime, or something similar, but honestly, he actually looked like Danial Craig. Yes, I know you all think I am making it up but I'm not. He really did appear to be the man himself. Did I ask for an autograph? Did I go over and ask him to sponsor me? None of those. What I did right at the point where I drew alongside the car was smack my head straight into a tree branch. Bang!

I felt a right twit. If this had been a cartoon I would have had little stars circling my head. Seeing stars from seeing stars. Anyway, I don't know who he was, or why he was there, but if the next 007 film includes a shot of a bandy legged jogger in an orange tee shirt running into a tree, that's me.

After fifteen miles I had almost reached the summit of the pass, and emerged on to a long plateau with extensive views ahead. The route was still going up really gradually. There was no shelter from the wind now which was noticeably stronger. I put on a windproof jacket and trousers, hat, gloves and for good measure pulled the buff I had bought the day before over my nose and mouth. I was toasty warm but wouldn't have wanted to stand still for long. Despite the wind, the place was stunning. The mountains ahead were topped with snow, and below the summits were adorned with a line of low clouds that stretched around them like a scarf around a snowman. Above the snowy tops was a cloudless blue sky whilst in the foreground, the sun shone brightly. I passed fields turning from the subdued beige of winter to the promising green of spring, and the scene was completed by the river Garry, making its way down the valley. It was picture postcard stuff, like the lid on a jigsaw.

With around nine miles to go to reach the next place, the village Dalwhinnie I pressed on. I'd been assured there was a café and I was eager to take on much needed calories. The route left the narrow road and moved right to the side of the A9 where a purpose-built tarmac cycleway had been created. A series of wooden posts had been erected, and each post was topped with the carving of an owl which had been painted white. Fixed to one of the posts was a sign made of slate, with lettering engraved into it. The letter was also painted white enhancing the writing that read:

'In Sun Rain or Snow Aviemore 43 Miles'.

With those words of warning I pressed on, covering the remaining nine miles in ninety minutes, arriving at what felt like an oasis in the wilderness. I had run Twenty-four miles in four hours and forty minutes most of which was uphill and into a strong headwind. I was really pleased with my morning's work, buzzing as I entered the snappily named 'Snack Shack.' It was 11am.

I went through the usual routine of ordering my food, finding a table with a plug, plugging in the phone, then heading to the toilet for a quick wash and brush up. I then put on my down jacket, before firing what was left of my water and settled down until my meal arrived. After devouring the food in less time than it had taken them to prepare it. I would send or reply to messages or social media posts before ordering a second pot of tea and piece of cake whilst asking the café owner or serving staff if they would refill my water bottles. After eating the cake I would usually start to feel sleepy and knew it was time to get going. If I stayed any longer than forty-five minutes I was likely to fall asleep, despite it being the middle of the day.

This has happened to me many times including during long races where we may have had an early start. My running buddies Andy Nicoll, Dave Stephenson and Robin Lawrence could all recount tales of times they've kindly waited for me to have a power nap in the middle of nowhere. This has even happened to me in solo races, one example was a race called 'The Lakeland Hundred.'

As the title suggests, it's a race of one hundred miles in the Lake District. Starting in the village of Coniston at 5pm on the last Friday in July, competitors run through the night in a large loop around most of the Lake District National Park. Runners have until around 2pm on Sunday afternoon to finish. The elite runners usually manage to finish within twenty-four hours. I'd run all night and all the next morning but began to get really tired as the clock approached 1pm. My aim was to finish on Saturday but I still had about thirty miles to go. I knew at some point I would have to sleep but was trying to make it to the next checkpoint. Unfortunately, tiredness won and I started to fall asleep as I was running. It became a matter of urgency and I was not going to reach the checkpoint unless I had a power nap. It was a nice dry day so I stopped, stepped a few metres off the path, put on my rain jacket and trousers, hat and gloves, and laid down on my rucksack in long grass and was asleep in seconds.

I woke up about twenty minutes later and could hear voices close by. I was now wide awake but decided to wait until the people passed before emerging from my hideaway, so I stayed laid down in the grass. After a few minutes it became clear the people were not passing by but were sitting having a pic-nic. I lay there for a few more minutes, pondering what I should do, but knowing that I couldn't lay there indefinitely. Eventually I just sat upright.

"Aaaaargh!" Sandwiches and cups of tea went in the air as the poor family seated right opposite screamed and stared at me open-mouthed.

"Hello. Sorry if I shocked you but I really needed to sleep. Bon Appetit." and I ran off down the path. This memory crossed my mind as I relaxed in the Snack Shack. There were a number of families with elderly relatives so I left at 12:15 to continue the last eleven miles or so to Newtonmore. I didn't want to be seen rising like the grim reaper with all those elderly people enjoying their Sunday lunch.

I continued through this tiny village that earlier I'd described as an oasis. At the end of the village was a distillery which seemed out of place surrounded by wild hills. An oasis with a distillery, now there's a thought.

My route went around a sweeping bend before turning right to follow the line of the railway line down the big open valley that narrowed as I got lower down, and acted like a funnel channelling the wind into my face. It was bright and sunny and I would have welcomed sunglasses but the wind really took the temperature down and battered my face. I was glad I had bought the buff in Pitlochry and pulled it up over my nose again. I must have looked strange to any of the few motorists who passed me, snuggly cocooned in their sunshine shrouded vehicles, as I ran along wearing gloves and covered from head to toe in windproof clothing with only my eyes showing. A Ninja Warrior.

The road went gently down the valley and progress should have been easy but was anything but. I was surprised by how hard it felt running into the headwind. At the bottom of the valley the route crossed the railway line and river, going into a thin line of trees that afforded some shelter from the wind and the running became easier for a short period. I was now on another purpose-built cycleway, less than three metres wide and only ten metres from the side of the A9. The track continually rose up and down sapping my depleting energy, but was certainly not boring. Each undulation was only a few metres high, but I could imagine how challenging they must be for cyclists with heavy panniers and I was grateful I'd only myself to propel. After a few miles the line of trees ran out and the track dropped below the level of the road, creating a steep banking and reducing some of the traffic noise which must have washed over the top of my head.

Every so often the track became strewn with discarded litter for very short stretches. I would go for a couple of miles enjoying the stunning scenic surroundings then suddenly there would be beer cans, plastic bottles, take away wrappers, coffee cups, and then nothing for another twenty minutes, before the sad sight was repeated. I was puzzled until suddenly there was a wheelie bin laid on its side, halfway down the embankment with its contents spread out on the ground below its open lid. I realised each pile of litter coincided with a layby along the busy road. This illuminated another thought in my brain, that my route in Scotland had been largely free of litter despite me having run on a lot more roads since crossing the border. In England I had run on lots of canals, old railway lines and cycleways but where my route was on a road, it tended to be a major A road, like the A38 and there had always been littler. Lots of it.

Litter was the one negative thing about the run through England but I had forgotten about it as I ventured through Scotland. This stretch, adjacent to the A9, brought back memories of running alongside any number of trunk roads in England, all of which had a surprising number of plastic bottles, half filled with a dark yellow, almost orange coloured liquid. I feel totally stupid telling you that for a few days I wondered why so many people bought coca cola only to half refill the bottle with Fanta, then chuck it out of their window. Maybe some of that is understandable if people are desperate, but it's obviously only one half of the population, unless the female of our species has developed some kind of ingenious way of relieving themselves into a plastic bottle whilst driving along the country's major roads, or am I being naive.

Another staggering observation is the actual amount of rubbish in general. You can't travel fifty metres along a trunk road without seeing a piece of discarded litter in this country and that is an extremely sad testament to our society. Why do people do this? It also seems that much of the discarded rubbish bears the same branding all over the country, or at least the line I ran on. There are empty cider cans and the arrows in the branding will give you an idea of make. A brand of a high energy drink that sponsors a formula one team and seems to be consumed as a replacement for breakfast by some. A brand of larger beginning with the letter C. Not the one from Scandinavia. Many brown paper bags or red boxes with a big yellow arched m. Lots of those burgundy-coloured coffee's cups, the contents having cost a princely sum. That accounts for a large majority of the roadside litter I passed on my journey.

There is a really simple way to combat this, and that is to impose fines on the brands. If their product packaging is found discarded at the side of the road the manufacturer should pick up the fine. I genuinely believe it's down to them to ensure the packaging containing their products is legally disposed of. It really is that simple. If one of the companies I have hinted at, or any other of the big brands can't ensure their packaging is not strewn all over the roads of the country, they should either not be allowed to sell it, or make a substantial contribution to the cost of cleaning up. I know many of you will feel that's not practical or is extreme but please consider this question. Have we become oblivious to much of this litter as we drive by? Littering is just one example of how a growing number of people seem to have little respect for the law, the environment as a whole, nor the people who have to share it with them. In between finishing my run and finishing this book I have seens signs on various roads asking people not to drop litter with the wording "Please don't be a tosser."

Three miles before Newtonmore I met a cyclist, Patrick from Stockton on Tees. He was supposed to be cycling from John O Groats to Lands' End, but Scotrail apparently messed his booking up and would only take his bike as far as Inverness. Not to be deterred he was going from Inverness to Penzance. We each took the all important selfie, then wished each other well and we're on our way. As I entered Newtonmore there was a sign advertising a shinty match that afternoon. I had never watched a shinty match which I understand is like a Scottish version of Ireland's hurling. I had watched a hurling match and found it a privilege to be watching. That is not a game for the faint hearted. Those lads don't fall down because they've tweaked an eyelash.

I arrived at my hotel just before 2:30 and they let me have an early check in. Once I discovered there was no shower I was lured from my intended afternoon of Scottish sport by the bath and once I was soaking in the warm water, I fell asleep again. I woke up shivering and hungry so trotted down the road to see what was available. I was pleased to see a Co-op and gorged on a large Mexican Chicken Pasta salad and a 200-gram bar of Cadbury's fruit and nut chocolate. Other chocolate brands are available if you want to settle for second best but it's Cadbury's for me every day of the week, and sometimes twice on Sunday. Refilled I realised the game would be over so walked back to my hotel and couldn't believe what I was reading on the BBC sport website. Bradford City had won 2 – 1. What an unbelievable day. Bradford City had won, and I'd run thirty-five miles. Both seemed impossible at the start of the day and I began to really believe it could have been Daniel Craig in the Aston Martin.

23 days done, 5 to go.

CHAPTER 30

Moments of Pleasure

Day 24 – Sunday 24th April 2022 – Newtonmore to Carrbridge

My normal routine each morning was to post a brief summary of what the day had in store on social media. I hadn't posted anything on this particular morning. I just wasn't in the mood. I had overslept and although I'd jumped out of bed when I realised it was 8:15, I was really not in the right frame of mind. Despite eleven hours of unbroken sleep I was still tired as I left the hotel at 8:30 with another long day in prospect.

Although it was light it didn't really seem like morning at all. I had to check my watch and phone several times because it didn't seem light enough to be 8:15 It was a cold grey morning and I kept my down jacket on as I ran through the town in the direction of Kingussie, where on arrival, I turned right and off the main road. I had been heading north, but suddenly I was heading southeast, and everything just seemed somehow wrong. I really just wanted to go back to bed.

As the road began to climb at a collection of buildings called Ruthven, the route turned north again, hugging the contour of the hill. Suddenly a castle-like building came into view at the top of what looked in early times to have been the site of a motte and bailey style castle.

I thought about taking a photo but in my morose state dismissed the idea. Then I had to go through a gate, so having stopped, I decided to take the photo after all. This did actually improve my mood a little, as did removing my jacket a mile further on as the road climbed and entered woodland. However, what really brought me around was the sight of another red squirrel which I spotted as I was putting the jacket away. I pulled out my phone and dropped everything else on the floor to try and photograph the little fellow and immediately christened him 'Tufty.' You have to be a child of the sixties to understand that reference so for those of more recent vintage who've no idea what that refers to, it was Tufty who taught us how to cross the road in the 1960's. I hope that's cleared that up for you, if not there is always google. I managed to get a picture and although it won't win any awards, I did capture 'Tufty' in profile climbing a tree and there is no mistaking it's a red squirrel. although it was only tiny in the shot I was euphoric. I laughed when I zoomed in closer as it looked more like a koala bear.

I picked up my bags and put the phone away with a huge smile on my face. Suddenly, cheered up, I was back in the running groove. I was doing one of my favourite things in wonderful surroundings and life doesn't get much better. The route continued to weave its way along an almost deserted road in the Spey Valley. Although the woodland restricted the view, occasionally on my left I could see the river and large areas of marshland which reminded me of the 'glen of tranquillity' from one of the TV adverts for whisky.

Passing through a water sports centre I spotted a restaurant but decided to get a few more miles on the clock before my first stop particularly as I was now moving well. However I caved in when I arrived in the small village of Kincraig and smelled the aroma of fresh ground coffee emanating from the Old Post Office Café. It transpired, the owner had previously cycled LEJOG and refused to let me pay for the coffee and the giant piece of cake, saying he had a good idea what my body must be going through. The place was wonderful, the food excellent, the staff friendly and is another of the places I ate at, that I would like to revisit someday.

As I was leaving, the chef brought a large urn of home-made mushroom soup and I got a cup to take with me that I drank over the next mile, as I walked along an undulating footpath through woodland. Once I had finished the soup, I stuffed the cup in a small plastic bag I had tied to the side of my bum bag for rubbish and started running again. The track ran alongside a railway line, and I went on mile after mile with the line of my left whilst on my right woodland alternated with open fields. I realised that since I had arrived in Scotland, apart from a short section after Pitlochry, my route had almost entirely been on tarmac. Even the cycle paths were tar mac. I know it was invented by a Scot but no wonder my legs felt battered. At some point I realised the railway line was probably the one that would be taking me home in less than a week's time. Suddenly I became homesick, before telling myself to, "man up son, you will be home before you know it and then be longing for adventure."

I pressed on to Aviemore and reached the tourist hot spot at around 12:30. It was Sunday and the town was very busy. I passed several cafés, all of which were full and was starting to get concerned that I was going to have a long wait. I had decided I needed more calories and that had been the reason for my grumpy mood earlier in the day, so today was officially a two-cake day. I peered through the window of every café and eating establishment on Aviemore's main street for an available seat, without success. Eventually I arrived at the last café on the road where I spotted a table with eight seats being occupied by three couples. Surely, they would allow me to sit on the end of the table I thought, so I went in hopefully and put on my best Yorkshire smile and poshest voice asking if they would permit me to sit at the end of their table.

"Ey up! Na then. Does thi mind if a park mi bones ere?

This seemed to do the trick, and they moved along the bench creating space for me. The usual questions ensued about how far I had run, what I was doing and was it for a charity etc and we chatted for a while after they had finished their meal. They were in no hurry to leave and each couple asked me for the details of the charity. When my meal arrived they wished me good luck and went on their way. A few minutes later I received friend requests on Facebook from two of the group and sent them replies in between mouthfuls. After I finished a plate of Lasagne and chips I ordered a portion of sticky toffee pudding with ice cream and returned to my table to see a message had come through from one of the group. They thanked me for what I was doing and then told me their dad had tried to take his own life when they had been a teenager. They explained how it had impacted on the family. The person concerned hadn't wanted to say anything in front of their friends but wanted me to know that they felt what I was doing was really important and wished me good luck again.

It was another sobering moment and I left the café feeling emotional. I had about eight miles to go for the day. It was 1.40 and I estimated I would be in Carrbridge not long after 3pm and set off up the road just wanting to get today finished. I had opted to leave the cycle route and continue along the road, the A95, thinking that because it ran parallel to the A9 it would be pretty quiet. Once I arrived at the A95 it was evident that was not the case. I waited a few minutes and watched car after car leave the A9 and then take the A95. There was no path along there at this point and I decided the road was too dangerous to contemplate running on. I didn't know if there was a path up ahead or if so, how far ahead it was so I began to retrace my steps back to Aviemore. The revised plan was to follow the much longer cycle route to Carrbridge, which did nothing at all to improve my mood.

I studied the map as I headed back and found a small, short cut that probably saved me a mile, and took me around the edge of a small wood. I tried to lift my spirits by telling myself this was much better than the road option. I arrived at a railway line where the path went beneath the tracks via a tiny tunnel. This had a small stone arch built at the front and reminded me of something from Alice in Wonderland. Was this the gateway to some enchanted kingdom on the other side? The tunnel was very narrow and yet in addition to the footpath that ran along a ledge, there was also a small stream running through it. This looked like a recipe for disaster as I was going to have to stoop to get through the arch. I am not the most flexible of people and I had visions of falling off the ledge as I tried to shuffle along. I decided to take a photograph just in case this is where it all went wrong and was lining up the shot when a figure appeared at the other end followed by a Jack Russel photobombing my picture.

The man eased his way through the tunnel, unfolding himself in front of me and we laughed at the timing. It was another comical moment. The man's name was Thomaz and he was originally from Poland but now lived locally. He took the details of my charity and we chatted for a short while, then after a selfie I was on my way. I struggled through the tunnel wondering how the cyclists got through here, until I remembered I hadn't reached the cycle route yet, this was my 'little' shortcut and laughed at my own joke.

A few hundred metres further on I reached the cycle route as it turned northeast following the line of the railway line. It was a wide forest trail and I met several families enjoying their Sunday afternoon. The route emerged from the tall trees and went through a large area that had been replanted allowing stunning views to the North and East. There was a lady working hard as she pedalled her bike up a hill towards me. She was towing a yellow trailer in which a small child sat surveying the surroundings. She crested the hill just before reaching me and breathed a sigh of relief as she began the downhill.

Maybe that was something I would be doing with my grandchildren in years to come. The route went back to the other side of the railway line, this time under a proper human sized tunnel, not one built for a Jack Russel. Here a sign read it was two and half miles to Aviemore. My watch told me

I had run five point four miles since leaving the café and I tried to put a positive spin on the extra mileages by the fact that this last section had been the best bit of the day. A few hundred metres further on was a house with a bird feeder in the garden. Even from a distance away I could see small birds flocking to it. Blue tits, gold finches, robins, sparrows and other birds I didn't recognise. I could have happily stayed and watched for the rest of the afternoon but Carbridge beckoned and it was still five miles away.

The gravel track became a surfaced road flanked by houses on either side. Big grand expensive looking houses, all immaculate. I could see CCTV cameras and signs on gates telling me I was being filmed. Oddly it was at that moment that I suddenly had a desperate urge to pee. I was on the outskirts of a small place called Boat of Garten and trotted along the road in the hope of finding a public toilet. The road seemed to go on forever and each step seemed to jar my bouncing bursting bladder. I reached a T junction. My route was to turn left but the signpost informed me that the railway station was to the right so I went right in the hope of relief. I asked a couple of passers-by if there were any toilets nearby but they informed me they were not local. I couldn't find any at the station which seemed to be locked up anyway. Somewhat frustrated I retraced my steps to the signpost and set off at a trot in the direction of Carbridge. The village was still far too busy with houses all along the road for the next mile but it was becoming a matter of some urgency. Eventually I passed the last house in the village, at which point a footpath and cycleway started, with a small line of trees between it and the road. This gave me hope that the discomfort could soon be over.

Fifty metres ahead was a small wooden bridge over a ditch where I dropped off the path. Standing on the camber of the ditch I went as far down as I could, but my head still protruded just above the level of the path. It would be visible above the bridge floor to anyone passing by. It was not an ideal situation but I was desperate. I looked up and down the track and could see almost one hundred metres in both directions. No one was in sight.

"What the hell, needs must," I said and began to relieve myself in what was undoubtedly a moment of relief, pleasure almost. However, it was short lived, because no sooner had the floodgates opened, than a couple came cycling around the corner one hundred metres away. I tried unsuccessfully to hurry the process along. My eyes were firmly focused on the cyclists, a man and woman. My head stuck out like I'd been buried up to my neck. Luckily part of the structure partially hid me from view and they passed by and didn't appear to have spotted me. After they'd gone and I was securing everything in its proper place I heard the lady say,

"Did you see that chap having a pee?" Thankfully they didn't look back and I emerged red faced but relieved, then laughed at the comedy of it all.

I ran the last few miles to complete a challenging day littered with many moments of pleasure. I struggled up the steps to my room feeling exhausted. I just wanted to sleep. However, I was overjoyed when I saw the biscuit next to the kettle. A Tunnocks caramel wafer looked up at me from its nesting place on the top of a useful sized mug. I ate this little bar of delight, I read through my messages. My spirits rose again when I read about the running success of one of my young club colleagues, Rebecca Flaherty. Earlier in the day she had finished 2nd in the World Schools Cross country championships. Well done Rebecca, Great Stuff. A very nice end to the day.

24 days done. 4 days to go.

CHAPTER 31

Made of Sterner Stuff

Day 25 – Monday 25th April 2022 – Carrbridge to North Kessock

If yesterday was a struggle, today was different. I woke up feeling refreshed after a great night's sleep. I'd enjoyed an excellent meal the night before accompanied by a pint of Guinness. Maybe it's true what they say. Guinness really is good for you.

It was an uninspiring damp morning, but I was buzzing as I ate a continental breakfast the hotel had left out for me and couldn't wait to get going. Leaving at 6.30 I spent a few minutes dithering as I took a photograph of the ancient bridge giving the village its name.

The first part of my day involved running along a road that ran between a railway line and the A9, as it climbed up and across Slochd Mor (local spelling). This was another exposed place so I was glad it was warmer than the day before or the persistent drizzle would have undoubtedly been snow. As I was running up the hill I worked out it was the first day I had seen rain since Day 12 when I ran from Stoke to Manchester, which for April was a surprising bonus. The climb was gradual, but the higher I climbed the heavier and more persistent the drizzle became.

I passed a deserted Ski Centre halfway up, which made me think I had underestimated the route and I questioned if I'd brought enough kit. About one mile after the Ski centre, the road ran out becoming more of a track. It appeared to be an old road, now disused and was broken up, with weeds and shrubs poking through its metalled surface. Despite these feelings of uncertainty, I was never cold and still had additional clothes to put on. The old road became narrower and closer to the railway line, and as I reached the top of the climb the three routes were all within fifty metres of each other. At this point the drizzle got lighter, becoming pockets of mist that swirled around in a light breeze. This enabled me to take a photograph of the summit itself. When I say summit, it's not the summit of a peak, but the summit of the railway climb, and probably the road climb also.

After this, the cycle route got very narrow for a few hundred metres as it passed a section of rock. Here it ran alongside the main A9, only being separated from it by a barrier made of one single steel cable. The speeding morning traffic threw up clouds of spray, some of which came in my direction. Not long after this, the cycleway joined a B road that led from the A9 downhill to the village of Tomatin. This offered faster running and suddenly I was out of the mist. The drizzle had stopped but the weather still didn't seem to know which way it wanted to go as I crossed Findhorn Bridge at just after 8 am. I ran through the village and was excited to see a sign for a café but alas it was closed at 8:15. According to my map at the Northwest end of Tomatin village, the surfaced road would run out and become a track as it passed a line of houses. The track would run for almost a mile until it reached a parking area on the south side of the A9 near a place called Dalmagarry.

Up ahead I could see construction vehicles and when I arrived at what should have been the start of the track, there was a road closed sign. A line of cones stretched across the road, tied together with plastic bunting. I looked ahead and could see what seemed like fifty workmen standing watching two men lay tarmac. I took my phone out and looked at the map. I thought there may be a possible route via an underpass under the A9, but it would add a significant distance to the day's total which was already far enough. As no pedestrian diversion appeared to have been put in place I stepped over the cones and prepared to do battle with the work man as I set off running in full 'Forrest Gump' mode. Shouts of abuse rang out from onlookers as they stood resting on shovels but we're all walking or standing on the same stretch of unsurfaced road I was running on. Three men stood leaning against a tipper lorry and one of them poured a hot drink from a flask. I cheekily asked if he had any to spare but I think the answer was no. At least that's what I interpreted "F*<k Off" to mean. Undeterred I kept going, taking care to avoid hot or newly laid tar. After a few minutes of heckling I was clear of the workman. It was definitely worth the effort of running fast as I arrived at the parking area in under seven minutes avoiding the long diversion.

The route now crossed the A9 and ran along the northside of it for half a mile before turning onto the B9154. After a few hundred metres there was a wide path and I passed what looked like a country estate. A few miles ahead I met a cyclist called Simon from Edinburgh who apart from the hostile road crew was the first person I had seen.

One of the things about getting up early and running such distances alone is that you lose track of time, particularly on a day when the weather is unsure of itself. I thought it was nearly lunchtime but Simon told me it was not yet 9am. At least I knew what day it was, just.

Simon headed off south and I continued my run north, just as the route went under the railway line and headed into an area of forestry land. This section of the road was perfect for running and cycling with only small manageable undulations and no major climbs. After two miles the road descended, gradually at first and then steeply, going through the village of Craggie. As I descended the rain started, but as luck would have it there was a bus shelter at the bottom of the hill. I took the opportunity for a few minutes there to check the map. I munched on a few wine gums and drank some water.

Someone in that big cake shop in the sky was looking after me again, as right opposite the bus shelter was a narrow lane. This was in fact where I was turning off, however if the rain hadn't started I could easily have missed the turn because the road was hidden by long grass. I only noticed it when I sat down in the bus shelter and had the rain not started I would have probably ran straight by.

I headed up what at first was a short sharp hill but gradually became easier again. It was a lovely route, gently undulating as it passed field after field of newborn lambs. Near the small hamlet of Cottatoen I met another cyclist enjoying this wonderfully scenic route. This lady, who could have easily been seventy-five or even older, said she had set out from Inverness that morning to cycle to the North Yorkshire Moors. She told me she was part of a cycling organisation where you allow touring cyclists to stay with you and then you can stay at the homes of other cyclists when you are touring. When she heard what I was doing she said,

"Last night I had two gentlemen cyclists stay with me. They'd cycled from John O'Groats to Inverness in four days. They were supposed to be going all the way to Lands' End but gave up this morning and headed for the train station."

"They were obviously not made of the same stuff we are," I said smiling.

"No, we must be made of sterner stuff," she said, returning my smile. Wishing each other good luck, we went our separate ways.

The route descended sharply and crossed the river Nairn in the bottom of the valley, where a turn brought me to an ancient standing stone and 'The Clava Cairns.' These were described on the map as chambered cairns. I took a few moments to photograph the standing stone and circular rock formation, which appeared on the photograph as basically a pile of limestone rocks. As I looked at the picture I said to myself, 'That's not likely to impress friends back in Yorkshire when we've got Malham Cove on our doorstep.' However it could actually have more to do with my lack of photographic ability.

The road now climbed steeply out of the valley and as I struggled up the hill a car pulled up beside me asking for directions. The people in question were looking for another historic site, namely the battlefield site Culloden. Between gasps I explained it was at the top of this hill, somewhere on the left, and the car drove off leaving me in a cloud of blue smoke. I could have done without breathing in the petrol fuelled fog, so I decided to walk a few metres so I could take shallow breaths. The route flattened out and I passed the small village of Leanch, and then passed between New Culloden and the site of the battlefield. My niece used to live in Culloden and I'd visited before, so I was not persuaded to have a second look. Instead I was drawn straight ahead by a need to eat. The road began a gentle descent that would eventually take me to the sea and Inverness but first I stopped at the Co-op in Balloch where I fuelled up on chicken pasta, a snickers bar and a litre of water.

After a fifteen-minute break, sitting on a wall whilst I ate, I was on my way again. An hour later I'd bypassed Inverness and was trying to find my way across the Kessock Bridge. I knew there was a walkway on either side of the A9 as it crossed the bridge high above the Beauly Firth. The two paths are separated by a dual carriage way which seems to be busy all the time. I set off from the roundabout using the path next to the northbound carriageway, only to find as I reached the bridge itself that this footpath was closed. It was impossible to cross to the other path at this point as this would involve climbing over three cash barriers and crossing four lanes of speeding traffic. I had no choice but to retrace my steps back to the roundabout and cross to the path at the side of the southbound carriageway. Another wasted mile that I could have done without but C'est la vie.

Once I had negotiated the bridge I crossed back over the A9 at a crossing point where a small snicket took me down a stone ramp, bringing me to sea level at the side of the Firth. The view was stunning but I was seduced by the sight of the North Kessock Hotel a few hundred metres further on where after a jacket potato with chilli, a sticky toffee pudding with ice cream, and two tea pots of tea, I did actually fall asleep in the bar, much to the amusement of the staff.

After paying my bill and booking a table in the hotel restaurant to eat later that evening, I set off to walk the last few hundred metres to the small B & B I was stopping at. This was recommended in the cycling book by Royston Wood but they didn't do evening meals.

The B&B, when I eventually found it, was homely and the old couple, Jean and David, who ran the place, were really nice. It was like staying with your aunty. I walked past the place twice, eventually resorting to google maps for help. This too brought me back to the same bungalow at the top of the same dead end. There was no sign or name identifying the place so I walked up the garden path and knocked on the door to find I was in the right place and was given a warm welcome. David showed me to my room and seconds later I was enjoying a nice warm shower.

I returned to the hotel at 7pm to find the restaurant was really busy which surprised me on a Monday night in April. I was glad I'd booked. The waitress came to take my order and then returning with my drink and cutlery said,

"Are you the guy who fell asleep in the bar this afternoon?"

"Fame at last, yes that was me." I replied.

"So, you're running from Lands' End to John O' Groats?"

Having confirmed that I was both the dozy dozing diner, and the relaxed roaming runner she asked me if I was running for a charity. This of course led to the usual conversation about Andy's Man Club. She went to serve another customer, but came back as I finished my meal. As she cleared the plates away she told me that men's mental health in and around Inverness was a big problem, informing me that only a few weeks ago a teenage boy had hung himself off a nearby bridge.

The local authorities were trying hard to get people outdoors and said she would look up the charity and my details on facebook and wished me luck.

As I walked back to my B&B, l began thinking about the boy. What had driven him to put a noose around his neck and throw himself off a bridge? How low does a person have to be to do that? I thought about my own boy. Had he experienced such troubles in his teenage years. The fact that I didn't know concerned me and once back in my room I phoned home and spoke to Angela. Tears welled up as I enquired how they all were. I tried hard to disguise the emotion I was feeling as I realised how lucky I was. I finished the call and turned the light out. What a day. It had been an exhausting rollercoaster of a day, both physically and emotionally. I was drained but I had now passed Inverness and was surely on the last lap. 123 miles to John O' Groats.

25 days, 3 days to go.

CHAPTER 32

The Pilgrimage of Cake

Day 26 – Tuesday 26th April 2022 – North Kessock to Tain

I started the day a bit later having had breakfast with my hosts and leaving at 9:15. The reason for the late start was that I was planning to visit a relative around 5pm. My route virtually passed the front gate of one of my nieces as it entered Tain but if I arrived too early she would be on the school run, and my lodgings were one and a half miles after her house, so I didn't want to pass by and have to retrace my steps.

I had three big days left, starting with today's run of thirty-six miles to Tain. There was not really a suitable place to break the journey halfway, so I'd decided to split my day into three. Twelve miles from North Kessock to Dingwall, twelve miles from Dingwall to Alness and finally twelve miles from Alness to Tain. I should have no problems getting refreshments and I needed to eat lots today because tomorrow would be longer than today, and the final day was set to be a real monster.

The morning was clear and bright with wonderful views across the loch. During breakfast my hosts pointed out a white building on the far bank, the Loch keeper's cottage, and reminded me this was the end of the Caledonian Canal.

I set off up the road and used an underpass to negotiate the A9 which was ridiculously busy with morning traffic. Once on the other side, the route went up some steps, emerging on a small lane that went steeply uphill for fifty metres to the village of Croftnacrech. This was national cycle route number one and once through the village it turned right onto a B road, Fifty metres later the route turned left onto another quiet lane. Ahead I could see daffodils growing in the grass verge outside a house whose roof had more grass on it than the area of my own three lawns added together.

Despite the day's bright start, it started to drizzle and once again I was running into a headwind so on went the rain jacket. Although the rain stopped after ten minutes, probably blown away by the wind, the jacket stayed on as the wind was cold.

After passing the tiny village of Tore I crossed the A9 again, via a cycleway at a roundabout then headed west alongside the A835. This was followed by a not so pleasant two miles as I fought a cross wind, and because I was so close to the road, the strong downdraft from the many trucks that passed, each almost stopping me in my tracks. I was pleased when I turned off the A road, opting for a much quieter road that ran parallel.

It was downhill for the next two miles as the road dropped from an altitude of one hundred and ten metres to sea level as it brought me back to the main road. Here, a bridge took me over the river Conon at the end of the Cromaty Firth. Halfway across the bridge was a bank of flowers fastened to an undamaged safety fence. There didn't appear to have been a car crash and I wondered why there would be flowers there. Then it struck me. Was this the place where the boy they lady from the night before had told me about had taken his own life. It was another thought-provoking moment. RIP young man. I hope you and your family have found peace.

I ran into Dingwall in search of a café and found a Wimpy. The small hamburger chain that used to be prevalent in the UK and forerunner to Burger King.

Wimpy was somewhere I had enjoyed many meals, particularly from the dessert menu. Even the thought of the names banana longboat, brown derby and king of them all, the knickerbocker glory had me salivating. The name

Wimpy was actually taken from a character in the Popeye cartoons called J. Wellington Wimpy who was always eating hamburgers. A company called Grand Metropolitan, the owners of the Burger King brand, bought the Wimpy brand in the late 1980's. Wimpy had two different types of store. They began with smaller diner style table service restaurants, then after McDonalds arrived in the UK, Wimpy opened the larger counter service type of store, to try and compete with Ronald and his happy meals. Eventually having been bought by Burger King's owners, the Wimpy management team in the UK bought back part of the company, so they could continue trading with the older style restaurant. I had spent three years managing one and owning a share in the franchise with my mum and dad, so seeing one in Dingwall really did bring back old memories. I would have eaten there but much to my disappointment, a note on the door said it was closed for a staff meeting.

Further along the street I found a nice café with a bakery attached, and enjoyed a ham salad sandwich, pot of tea and cream cake, two cream cakes actually. In doing so I told myself this was 'Two Cake Tuesday' leaving Dingwall suitably stuffed at 1215 for the next stint to Alness.

The route climbed from sea level to one hundred and fifty metres in altitude. This was no problem at all as I was walking to let my lovely lunch find its level. The road turned north again and provided excellent views across the Cromarty Firth to what is known as the Black Isle. Further up the coast I could see the oil terminal at Nigg. The large structures looked out of place and like something from a sci-fi film.

I was now contouring along the hillside. Unknowingly I had picked up the pace and for a while I did some of my best running along the entire route. I was amazed to see that I had run several consecutive miles in under eight minutes. I felt really good. For some reason the view of Cromarty Firth made me think of a book I read years earlier. 'The Unlikely

Pilgrimage of Harold Fry' a fictional story by Rachel Joyce. I found it to be a wonderful story with lots of humour yet having a dark undercurrent. It was one of those occasions when you buy a book in haste because of the title whilst having no idea what it's about. I was in an airport about to go on holiday and in a queue in W.H. Smiths when I spied it on the shelf.

In the story Harold, a man of mature years who lives somewhere in the Southwest, has a disagreement with his wife as he is going out of the door to post a letter. After a conversation with a girl in the shop he decides not to go home and sets off walking north. As he walks he meets people along the way, some of whom join him and the whole thing gathers momentum. At some point he leaves the group behind but I couldn't recall how far north Harold got or even if he reached his destination, but the thought of the book made me smile. I thought about my own journey. It had in some way become a kind of pilgrimage and I decided an apt name for my journey of discovery so far would be the 'Pilgrimage of Cake.'

I arrived in Alness at 2pm, again on the lookout for somewhere to eat. Half a mile into the town my route turned left off the main street but I ignored the turn and continued along the main street. It was important that I get something to eat and more water. I was two thirds of the way through my day, but still had twelve miles to go. I was not just eating for today though, I was eating for the next two days and any shortfall in my calorie intake today could come and bite me later. Fifty metres further on was a co-op which would do, but I really wanted to sit down for ten minutes and rest my legs.

As I stood on the pavement across from the co-op I must have looked lost because a lady approached carrying a two-litre carton of milk and saying,

"Are ye alright?"

"I'm looking for a café."

"There are three cafés in town" and she pointed up the street where I could see two different cafés but both were closed.

"There is another one just around the next corner." She said. I smiled at her and jokingly said,

"You're not sending me on a wild goose chase are you, because I've already run 24 miles today and I still have to run to Tain" You can guess this prompted her to ask about what charity I was running for.

" Oh right well If you find it's closed, come back here and I will make you a cuppa." Then she opened the door to what I thought was a hair salon. I carried on up the road and found the café but this was also closed, so retraced my steps to the salon. I looked through the door to see a crowd of people standing around chatting and drinking cups of tea, so I went in.

The lady I had met outside immediately came over from the crowd. Taking my arm she called out to the group introducing me.

"This is the chappie running to John O' Groats" She brought me a cup of tea and sat me in a chair next to a small table on which were two plates. One was of sausage rolls and the other was of chocolate chip muffins. She told me to help myself. Her name was Helen Ross and she explained this place was actually a young people's drop-in centre where teenagers could come for help, advice, or just to chat. The place was simply called 'The Place' and it transpired that those inside were organising and supporting the family of a teenage boy who had been missing since the previous Friday night. It was Tuesday.

She went on to tell me that it was hard for young people locally as there was not a lot for them to do. Many end up with mental health issues or fall into drugs. I told her of the story recounted the night before about the boy who hanged himself, and incredibly she said she knew of six boys who had hanged themselves. It was harrowing. I just didn't know what to say. I wanted to speak to my own children to make sure they were OK and to ask my friends to do the same. Later that day I put a message out on social media telling people about the missing boy, adding 'Mothers and Fathers among you. Give your kids a hug or send them a kind message today to tell them what they mean to you. Do we really know what they are going through?' After thirty minutes of being moved to tears punctuated with tea and a chocolate muffin I was on my way again.

After the initial climb up the hillside to Alness golf course, progress was good. I sped along the road like a man on the run, trying to escape the feelings of uselessness, attempting to put behind me the emotion of the previous stop. The miles seemed to fly by as I passed through and close to places, the names of which I struggled to pronounce. Badachonacher, Dalnaclairach, Dalnachlach, Brenachie, a few examples. Around the area of Marybank and Lamington I passed and re-passed the local school bus on the narrow country lane in what seemed like a race between the two of us to reach Tain. About one mile outside the town a man on a bike came up behind me and shouted

"You've had a long run today."

"Yes, I've come from North Kessock."

"Aye I know. I drove past you in the car at about 10am. I recognised the words 'Yorkshire Runner' on the back of your shirt. Are you running to John O Groats?"

"Not today" I laughed cheekily then added "Yes I am, but first I am visiting my niece in Tain".

He asked my name and when I told him he said.

"Is it Melissa you are visiting or Maria?" These were the names of two of my nieces. It turns out he was a retired schoolteacher, Jimmy McClain and had taught both Melissa and Maria, who were my brother's daughters. A further connection was that he was now involved in a music group in which a third niece, their younger sister Shannon played the violin. It's a small world. We took the compulsory selfie, nearly getting knocked down in the excitement. I was actually visiting a fourth niece, Gabrielle, the daughter of one of my sisters, Angela, and I arrived five minutes later telling her the story of the teacher.

After the awful news at the drop-in centre in Alness, it was cathartic to spend time with my niece and her children. I enjoyed watching the boys play football with other lads on grass at the front of their house and listening to the sibling banter around the kitchen table as they ate their evening meal. Gabrielle invited me to stay for tea but I could see she had more than enough to do, especially when I heard she was heading out to work the night shift on the dementia ward of a nearby care home. It was really nice to catch up and see her again but after an hour and a family photo I knew it was time to go. I still had a mile and a half to my B&B. I arrived just before 7pm and was shown to the most immaculate room. It had an absolutely stunning view over Tain Sands and the Dornock Firth. It was undoubtedly the best view of any of the twenty-six rooms I had stayed in so far.

88 miles and 2 days to go.

CHAPTER 33

Taxi for Fry

Day 27 – Wednesday 27th April 2022 – Tain to Helmsdale

I was woken by the morning sun shining through my window as if it was calling me to get going. I shook my head at the thought of the thirty-eight miles to Helmsdale, knowing it was going to be another tough day. I also knew it was going to be another emotional day, even if I didn't meet a single person as it was two years to the day since my dad had died.

In April of 2020, my dad was on the dementia ward in a care home when he caught Covid, only five weeks after the first lock down. I went to visit him at the hospital which was what I can only describe as a truly dreadful experience.

Before going to see him I was told that only one person could go, and that person had to bring a complete change of clothes and a bin liner. After seeing my dad I would have to strip off completely, change my clothes immediately and put them on a boil wash when I got home. I was also told that I wouldn't be allowed back once I'd left. It was a one time deal.

On arrival I was given gloves, a full-length heavy apron, a face mask and plastic goggles which went over my eyes and nose. All the doctors and senior nurses were covered head to toe in PPE. It was how I imagined it would be to work in a nuclear plant. Two young nurses showed me the way to a room where my dad was lying in bed, wired up to monitors. He had a cannula in his hand and an oxygen tube that should have been in his nose but was dangling under his chin.

The nurses announced my arrival to my dad and then left. My dad didn't acknowledge me but instead kept staring at the wall in front of him. I spoke to him trying to make small talk and trying to put the oxygen tube into his nose, but he kept taking it out. I sat holding his hand and trying to engage him in conversation but at no point did he answer me or look me in the eyes. After ten minutes one of the nurses came in and I asked if she would put the oxygen tube in his nose. Before she even got hold of the tube, dad pulled his hand away from mine and grabbed the nurse's hand, forcing it onto the bed. I had to prise his fingers away with both hands so she could remove her own hand. I realised why he couldn't look me in the eyes. He had decided his time was up. I held his hand again saying "Oh dear, it's like that is it. You've made your mind up then." He still didn't acknowledge me, so he didn't see my goggles fill with tears, nor see me pull them forward to let the water escape. I had to repeat this process several times as we sat there in silence for what seemed an absolute age.

All kinds of thoughts went through my head as the afternoon wore on, but I kept coming back to the same one. I didn't want to watch him die. Eventually he fell asleep. I stayed there for a while longer holding his hand, periodically emptying the flooded goggles. One of the nurses came in to change the drip and I asked her what his chances were. She skirted round the issue but said it was not good and I should prepare for the worst.

I didn't want to go through the rest of my life remembering him as he breathed his last breath. I had seen my mum's body just after she had died, a grey figure with a green tinge and lifeless eyes that looked more like cardigan buttons than the bright pools of blue I remembered. She bore no resemblance to the mum I knew, the cheeky smile, as totally out of character, she had told me about attending her first keep fit class for the over sixties, and how as they all bent and stretched, the room was filled with the sound of involuntary flatulence. Or of how when telling such a tale she would laugh uncontrollably, unable to get her words and then eventually cry.

No, I didn't want to remember my dad in the same lifeless way, I wanted to remember him as the broad-shouldered former judo instructor who carried me on his shoulders up the hills and across the moors of the Yorkshire Dales. A big friendly bear who would wrestle me and my four siblings all at the same time, on the carpet in front of the fire on winter evenings, like the playful wolf cubs from Jungle book. That's the image I tried to focus on as I sat there weeping.

After a while my mind was made up and I walked around the bed to take a last look at him. He looked peaceful and I decided it was the right time to leave, and like a coward before a battle, I silently slipped away.

After getting changed I walked along the endless corridor and outside to the car park, thinking back to times shared with dad and some of the things we had done together. I thought of the last time I had seen him in February, just before the care home announced their self-imposed lock down. Of how we had gone through our twice weekly ritual of sitting in Ilkley park eating ice cream, even though it was a cold dark night. I sat in the car until I could stem the tears long enough to drive home where I immediately put on my running kit and tried to run away from my helplessness, my grief, my guilt.

At 1.30 am on the next day, 27/4/2020, the hospital called to tell me he had passed away. I do feel guilty about not being there for him at the end. For leaving him to die alone but you can't turn the clock back. You have to live with the decisions you make and the consequences they bring. I draw some small comfort from the fact that if I was in that position again now, I would probably make exactly the same decision because given the choice, why would any of us want to watch someone we love die? I don't think he wanted me to see it either.

So exactly two years later I knew I was in for an emotional day as I left Tain. My dad loved to sing and as I ran along at the side of Glenmorangie distillery, I sang rousing hymns in his honour as loudly as I could.

The sky was blue and cloudless and I couldn't deny it was a really beautiful day. Far too nice to be melancholy. My stiff legs took a while to wake up but the rhythm of the marching hymns helped. It wasn't long before I was running at a good pace, covering the first two miles to the Dornoch bridge in twenty minutes. Here I saw my first road sign showing the number of miles to John O Groats and stopped to take a photo as a cyclist passed by. It occurred to me that I should have asked him to watch my back across the bridge as there was no proper foot way. At that moment he stopped for a picture of the Firth. I caught up with him and he agreed to ride behind and escort me over the bridge. It transpired he was originally from Bingley, attending Bradford Grammar School as a boy. He was called David Taylor and was in the same class as one of my running club's legendary runners, Richard Nuraker who became world marathon champion.

David very kindly was my wingman across the bridge and for a pretty hairy section of the A9 to the turn off to Dornoch village. We stopped for the obligatory selfie, exchanging twitter details. His help was invaluable and another indication that someone somewhere was watching over me as help seemed to arrive whenever I needed it.

The next ten miles were on quiet roads through Dornoch village, then along the side of the firth. I headed in the direction of Embow and the nearby village Skelbow. The views were stunning and the running effortless as I covered my first nine miles in ninety minutes.

Eventually I came back to the A9 which was the only route across the next loch, Loch Fleet where I had a hair-raising few minutes. The traffic whizzed down the hill towards me as I crossed a bridge called the Mound. After this, it was a further four miles to the village of Golspie, and no alternative but to stick to the main road. For much of the way there was some kind of verge but this was generally lumpy, bumpy, rocky or overgrown so instead I ran on the road, choosing to step off when cars approached. The strategy worked but demanded a high level of concentration, so I was again relieved when I arrived on the outskirts of Golspie and able to use a proper pavement. I reached the village centre at exactly 12.00 a full hour earlier than planned and went in search of the village co-op. I knew the village had a co-op because my sister Angela worked there. I planned to surprise her in the hope we could eat lunch or at least have a cup of tea together as we hadn't seen each other for around five years. It transpired that Angela worked a half day on Wednesday and wasn't starting until 2pm. Having covered over eighteen miles I couldn't wait for another two hours to eat so I went to check out the nearest café. Whilst there I spoke to a group of local walkers who told me there was a path along the coast for the next six miles to Brora and I should not run on the A9 as that section was particularly dangerous. One of the group was a keen cyclist. He asked me which route I was taking after Helmsdale. He explained that the pandemic had led to the closure of shops in the smaller villages away from the coast, so I would find it difficult to obtain food unless I carried it with me. I thanked them for the vital information then after my meal, and just the one piece of cake, returned to the Coop.

One of the staff I'd spoken to earlier pointed out where Angela was working. I walked up behind her asking,

"Excuse me, can you tell me which aisle I go down to get a hug please?"

She was taken by surprise, announcing to her work colleagues, and the whole store, that I had run all the way from Lands' End to see her. I felt like a celebrity. The supervisor kindly let her go for a short break even though she had only just started and we chatted for half an hour which proved to be another emotional rollercoaster. It was nice to catch up but it was clear that life in this part of Scotland was really difficult for the young people. She told me of two local girls who had tried to overdose. I could see she personally wasn't having an easy time and we both became emotional. Nevertheless, it was nice to see her and spend a precious thirty minutes with her before going in search of the coastal path.

This well-trodden route was like running on a soft grassy carpet taking me across land at the back of Dunrobin Castle, Madonna's wedding venue. The magnificent castle looked like something out of a Walt Disney film and I did my best to capture its splendour with my phone. The pathway was excellent for the first three miles but as I got nearer to Brora the path became much narrower, eventually dwindling to nothing more than a small sheep trod amongst tussocks of grass. It ran along a narrow strip of land between a boundary fence and the shoreline that every so often had broken away. Suddenly I was constantly down and up avoiding these patches of erosion. I was forced down to the shoreline where seas of large pebbles and steep soft sand dunes made running absolutely impossible. Even when there was a beach of sorts it wasn't a beautiful length of golden sand that I could have run on, instead it was broken up with slippery seaweed covered rocks and rock pools, perfect terrain to break an ankle or twist a knee. Eventually that's exactly what happened, I twisted my knee half a mile from Brora, which I limped into at 4.45.

I still had eleven miles to Helmsdale. If I could get running it would take me two hours. If is such a small word, but at that point came with a very large question mark. As I left Brora there seemed little chance of me running properly any time soon. As I left the town I met a man carrying a massive rucksack. He was about six feet four inches tall and his bag seemed bigger still. I asked him if he had come from John O Groats and if so, why wasn't he walking on the coastal path. He was American and confirmed he had come from John O Groats and that he started on the coastal path but the constant undulations and terrain had injured his knee, so he was now sticking to the road, He said it wasn't too bad, as there was a grass verge all the way from Helmsdale.

When the pavement ran out I moved onto the verge but once again it was not nice smooth grass, but uneven and full of debris, nettles or other thorny vegetation. I decided to try and run thinking that I could alternate walking and running as I had done previously. I didn't even get ten yards. It was excruciating. There would be no running for a while so I settled into a brisk walk. Eventually that too became uncomfortable. It would take me longer than two hours to reach Helmsdale. I tried walking as fast as I could, covering the next two miles in forty-eight slow and painful minutes. Another problem now was the sun. The verge being far too lumpy, I was walking on a main road with the sun setting behind me. I could see my shadow on the ground in front of me and it was clear some of the car drivers were not able to see me so, every time a car came I had to step up off the road on to the verge. Each time I did this the pressure on my knee was torture. At this rate it was going to be 8pm before I finished. All kinds of thoughts went through my head. Will it be dark, will the village shop be open? What time do they stop serving food in the pub? And how on earth was I going to run fifty-three miles tomorrow to the finish?

Because of the enforced shorter day around Blair Atholl, I had not been able to split the remaining days evenly to ensure I finished on the 28th without having a really long day at some point, so in my planning had decided that the only way would be to try and cover the remaining fifty three miles from Helmsdale in one go. It sounded like a big task, but almost every day I had finished by early afternoon. I decided that on the last day, if I could get away at 6am and run thirty miles by 2pm, I should also be able to cover the remaining twenty three miles in no more than seven hours, finishing at 9pm. That meant it was possible to have a taxi waiting in John O'Groats to take me to the Hotel in Thurso. I would be there before 10pm at the latest. So that had been the loose plan but as I hobbled along the road like a tortoise with a broken leg, I had to reassess things.

I phoned Angela, my wife not my sister, and we discussed my options. She then began hunting for some accommodation at Lybster and found an Airbnb. Once that was arranged she phoned the hotel in Thurso, persuading them to push back my booking for Thursday night by twenty-four hours. She phoned me back to say everything was sorted but since our earlier call the pain had worsened, my pace had slowed, my mood had worsened and I had become hangry. So when she cheerfully announced,

"It's all sorted," I probably appeared less than grateful, and snapped at her saying.

"It's not sorted yet because I can hardly walk."

She did what she does best and politely put me in my place by pointing out that I had thought it was all over when I reached Perth, and yet here I was, two hundred miles further on and calmly instructed me not to worry. As if reading a message from a mug, she told me to,

"Keep Calm and Carry on," and then put the phone down.

It was 6:30pm and I was still almost eight miles from my lodgings. I was mentally and physically spent. I sat down on a wall and considered phoning a taxi. As I was now having a shorter day tomorrow I could rest up tonight, get a taxi back to my current position and add the last eight miles of today to the twenty-three miles of tomorrow. This seemed a workable option.

As I sat pondering, my phone pinged with a message from Andrew Nicoll. He told me that my post yesterday, about the missing boy, had made him think. If you're enjoying life, it is easy to assume everyone else is and miss signs that someone else may be struggling. I sent a message back that read,

"Well, I am £*<$!&* struggling. 8 miles to go and my knee is kaput. Moving at under 2 mph, thinking of calling a Taxi."

He replied with the sympathy I deserved and is only afforded to such close friends. In his usual style of using the fewest words possible, he managed to question my parentage, my sexuality and indeed my Yorkshire birthright all in the one sentence. He was right of course. Paying for a Taxi! It's amazing how much pain a Yorkshireman will tolerate to avoid 'parting wi't brass.'

"Lazarus. Pick up thy crutches and walk," I told myself, and I set off determined to get to Helmsdale before it got dark. I thought about my running action and how I try to instil in those I coach to take shorter strides and land on the front half of the foot. Although walking, I started to take shorter strides and mimic the running action. I got into a good rhythm singing the song I'd written for my dad's funeral and soon my watch announced I'd walked the last mile in under seventeen minutes. Brilliant, easily the fastest mile since the beach before Brora. I batted on, constantly looking at the watch's pace setting. Eventually I saw Helmsdale about one mile away. It was 8.15pm. I messaged Angela.

'Now it's all sorted. Helmsdale one mile. Should be there in twenty minutes.'

As I pressed send I realised that would mean arriving after 8.30 and I suddenly had a horrible thought, What time do they stop serving food? I phoned the B&B. They told me it was too late in the pub now and the Fish and Chip shop shuts at 8.30. I explained I was on foot and had come from Tain and needed to eat. She said she'd phone the chippy and order me a fish supper, but I should hurry. I ended the call and said to myself,

"Hurry! – Easy when you're driving, but not when you're on your last leg!"

I began to sing faster and in doing so my speed increased and I entered the village at exactly 8:30. Up ahead I saw a man and women in the pub car park getting in a car and hurried over to ask directions.

"Can you tell me where the fish and chips shop is please?"

"No. I am French," he said.

Now I don't speak French but I do remember a few words from my school days, and I wasn't about to give up my fish supper without a fight. So, casting my mind back almost fifty years I replied with

"Ou et l'emporium de poisson et pomme frite, s'il vous plaît?"

I thought it was a good effort on the spur of the moment but it didn't work. What I should have said was,

"Vous et un grand tête choix fluer avec petite ballons," because his reply to my perfectly pronounced plea, was to just repeat, "No. I am French." Surely he should understand 'Pomme Frite' no matter how bad my pronunciation. I gave up and decided not to waste time or energy on Anglo French relations, so went straight to my B&B where the nice, kind landlady told me she had ordered the food and I could pick it up at 8:45.

Another day ticked off and although I would no longer finish on the 28th as I wanted, at least I was thirty-eight miles nearer to John O' Groats than I had been at breakfast.

27 days and 890 miles done. 2 days and 53 miles to go.

CHAPTER 34

Bonus Day

Day 28 – Thursday 28th April 2022 – Helmsdale to Lybster

I think it's fair to say I was a bit disappointed when I woke up but tried to remain philosophical about the situation and look up on it as a bonus day. However, it was my son's birthday and in some small way I felt I was letting him down by not finishing today. That said, I knew attempting to run 53 miles in one day with only one good knee and after what I had done so far, was just beyond me. In fact, I was concerned as to whether I would make it up the first hill, knowing I wouldn't have long to find out.

Fuelled on a full Scottish fry up, I stepped apprehensively out into the morning. My mood was lifted a bit when I looked up the street and saw the hillside of bright yellow gorse that overlooked the village. A golden glow that seemed to go right to the top of the one thousand feet climb I was about to attempt. I wasn't sure how the knee would react. Like its owner it moaned and groaned as the road began to ascend but settled down after five tentative minutes.

Almost every morning so far I had posted a message on social media with a brief summary of my journey but hadn't done so this morning. I just wanted to get on with it, but as I climbed the hill my phone began to ping at regular intervals with messages of support. Part way up the hill I stopped to look at the view and took out the phone to read the messages. I was blown away by the kind comments and support, mostly from family and friends but some from total strangers who had heard about it from someone I met or the friend of a friend. I now had a significant number of strangers following me on twitter. I recognised some names as being respected sports coaches or athletes of note, all following me. I was nothing special, just a little lad from Lidget Green in Bradford, the son of a wool sorter who had started school wearing short trousers and I was being cheered to the finish line by all these invisible people. It didn't seem real.

I passed a house with a big bay window looking out to sea. It was a splendid view, and I noticed an elderly lady sitting in a high-backed chair with a morning cuppa. I waved and she waved back. Then I looked at the view and looked back at her, moving my hand in a sweeping movement towards the view. She raised her arm level with her shoulder and gave me a big thumbs up. It was as if she too knew what I was doing and was also wishing me success. It occurred to me that many of the people messaging me couldn't do what I had been doing and that somehow I was carrying their hopes and dreams on this journey too. I realised that I was drawing energy from this support. It kept me going when I needed a mental lift as if they were pacing me or carrying my bag along the way.

The road seemed to go up forever, eventually following the contour around the head of the valley called the 'Ord of Caithness' and here I crossed into the county of Caithness, the last county of my run. The homestraight. It seemed an age since I had celebrated leaving Cornwall and I reflected on the journey. I stopped to take a few photos, firstly of the Caithness sign and then the view from a car park overlooking the sea. This proved to be a mistake as each time I set off again the knee pain flared up all over again but ceased after a few minutes of movement. It was clear that slow and steady was to be the mantra for today so I tried to march along at a consistent 3.5 mph and repeat what had worked after I had suffered going into Perth. I would walk all day today and hope my leg recovered enough to allow me to run tomorrow. I had estimated I had 23 miles to cover today and a further 30 to cover tomorrow so it was still not cut and dried.

Having climbed from almost sea level to above the two hundred metre contour in the first one and a half miles, the road then descended for the next seven miles, I kept a nice rhythm and my spirits high by singing as I marched. Firstly, my old School Hymn, followed by other hits from the 19th century such as Jerusalem, Bread of heaven, For all the Saints and other (not so) well known classics. After eight miles I arrived back at sea level in the village of Berridale. The road then ascended another punishing one hundred and fifty metres in half a mile. The hill was known as 'Berridale Brow' but before attempting the monster climb, I took the decision to stop in a café in the valley bottom for a much-needed pot of tea and an early lunch. I recalled the words of the old cyclist in Golspie about all the places that had closed following the pandemic so I decided to follow Jack Reacher's advice once again and eat when food was available. As I was paying my bill, I noticed a fancy tin next to the till. In the tin were bars of peanut brittle standing upright and just waiting to be picked. I fell hook line and sinker for the seductively stationed sweets and paid what I felt was an inflated Three Pounds fifty pence for a single bar. Seriously! Whatever happened to the penny tray? It was to prove a wise investment.

I set off to negotiate the climb with short staccato steps that slowly propelled me up the hill. Near the top I met a Swedish lady of similar years walking down the hill. The large rucksack told me she was not just a day hiker and she confirmed that Lands' End was indeed her destination. We chatted for a few minutes before taking the obligatory selfies then wishing each other good luck. The afternoon seemed to drag on. I became weary not through tiredness but through boredom. My pace slipped to 3mph which somehow seemed massively different to the jogging pace of 5 mph thus making progress really slow.

My spirits were lifted when I reached the village of Latheron late in the afternoon. Here the A9 turned left and headed for Thurso and Scrabster. I carried straight ahead in the direction of Wick and John O' Groats. There it was displayed as a main destination on the sign. This was another significant milestone. Just around the corner another road sign read,

'Wick 18, John O' Groats 35'.

I really was getting near the end of the journey but still had five miles left in my day. Another two hours at this pace. It had been four hours since my lunch and hunger was creeping in. I took out the peanut brittle and broke off a small piece. I ate the bar over the remaining five miles, eating the last bit as I arrived in Lybster. I had not passed one single place to buy food since leaving Berridale and suddenly three pounds fifty seemed to be money well spent.

My accommodation was in the old school and I turned off the main road on the lookout for such a building. I found it after four hundred metres and called the number on the door. Five minutes later a small hatched backed car arrived. A small lady of oriental origin with impeccable manners and a cheerful disposition, showed me into the school. Entry was via a door and small entrance hall at the back of the building. The school had been converted into a series of small apartments equipped with everything needed for a short stay. It was perfect. The lady left after showing me in and told me to leave the keys on the kitchen worktop when I left. I showered then washed all my running kit before placing it to dry on the most fantastic towel rail I had ever seen. It was a huge square coil that stood upright from the floor and was almost as tall as me. With that important job done I sauntered a few hundred metres down the road to a small store and bought food for my evening meal and for breakfast before returning to my room.

During the evening I did various stretching exercises and before going to bed rubbed voltorol cream all over both legs. Everything was packed away and my running kit which was now dry was placed on a chair ready for the morning. I climbed into bed and wrote up the details of my day's journey before turning the light off.

28 days and 913 miles done. One more sleep to go.

CHAPTER 35

What Would You Say to Your Hero?

The need for a noctural bathroom trip meant I was out of bed at 2am and once awake I couldn't get back to sleep. It was as though I was a child again on Christmas Eve. Thoughts went through my head about the journey, the places I had been and the people I'd met whose stories had moved me.

I wondered about the old lady in the house on Bodmin Moor who refilled my water bottles. Was she still out in her garden watering her plants? How was the lady at the tea rooms in Berkeley coming to terms with life? Had she managed to persuade her son to cycle with her. I thought about the girl on the horse in Worcester. Was she coping with life without her dad? How far had the old lady who was cycling from Inverness to the North Yorkshire Moors got, and had they found the missing boy in Allness?

I thought about my own family and friends. I was looking forward to finishing and having a rest. I decided I would organise a party to celebrate my achievement. In my head I drew up a list of the people I would invite. I thought about my mum and dad and how proud they would have been of me. This led me to think of who I would have really liked to be there and talk to if I could invite anyone at all, living or dead. Famous people or my heroes like George Best, Ian Stewart, David Bedford, Joss Naylor, Ranulph Fiennes and Ian 'Beefy' Botham then saying to them,

"Hey look what I have done, you inspired me to do it, Thank You"

I thought about those people who had made a significant impact in my life like the man who caught me when I fell down Otley Chevin and what I would like to say to him. That led me to think about a lady called Margaret Rhodes. What would I have said to Margaret Rhodes?

I was born with a twisted testical, so when I was six or seven, I had to go into hospital to have something done to keep it in the right place. I don't know the correct medical term for the procedure but do know it was major surgery. A full-blown operation with anaesthetic, masked men and women with sharp tools cutting me open, moving stuff about and stitching me back up again with a needle and thread. After the operation I needed a few weeks of recovery and was confined to bed for the first week in the children's ward of St Luke's Hospital.

The sister in charge was a lady called Margaret Rhodes. She became another of my unsung heroes I would like to have spoken to in later life. Annoyingly I did actually meet her when I was about forty five but didn't realise who she was until it was too late. I am sure she knew who I was though, but never brought up the subject of our earlier encounter, probably because what she did for me was all in a day's work to her. After all, that's what hero's do. They save the world, or their own little patch of it on a daily basis. No fanfare, no medals. They just get on and do it.

Whilst in hospital, I met a lad called Colin. He was six years old and was a really likeable, lively lad, full of beans as they used to say. Colin had been unlucky. When he was four, he was playing in his kitchen. He reached up above his head and pulled the handle of a pan, tipping the boiling contents all over himself. He had been in hospital for two years having skin graft after skin graft. His face resembled that of a war veteran or a smaller version of Nikki Lauder. Colin was allowed out of bed and would come to see me and play cards or board games. We got on really well and he would make me laugh lots. He was a proper clown and one of his favourite japes was to sit on top of the vacuum, as the cleaner towed it around behind her, wheeling it around the ward.

This caused two problems. Firstly, it got harder to tow so the cleaner would put the large hose over her shoulder and haul the machine as if she was pulling a cart without looking behind her. The second thing was that sitting on top of the vacuum covered up the air vent which stopped it from picking up the dirt. The cleaner would inspect the head of the hose for blockages but would then chase Colin around the ward with a wet cloth or duster. The cleaner was a large West Indian lady with an infectious laugh and I think she liked Colin. I'm sure she knew he was going to do this, but it was all a kind of pantomime and her way of helping Colin in what must have been a traumatic time. It was great fun for the rest of us and we would cheer Colin as he ran around the ward until Colin and the cleaner were chastised by one of the staff nurses or sisters.

Also on the ward was a nurse who called me Little Stevie. Each morning she would wake me to take my temperature and pulse by singing 'wake up little Stevie' like the song wake up little Suzie. I seem to remember she was called nurse Lee. We also had our temperature and pulse taken after lunch and it was as nurse Lee was taking my temperature one afternoon that this incident began.

Colin ran over to my bed and took my pack of cards. By this time I was allowed out of bed. Colin was messing about and knew I would chase him to get the cards back, which as soon as nurse Lee had finished I did. I caught up with him and pinned him against his bed and tried to recover the cards. We were in a friendly kind of scuffle, me trying to wrestle the cards back and him trying to hold on to them. Suddenly he kneed me in the groin, and I passed out.

When I came around nurse Lee was standing over me. There was a lot of blood. Sister Rhodes had just come back onto the ward and was still wearing her nurse's cape as she came running over. Colin had inadvertently kneed me right in the scrotum, splitting the stitches holding the scrotum together and possibly dislodging the contents. Nurse Lee had come rushing over and seen blood seeping through my pyjamas and screamed for help. The timing of this was significant as it was 1.30pm, meaning visiting time had just started and there I was, laid on the floor in an ever-increasing pool of blood. Let's be honest, no visitor wants to see blood oozing from the private area of a young child's pyjamas as they are carrying bags of over ripe plums or grapes for their loved ones.

Sister Rhodes scooped me up in her arms. She ran as she carried me through the ward just as my mum walked in through the visitor's door. All this is true. Nothing guessed, nothing made up. However, in my mind's eye, I imagine what my mum must have seen. Picture the scene if you can. Sister Rhodes running in front, her hero's cape flowing behind. Nurse Lee, running after us trying to keep up, hands held out in front, each hand clutching something. From my pyjamas blood is dripping but also two thin pieces of dental floss like thread are trailing back to Nurse Lee's hands. One going to her right hand and one to her left, each 'floss like' ligament linked to one of my testicals!

Some kind of emergency surgery was performed. Things were counted and put back in place, checked and double checked and my scrotum was stitched back together again. Eventually I met Angela and we had two children which may not have been possible if it had not been for the speed, dedication and professionalism of Margaret Rhodes.

So back to my question. What would you say if you met one of your hero's. One who, like Batman, had run to save you with their cape flowing on behind. I did meet Margaret Rhodes in later life, only at that point I hadn't been aware of my hero's first name. To me she was Sister Rhodes. So, forty or so years after the scrotum splitting soirée, when a lady was introduced to me as Margaret, I had no way of knowing she was my caring caped crusader. It turns out she was a friend of my aunty Eileen.

Aunty Eileen was a sister in the N.H.S. all her working life. Over fifty years. We used to go see her every Christmas, usually on Christmas Eve. We all loved Aunty Eileen. Both of my children and my wife all thought she was great. She was a lovely lady who was always interested in you and in what you were doing and loved to sit with you and share in what was going on. She was always a great hostess and would prepare a banquet whenever you turned up. One thing I remember is there were always lots of nibbles. Crisps, chipsticks, and all kinds of savoury snacks in dishes around the room. Her house was the first place I ever ate twiglets. I liked her for lots of reasons, one was when I was young she would allow me to pick the raisins out of the fruit and nut mix. My mum or dad would tell me off for this but Aunty Eileen would say "oh he's all right, it all has to be eaten," and would place her hand on my head and ruffle my hair as she smiled forgivingly at me.

So, in the lead up to one Christmas we arrived at Eileen's house to find she was entertaining a host of friends, all ex-nurses. I found out later these included Sister Rhodes. Since then I have often thought about what I should have said to her if I'd realised who she was. Given the setting, the fact that my children were with me and the assembled ladies, what could I say to acknowledge what she had done for me without causing embarrassment and all I can think of is,

"Margaret, would you hand me the nuts please."

CHAPTER 36

A Balti Breakfast and a Well Done Dear

Day 29 – Friday 29th April 2022 – Lybster to John O' Groats

The day started early for me. I woke up at 5:15, showered, got ready and ate a breakfast that consisted of a Chicken Balti pie! Yes, you read that right, and as I did so I thought of my old pal Andrew Nicoll and his 3 Peaks yacht race experience.

Having sailed on a yacht in rough seas around the coast of Wales, throwing up the entire way, he then ran a marathon up and down Snowden on nothing more than half a bag of crisps. He immediately got back on the boat and sailed to Whitehaven in Cumbria. Here he jumped on a bike and cycled to Ennerdale then ran over Black Sail Pass into Wasdale, up and down Scafell Pike in the dark and back to Ennerdale where he picked up his bike again to ride back to Whitehaven. I met him as he was cycling up a steep hill on the way back and he asked me,

"Steve, what time is it?"

"7 o'clock." I replied.

"AM or PM?"

That's what these endurance events do to you. I told him it was 7am, which was quite correct, and yet fifteen minutes later, he was back aboard eating a breakfast of Spaghetti Bolognese, followed by fruit cake and cheese. The body wants what the body needs, so fueled with my very tasty and enjoyable chicken balti pie, washed down with a half-litre of water and two Ibuprofen, I set off at 5:45 am.

Progress was good and I soon got into my running. The knee had eased. The road was quiet, the day was dry but with a strange sky that gave no indication of what weather we were going to get. After about five minutes I heard the first vehicle. A big truck came toward me so I checked the road behind before crossing to the left-hand side so I could continue to run. I did this several times for three of four trucks and several coaches to ensure I was well out of their way. There was a small strip of grass and a one-metre-wide strip of granite chippings, so I would be quite safe if I needed to jump out of the way but felt safer on the opposite side of the road and would move back to the correct side after the vehicle had passed by.

I had decided to heed the advice of the old cyclist in Golspie and stick to the coast road. I could have taken a less busy route inland but was afraid I wouldn't be able to get water. Thirty miles was a long way to go on one litre of water and if I was unable to run it would take me ten hours. So, although there would be more traffic, the A99 was the route of choice.

I was ticking along nicely and having to tell myself to slow down. My legs felt fine, and I covered the first four miles in under thirty-six minutes. This was a world away from the day before and the journey to Helmsdale. The road was long and straight. The surrounding area was mile upon mile of empty fields, punctuated with the occasional croft and I could easily see for about a mile in both directions. Another large truck approached and once again I crossed to the other side of the road, and listened carefully after it passed. As it disappeared into the distance I looked back to see if the road was safe to cross.

As I turned my head suddenly something large reared up from the granite chippings a few feet to my left. It let out a horrible, piercing shriek that made me jump to my right and stopped me in my tracks. It was a large stag and appeared to be quite badly injured. It was trying to stand but couldn't. At the same time, it was trying to defend its territory, territory that I had encroached on. I was transfixed. I looked down at the poor injured animal and took a step towards it. It immediately reared its front legs and stuck out its antlers. I wanted to assess the injury but couldn't get near it. I stood there, hopeless, useless and helpless, seriously worried about losing solids from both ends and weighed up my options.

I should try and treat the injury in some way, but I didn't even have a blister plaster with me now, having thrown away everything I felt I no longer needed that morning. I should put it out if it's misery but had nothing more than a pair of nail clippers? I could flag down the next vehicle to help, but what would anyone else do? I am not sure what this says about my view of society, or about the public in general but I actually said to myself,

"If I do manage to flag a car down, they are more likely to get their phones out and start videoing it." I could phone the police but would have to wait until they arrived and that could be hours. I weighed up my options and decided the best course of action was to do nothing. I couldn't help the deer. It needed to be culled. I couldn't do that. It was too injured to move so wasn't a danger to traffic and if it did decide to move there was nothing I could do to stop it. I looked up and down the road. No vehicles about. No houses nearby, it was 6:30 in the morning and I was already starting to get cold just from standing for these few minutes.

I am not proud of my decision and there may be people who hold it against me, but those people were not there. I was the one standing in the middle of nowhere freezing physically and metaphorically, retching and feeling totally inadequate. I had to make a decision and given the same set of circumstances tomorrow I would probably do the same again. I ran. Fast. With tears streaming down my cheeks like the coward who walked from his dying dad's death bed two years earlier, I left the disabled, defeated deer to fend for itself.

I covered the next two miles in fourteen minutes, weeping all the way. It started to rain so I stopped to put my jacket on but before I did, I doubled over at the roadside retching and blowing the dangling snot from my nostrils. I cursed this whole thing. Why had I set out on this bloody journey? What the hell had I been thinking? I wanted to be sitting on the sofa with Angela watching the shows she loves. The same shows I moan about all the time. I didn't want to be on a road to nowhere in the back of beyond, shirking my responsibilities as a caring human being, but alas that's where I was, and that's what I had done.

There's an old saying. It's no good crying over spilled milk. It was too late to change my decision and sit by my dad's bed side. I had to live with the memory that I left him there to die alone and had today repeated the cowardly action. It's done, move on but be prepared to stick your chin out and take what's coming. We all have to be responsible for our actions.

I ran the remaining eight miles to Wick and spoke to the first man I saw who by coincidence was also a runner but was on holiday from Winnipeg. I told him what had happened and asked him what I should do, he said he didn't know but added that it happens all the time in Canada, then said you have probably done the right thing, someone will report it and the police will sort it out.

I carried on running towards the centre of Wick and came upon a bakery. I went inside for a bacon sandwich and cup of coffee. It was busy and quite a few workmen came in. I told two of them what had happened, and they basically said the same thing as the Canadian guy but one asked me If I would have been able to lift the deer.

"Not a chance, it was twice as big as me" I said.

"Well, if you couldn't lift it your only other option would have been to phone the police and wait there until they arrived which at 6:30 could have been a while."

This gave me a small crumb of comfort as I left the bakery and with my guilty burden slightly eased. I phoned Angela to tell her where I was but didn't mention the deer. I walked a half a mile through the town to let my second breakfast settle as I drank the remnants of my coffee and then began to jog again. As I passed Wick airport, I came to a sign showing sixteen miles to John O' Groats and tried sending a picture of it with a message that read "Hope to finish by Lunch time" to family and friends but there was insufficient wifi. Instead, it seemed to jam up my phone.

Running was still easy. The road was still flat, and I was still flying along on emotion as I passed through a few small villages. The names all seemed to me to be Germanic in origin: Reiss, Keiss and Nybster, each of which had a sign showing the distance to my destination. With each sign I saw the distance ticking down. Twelve miles, nine miles, five miles, I was closing in on the prize.

Two cyclists passed me as the route went slightly downhill to where another road sign read, John O' Groats three miles. I resolved to catch them up the climb that was ahead but as I started to work up the hill my knee gave way again. I looked at my watch and saw I had run twenty-six point six eight miles in four hours and fifty-eight minutes. This included the stop in the bakery where I forgot to stop my watch. Alas the legs had decided they had taken enough punishment and I was forced to walk up the last hill. It took me almost fifteen minutes to cover that half mile, but from the top I could see the Orkney Isles. It was a wonderful moment and I stopped to make a short video and take in the panoramic vista.

There was now only two miles to go, and it was all downhill. I had wanted to finish in style by running at speed right up to the famous signpost, but my body had decided that enough was enough. I looked down at my knee and saw my leg was bruised all down one side from the quad, past the knee to the side of my calf. I decided to stroll those last two miles remembering that I had planned to finish singing a new song. My son Tom plays bass guitar in an indie band called Pretty Mafia. They were releasing a song that day called

'Slow Down'. Somehow the words seemed appropriate and I sauntered down the hill singing.

"I'll be the first to say it hurts, maybe we just need to slow down, got to slow down."

Eventually the small town came into view. I photographed the road sign. It was almost over.

A few hundred metres further on I passed a post office as a lady came out following a few paces behind me. She asked if I was all right because I was limping. She laughed when I replied,

"Absolutely bloody fantastic love." I told her what I had done, which brought forward the usual question,

"Are you doing it for a charity?" I told her about Andy's man club and what they did, she said,

"That's a wonderful thing to do. In this part of Scotland, the young people who die before reaching adult hood either die from drugs or suicide, so what you're doing is vital, well done. It must have taken a lot of courage to keep going when you're obviously injured."

"It's nice of you to say so but I'm on holiday" I said, and we both laughed. However, at that moment I did feel an immense sense of pride in what I had achieved. I didn't know anyone else who had done it.

The lady didn't sound Scottish and told me she was actually from London but now lived here and worked in the Edinburgh Woollen shop. I asked for directions to the famous signpost, and she told me it was just past the bus stop which led to me asking her what time the next bus was. I had planned or rather thought I would have to get a taxi to Thurso and the realisation that I would be able to get a bus and save some money was a bonus as I estimated the trip had already cost me over £2500 for hotel bills, train fares, food and other necessities.

Further down the hill I spotted a man in brightly coloured clothing walking towards us. Also seeing him the lady said,

"Oh, he's finally set off then. That bloke is going to Lands' End. He's been here all morning and had a photographer and reporter interviewing him earlier."

As he got nearer, I could see he was towing something as he walked. It was some kind of small wheeled trailer or rickshaw and had a lot of gear in it. We shook hands and I wished him good luck whilst he in turn congratulated me.

I had less than fifty metres to go and it was just a few minutes before noon. I had completed the journey in twenty-eight and a half days and felt elated. All that was left now was to get someone to photograph me in front of the famous signpost, treat myself to an ice cream and get on the next bus home. As I approached the sign, I held my phone out to an elderly lady who had just taken a picture of her friend. I asked her if she would take a picture of me, explaining I had just run all the way from Lands' End, to which as she took my phone from me and replied,

"Oh Well Done Dear."

CHAPTER 37

Worth more than Gold

The words 'well done dear' brought to mind images of a different deer and I had to force a smile as the well-meaning lady photographed me. After thanking her, I moved away from the sign but just stared out to sea. I wasn't looking at anything in particular, and for a few minutes I was in a kind of vacuum as for the first time in a month I had no immediate destination. I wandered aimlessly with no clear plan, before deciding to celebrate with a pot of tea and headed for a café. Once inside, the smell of home cooked food brought me from my trance-like state and I ordered a spicy bean stew, a pot of tea and a piece of courgette cake. I shared a joke with the lady serving me, telling her about how my wife blitzed up courgette, adding it to meals she made for my son because he refused to eat vegetables.

I phoned Angela to share the joke with her and tell her I had finished, ending the call when my meal arrived. The stew smelled delicious but was so hot it could have come straight out of a nuclear reactor. I was forced to leave it for a good five minutes before being able to take my first mouthful. This allowed me to check some of the messages I'd received.

People had been tracking me and were congratulating me, but I felt unworthy of their praise having run away from the dying deer. I sat there mentally beating myself up but realising that actually although I regretted the decision, it was the right choice, and I would make the same choice again but regretted being forced to make a choice.

Sometimes in life we find ourselves between a rock and a hard place as they say. We don't know what to do. In those cases, we usually have three choices: Do one thing, do another or do nothing at all. The worst thing is to do nothing at all, and whilst we may hate having to make either of the remaining decisions, once made we have to be big enough to accept the consequences and try not to let, 'what might have been' or the other people's opinion of our decision have a negative impact on us. In my case any critics were not faced with the same circumstances. Let them run 943 miles in my moccasins then they can judge me.

I continued to read more messages and came to a Facebook post addressed to me from Andy Nicoll. Tears flooded my eyes and ran down my face into my nuclear stew. The lady who had served me was clearing the next table and saw that I was an emotional wreck. She came over asking in a quiet voice if I was OK. I replied saying,

"I'm actually happy, I've just run the length of the country and this is what it does to you" and we laughed together.

I thought back to my dad and a piece of advice he used to give me about completing a task.

"You have to plan your work, and then you have to work your plan." It became his mantra.

In today's modern world it's easy to become bogged down in the day-to-day issues life throws up. If this happens we can sometimes just keep going along trapped on the hamster wheel of life, earning more money and accumulating more possessions, a bigger house, or better car, but just meandering our way through life, without setting any proper goals. Suddenly ten years have gone by, and we wonder why we are in a rut. In the past I have experienced many such times, and yet it is amazing what we can achieve if we actually challenge ourselves, and in doing so make our family and friends proud of our achievement.

I had set a goal to run from one end of the country to the other, and to try and do it inside one month. I had then worked out a plan as to how I could achieve this. I didn't really know if I could do it, but I had, and it was an immensely satisfying feeling.

I knew my family and friends were proud of me and I knew my mum and dad would have been proud of me. Alas they were no longer around to share my success so I will leave the last word to my friend Andy Nicoll and the Facebook post that had me melting into my meal. He can have the last words because, whilst we may at times be wounded by the opinions of others, isn't it what our friends and loved one's think of us that matters most? Don't we place the ultimate value on their favour?

According to the book of proverbs, 'God's favour is worth more than gold.'

If that's the case why settle for gold? Why waste the rest of your life accumulating wealth?

My memories and my friend's message are worth far more to me than that.

If there is a place called El Dorado I believe I have found it.

"Steve – today will be another day that you'll remember for the rest of your life – today is a day that you should think of all those that have helped you make this day happen – today you should think of all those you have already inspired to do more than they thought possible (I'm one of those) and today you can think of all those people you will help in the future through your fundraising – you sir are a very special person and someone I'm proud to call a friend"

The End

Or is it? Why not let the end of my adventure be the start of yours?

Don't Settle for Gold.

Acknowledgments

Most of the people I want to thank are already mentioned in the book but there are a few that aren't. My apologies if failing memory means I've missed you off.

The first Is Joe Balmforth. Joe rekindled my love for running and if I'd not met him, my life may have gone down a different path meaning, I would have missed so much. He persuaded me to join Bingley Harriers which is without doubt one the best decisions I've ever made, and he would have never tasted Coteafee. Thanks Joe.

The second is Steve Frazer. Steve is a wonderful human being and someone I have the utmost respect for. We have spent many hours in the hills and have lots of happy memories. His support and guidance has been invaluable, even if his interaction with Swiss Border Control needs some work.

I would like to thank all those who have run with me over the years, sharing their time on the trails. It's a long list, so not only but especially, Adrian Netherwood, Andy Nicoll, Dave Stephenson and Robin Lawrence. Thanks for listening, and for some fantastic times in varying weathers EG. OMM 2008!

To Barbara and Dave Weatherhead, Vic Wilkinson, Sarah Tunstall, Meryl Levington, Ruth Thackray, Ali Raw, Carol Morgan, Ali Dewhurst, Jo Buckley, Martin Peace, Andy Jebb, Jamie Robinson, Tom Gomersall, Simon and Denise Wright, Catherine and Becky Holmes, John Parkin, Gibbo, Kate Farley, Jason Feeney, Mark Westman, Robbie Williams, Sally Robinson, John Conroy, Jackie Hammond, Kerry and Rick Gilchrist, and all who've supported me in my many ridiculous runs, feeding me and keeping me awake along the way. Thank You.

To all those who have allowed me to coach them and believed me when I told them that running up Ghyllwood Drive is good for them. Thank you for your trust.

To all who've encouraged me in my writing, especially my walking friend and writing sounding board, David Slater. I've loved hearing the stories of racing against Dave Bedford, Brendan Foster, Mike McCloud and Julian Goater but also stories from both mill and boardroom. I'm looking forward to the play.

Thank you to Julie Howard and Laura Thornton who made me believe I could write something people would enjoy reading. You've proved to me that people achieve so much more from receiving kind words rather than criticism.

To Cathi Poole and Clare Brayshaw at York Publishing Services. Thank You for your help, professionalism and for your patience in my moments of recollection, excitement and passion. What a fantastic job you have done.

To Big Pappa Crow, Catherine and all the Flying Crowleys. I would like to say so much but words can't do justice to our friendship or the admiration I have for you and the brotherhood of the wheel.

To my siblings, Anne, Michael, Maureen and Angela, Cousins Colin and Adrian, and In-laws Jim, Maureen, Steven, Amanda, Philip and your families Thanks for indulging me in my passion for running and for letting me bore you with my adventures. I've even started talking myself to sleep.

To my children Vicky and Tom who impress me every day in what they are doing and achieving. I hope you are as proud of me as I am of you. Sorry about all the technology questions but it's all a mystery to me.

To my wife and partner in life for over forty years, Angela, I've loved every minute and it's getting better by the day. Thank You.

Lastly, Thank You to you dear reader. Thank you for reading my book. You've given me a wonderful gift, the anticipation of pleasure. The next time I introduce myself to someone, and they say, as they usually do, "Not the real Stephen Fry? It is going to give me enormous pleasure to respond in all sincerity;

"Stephen Fry the Author".

The purpose of my story is to inspire others to take on their own challenges so I was moved to receive this picture from eight year old Hetty Hey whose mum had been following my journey.

"J.O.G. Done" By Hetty Hey

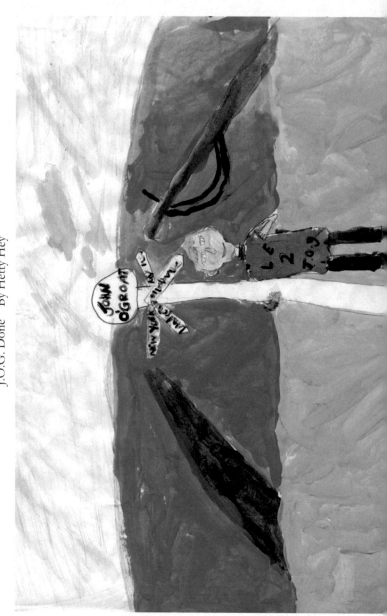

Scan the QR code to see photographs of Stephen
on his journey running from Lands End to John O'Groats
for Andy's Man Club